THE
UNCHARTED PATH

An
Autobiography

PRESIDENT
LEE MYUNG-BAK
PRESIDENT OF THE REPUBLIC OF KOREA AND FORMER CEO OF HYUNDAI

Translation by Kim Ilbum

Published by Sourcebooks, Inc.
P.O. Box 4410, Naperville, Illinois 60567-4410
(630) 961-3900
Fax: (630) 961-2168
www.sourcebooks.com

Originally published in 1995 by Gimmyoungsa.

Library of Congress Cataloging-in-Publication Data

Yi, Myong-bak.
  The uncharted path : the autobiography of Lee Myung-Bak / Lee Myung-Bak.
    p. cm.
  Includes bibliographical references and index.
(hard cover : alk. paper) 1. Yi, Myong-bak. 2. Presidents—Korea (South)—Biography. 3.
Mayors—Korea (South)—Seoul—Biography. 4. Executives—Korea (South)—Biography.
5. Korea (South)—Politics and government—2002- 6. Seoul (Korea)—Politics and gov-
ernment. I. Title.
  DS922.4642.Y47A3 2011
  951.9505092—dc23
  [B]

                                2011031824

Printed and bound in the United States of America.
BG 10 9 8 7 6 5 4 3 2 1

To my mother, who taught me to persevere, to serve, to love, and to hope
To my wife, Yoon-ok, my dearest May Queen
and
To all the unforgettables

NOTE FROM THE AUTHOR

The Korean War ended in 1953 when I was twelve years old. The country was ravaged. It is estimated that the war killed more than two million civilians, and hundreds of thousands were wounded or went missing. Families became separated during the war. After the armistice was signed and the peninsula was divided in two, many would not hear from or see their loved ones for more than four decades. With little left standing, the people had no jobs and nothing to do. They had nothing to eat. Many children, orphaned and malnourished, roamed the streets looking for food. For many of them, spring never came.

We were fortunate because we had my mother to take care of us. Although my family was extremely poor, we stayed together. My earliest childhood memory is of helping my mother sell small muffins filled with red bean paste in the local market. I can't remember not working; work was always a part of my life. But Mother's dream was never about escaping poverty, nor did she ever push us to become rich. Instead, her life was simple and honest. She was always thankful. She took one day at a time and held onto one dream at a time, such as sending my older brother to college or having the entire family celebrate one of her children's birthdays. Whatever she did, she gave it her all, believing that the Lord would take care of the rest. That's how she wanted us to live, too: to work hard, to perse-vere, to have faith, to serve, and to love others.

When I was young, I vowed to someday later—when I made lots of money—buy Mother a pretty dress, take her out to a fancy restau-rant, and go on a trip together overseas. Well, I now know that there is no "later." Although I was unable to do any of those things I prom-ised her, I hope this book—which is not so much about what I did as about what she taught me—can pay tribute to a great person. I think Mother would be happy.

Translator's Note: Endnotes have been added to the English edition of this book in order to provide the reader with historical background or further explanation when needed. All the endnotes contained within this book have been researched and written by the translator, who bears the sole responsibility for any inaccuracies and mistakes therein.

INTRODUCTION

All we had back then were a desperate yearning to live a better life and a fierce sense of urgency. And this is what allowed us to do what many considered impossible.

Today, the Republic of Korea (or South Korea) boasts the 13th-largest economy in the world. It produces cell phones and semiconductors and builds giant ships and luxury cars, along with the world's tallest skyscrapers and longest bridges. Its athletes, artists, musicians, and scientists are renowned throughout the world. And these remarkable achievements happened during the last sixty years, all while South Korea was struggling with North Korea. People have tried to explain this phenomenon. How did this tiny nation, which has been brutally colonized by one of its neighbors for close to forty years and ravaged by a devastating war, manage to become what it is today? Ask any number of people and you will get as many different answers, none of them right or wrong. This book is an attempt to create a small part in this giant and colorful mosaic that the Korean people have been collectively making for the last sixty years. I was privileged to have the opportunity to take part in this epic journey.

I spent twenty-seven years of my life at Hyundai, helping to transform a small local construction firm into a global corporation employing 170,000 people worldwide, with an annual revenue of more than $40 billion. As a thirty-five-year-old CEO, I roamed the world, from the deserts of Saudi Arabia, to the jungles of Thailand, to the Siberian tundra, seeking new opportunities and opening up new frontiers. I met with visionaries and statesmen as well as strongmen and dictators. Back home, I had to deal with an authoritarian regime, which was not only challenging but, at times, dangerous. Once I was almost killed in a distant land by a mob trying to rob our office.

Korea's history has been never easy. Colonization was followed by war, then military dictatorships, internecine struggles, ideological battles, regional divisions, and social unrest...the challenges at times seemed overwhelming. Being a businessman during such times was not just about making money, it was about making our country strong. Thousands of men went overseas as miners and construction workers to give their children a better shot at life; the money they sent back saved Korea from bankruptcy following the first Arab oil embargo in 1973. Thousands of women went to Germany as nurses so that they could send back money to help their young siblings go to school. These children later became teachers, musicians, and scientists.

Sacrifice—this is what makes our mosaic so beautiful and rich. I rarely had time to spend with my family. All we had back then were a desperate yearning to live a better life and a fierce sense of urgency. And this is what allowed us to do what many considered impossible.

This book was first published in Korean in 1995. In 2011 it was updated and expanded to include my life after leaving Hyundai. The purpose of this book is not to dwell on the past or tell others how to live their lives—instead, I hope it will help inspire people everywhere to realize their own dreams of becoming statesmen, entrepreneurs, and leaders of the future. I believe our world will become a better place as our young leaders explore the deepest oceans, find new cures for diseases, and develop new sources of clean energy. Challenges often kindle fear, but they also bring out the best in people. Our finest hour is still ahead of us. So, to all of our future leaders—good luck and enjoy the wonderful journey.

—Lee Myung-bak

1 | THE STRENGTH OF POVERTY

My very first memories are of my hometown and its marketplace, the pungent odor of fish entrails, the smell of the sea, and excruciating poverty. Poverty clung to my family like a leech, and it would be many years before we were able to free ourselves from its miserable grip.

Homecoming

In August 1945, with Japan defeated by the Allied forces, Korea finally gained independence after thirty-six years of colonial rule imposed by the Japanese[1]. In November of that year, my family—my parents, four older siblings, myself, and my younger sister—packed our belongings, ready to head back home from Osaka, Japan. We had some old clothes and a small amount of money that we had managed to save—this was all that we had to show for the years of humiliation, servitude, and hardship that we endured during our time in Japan.

We arrived at Shimonoseki, a port on the southwestern coast of Japan, and boarded a ferry headed toward Busan, Korea's largest port city, on the southeastern coast. We were all excited to leave behind a life of misery and dread. We were also worried, not knowing what to expect.

The ferry was teeming with people like us. The mood became more raucous and cheery as we got farther away from Japan and closer to home. Many of us suffered miserably from seasickness, but that didn't dampen our joy. We were just grateful to be going back home alive.

Unfortunately, our overloaded ferry was shipwrecked as it neared the island of Tsushima, 33 miles off the coast of Busan. Everyone had to jump overboard. Luckily, everyone was rescued, but all our belongings were lost. We were home, but with literally nothing except the clothes on our backs.

I was four years old at the time, so I have no recollection of my sea voyage or the shipwreck. Instead, my very first memories are of my hometown and its marketplace, the pungent odor of fish entrails, the smell of the sea, and excruciating poverty. Poverty clung to my family like a leech, and it would be many years before we were able to free ourselves from its miserable grip.

My father, Lee Choong-woo, was born a few miles from Pohang, where we eventually settled. He was the youngest of three sons. My grandfather was a farmer, but he didn't own much property. As was the custom back then, my grandfather gave the small plot of land he owned to his eldest son and the rest of his possessions to his second son. Penniless, my father left his hometown at an early age, wandering, looking for work, and scraping by on menial labor. He wasn't the only one. Under Japanese colonialism, many young men his age couldn't find proper jobs and had to make do with whatever they could find.

It was during this time that my father became a farmhand, learning how to raise cows and pigs. Soon after, he decided to try his luck abroad. With a few of his friends, he set off for Japan and settled near Osaka, where he was hired to tend a farm.

Life in Japan was arduous. The back-breaking farm work was

hard enough, but he also had to endure the deep prejudice that many Japanese held toward Koreans. The humiliation was painful, but he did what was expected of him and even saved some money.

After some time, my father was able to save enough money to come back home briefly to get married. His bride was a woman from the Chae family who came from a town near the city of Daegu. After getting married, my parents went back to Osaka and had six children. My youngest brother, Sang-pil, was born when the family moved back to Korea.

Upon returning to Korea, our life remained difficult. My father was able to secure a job before the Korean War broke out in 1950. He was hired to manage a farm that was owned by the chairman of the board of a local high school. Although the job was nothing much, it beat roaming around the countryside looking for work. Besides, Father knew a lot about tending livestock and had good managerial skills, so the job suited him nicely.

Father was a traditional man steeped in the teachings of Confucianism, which emphasized respect for elders and for others. Not surprisingly, he was a man who said very little. He showed us how to behave properly in different circumstances, such as the right way to bow. His teachings instilled in us the importance of adhering to and abiding by these various social customs. My siblings and I understood at an early age that such responsibilities are not a burden, but something that should be treated with respect.

It is always a challenge for any father with limited means to teach his children such values or to exercise and command respect within the family. Often, poverty will beat a man into submission; a beaten man often turns to alcohol or neglects his family altogether. However, my father did his best to keep his integrity intact. Despite being poor, my father never lost his pride or his self-esteem.

While Father was working at the farm, our big family was able to enjoy some semblance of stability. We were not well-off, but we had the basic means to carry on. And we managed to stay together. Unfortunately, when the Korean War broke out, our stability was shattered once again[2].

Pohang soon became the scene of a major battle between the South Korean and United Nations forces and those from communist North Korea. And when Pohang fell to the communists, we were forced to abandon everything and move to another town farther south. Father, however, decided to remain in Pohang so that he could take care of the livestock. It was a foolish (not to mention dangerous) decision, but he refused to leave. The owner of the farm was already gone, but my father considered it his duty to take care of the farm and the animals. When our troops re-took the city of Pohang, the rest of us returned home. To our great relief, Father was safe. But the farm was destroyed. He was jobless and we were broke, once again.

With Father out of a job, I was forced to work at an early age. I tagged along with my father to nearby markets. This was my first foray into the world of business. One of the many jobs Father did was selling fabric, a job he was able to obtain through the patronage of a North Korean refugee. In this business, profit depended on how one measured the amount of fabric. For instance, a widely practiced trick was to basically double-count slightly when measuring the fabric and to throw in the remainder as a bonus. Doing so leads the customer to believe that she is getting a few inches of extra fabric when in fact she is being shorted. When Father was told of this trick, he refused to go along. In fact, he measured out exactly the amount he was selling, and then he would throw in a bit extra. He would also let customers buy from him using credit. Unfortunately, my father never kept a ledger of any sort, so he had no way to keep track of who paid him and who didn't. Also, it was usually women who came to buy fabric, and for an austere man steeped in the teachings of Confucianism, it was unthinkable to ask a woman her name, let alone her address. If some of them failed to pay him back, he would soon forget who owed him money.

When Father was a young man, he attended church. However, when he was twenty-eight years old, he stopped attending after an argument with his pastor. During those days, churchgoers who had no cash would often bring food and other goods as offerings. One day, when the pastor singled out the people who gave offerings and said a special prayer for them, my father became very upset. "Why is the pastor saying a prayer only for those who gave offerings? Shouldn't he be praying earnestly for those who want to give but can't?" In my father's view, the pastor was distorting and tainting the teachings of Christ. Nonetheless, my father allowed the rest of the family to attend church. He also said nothing about my mother's deep Christian faith. Decades later, Father came back to the church. He told us he disliked big churches, so he decided to attend a small one. Although Father didn't have much, he later donated a portion of his wealth to the church and also became good friends with the pastor. He would often invite the pastor over for a game of chess, and did volunteer work at church. Shortly before he passed away, he was baptized by his new friend and pastor.

War

The Korean War broke out right after I entered elementary school, so my memories of the war are quite vivid. While Father stayed behind at the farm to tend the livestock, the rest of the family was temporarily staying at my uncle's house. I remember in particular a hot and humid summer day. My older sister, Gwi-ae, was taking care of my younger brother, Sang-pil, who was still an infant then. Sang-pil was crying, so Gwi-ae carried him to the front lawn to try to soothe him. Suddenly we heard a loud, shrieking sound above us and the thunderous crashing of what sounded like metal pellets on our roof. Instinctively I ducked. When I looked up, I didn't see anything. Then, all of a sudden, Mother, realizing that Gwi-ae and Sang-pil were not inside, ran outside. She found Gwi-ae and Sang-pil lying on the lawn. Both of them had blood spewing from their foreheads and backs; both had suffered horrible burns all over their bodies. Finding that both were still alive, Mother rushed into the mountains and brought back some mugwort, which was known to alleviate burn injuries. She ground the mugwort into a paste and began to rub it on their charred skins. It was impossible to take my brother and sister to a hospital with a war raging; there was no medicine, and besides, it was beyond our means. We later heard the village elders lament that the Americans were deploying fighter jets because they had obtained intelligence that there were communist infiltrators in our village.

For weeks, battles raged in and around our village. Mother finally decided that it was too dangerous for the family to remain there, so we were sent to a safer location. But Mother stayed behind to take care of Gwi-ae and Sang-pil, who were too weak to move. Mother nursed them amid continuous bombings and air raids. Sadly, however, both died after two long months, having endured what could only be described as horrible pain and suffering.

There's a phrase in Korean: "bury your loved ones in your heart." That's what we did. Mother was devastated and never stopped blaming herself for her children's deaths.

From then on, the Korean War was always very real to me. Seeing my own brother and sister lying there on the ground, their bodies burned, was a constant reminder of the evil of war and of communism. Later, when I became chairman of Hyundai, it was this untold, yet deeply personal story that drove me relentlessly to venture into the former Soviet Union and China. Perhaps it was my way of seeking reconciliation for my brother's and sister's deaths; or maybe it was my way of dealing with the guilt and the sadness.

Boy with the Long Arms

With Father unemployed, our family had to move once again. We ended up at an old temple site located at the foot of a mountain. Once, a Japanese monastery had been there, but now it was all but abandoned. The place had no running water or toilet, and fifteen families lived clustered together. We were all either day laborers or peddlers, and we considered it a good day if we could sell something. Poverty was raw and painful. All around us were sounds of children crying, adults fighting, and the sick dying. What was most difficult to endure was the constant hunger. The hunger became so severe that it hurt. Fortunately, our shanty was the least noisy, since the entire family was out working. Despite our collective efforts, we still had no money, and figuring out what to eat was a daily struggle. During those days, our meals mainly consisted of what we call *lees*, which is the dreg left behind after you brew rice into alcohol. Lees was cheap, and this was all that we could afford. As the youngest boy, my chore was to go to the brewery every day to pick up the lees. With very little money, we could only afford to buy the worst batch. Our family would eat this twice a day for weeks on end; I would walk around red-faced and slightly intoxicated because lees contained alcohol, albeit in small amounts. In junior high school, some of the teachers even mistakenly branded me as a misfit, since my cheeks and the tip of my nose were always red as if I were drunk (I was).

Taking lunch to school was, of course, out of the question. While other kids ate their lunches, I would go outside to the water pumps and fill my stomach with water. I remember drinking until I became bloated. That's when I learned that no matter how much you drink, water never makes you full.

On days when we had to pay our tuition, I would be told to go home and bring back the tuition. Whenever this happened—which was quite often—I would just wander around or go up the hill behind our school and stay there for some time. I knew that even if I did go home, there was no money I could take back. After some time, I would go back to school and ask my teachers for an extension.

We had no money for school because my father, ever since he had been working in Japan, sent money to his older brother back home so that he could send my older cousin to school. My father did this for many years, but when the time came for him to send his own children to school, he had no money. It sounds absurd and irresponsible, but that was my father. I don't blame him, but looking back, it was a hard time for a young boy.

Nonetheless, we never used poverty as an excuse. Instead, poverty strengthened us. If a poor man sits waiting for handouts, he will never be able to escape poverty. To such a man, poverty will be a festering wound, never able to heal. On the other hand, poverty helped me and my siblings strengthen our resolve. We were determined to never let poverty smother us.

By the time I was in fifth grade, there was little I hadn't done to earn money. I sold matches that I made myself by dipping the ends of wooden sticks into sulfur; I made *kimbap* (rice wrapped in seaweed) and sold them to soldiers near military barracks. Once, I was caught by a military policeman for selling sticky cakes made of wheat flour and was given a nasty beating.

I was constantly hungry, but I continued to go to school, walking four hours a day back and forth. My body became weaker, and by the time I enrolled in junior high school, my body was nearly broken. When I was in eighth grade, I became severely ill and was confined to my bed for three months. I still have no idea what caused this mysterious illness, but my guess is malnutrition. I couldn't afford to go to the hospital, so the best I could do was lie in bed and hope to get better. After three months of bed rest, I got up and resumed my daily routine of walking four hours to school and back.

Maybe it was because of this, but of all the men in my family, I'm the shortest at five feet six inches, while my father and two older brothers are close to five-foot-nine. If I had been able to eat normally, like other growing children, I'm quite certain that I could have become taller. However, my body made up for my short stature by growing arms that are at least four inches longer than the average person's. For this, I was called "the boy with the long arms."

Mother

Mother came from a family of devout Christians. My father's family abided strictly to Confucian customs and traditions. My father's relatives looked at my mother and her faith with disdain. However, were it not for my mother's unwavering Christian faith, I'm certain that our family would have succumbed to poverty and its hardships.

Mother was a tall woman with a narrow face. She had penetrating eyes, always sparkling and alert. My mother once told me she had attended elementary school, but I don't recall her telling me if she ever actually graduated. Although she had little formal education, she more than made up for her lack of book knowledge with her keen mind. She had an uncanny ability to remember all sorts of things, such as the birthdays and memorial days of long-deceased relatives and the addresses of friends. She even knew all the important dates of our neighbors. To me, she was the wisest person.

Our normal day would begin at 4:00 a.m. Mother would wake us up and make us sit in a circle to say our morning prayers. Mother would lead the prayer, and I recall her prayer being very consistent and unique. She would start off by praying for our country's well-being. Then, she would pray for our relatives. After that came a prayer about our neighbors and their families. She would remember what our neighbors were going through and what they were distressed about. She would know who was sick, who was going through trouble, and who had fought with whom. She would pray for them and also pray that all of them would believe in Jesus Christ. And then she would pray for her children. Throughout her prayers, I never once heard her pray for herself. Our lives were hard, but others always came first.

These early morning prayers were a nuisance for me. I was always tired from work and desperately wanted more sleep. I would sit in the circle, half-asleep, and would wake up, startled, only when my mother said my name. When my mother prayed for her children, her prayers would be proportional to our ages. In other words, mother would pray longer for my older brothers and sisters, while the youngest would get the shortest prayer. So my prayer was always short. In fact, it was always the same. Mother would pray, "Dear Father, we pray that Bak will grow strong. Amen." My short prayer was a reflection of my standing within the family.

Because my father worked as a manager at a farm that was owned by the chairman of the board of Dong-ji High School, both of my older brothers attended and graduated from Dong-ji High School. My oldest brother had a talent for business, so he left home at an early age. My second-oldest brother always excelled at school and was considered the smartest in the family, and so he was sent to

Seoul to continue his studies. As for me, I stayed behind in Pohang with my parents and worked to earn money to pay for my older brother's tuition.

When I was young, I felt envious of my older brothers for being able to continue their studies while I had to work alongside Mother. Mother always believed that it was more realistic to support her oldest son than to try to send all the children to school. In return, she expected the older ones to excel and to take care of their younger siblings. (For this, my second-oldest brother, Sang-deuk, always felt indebted to me. He would later encourage me to study so that I could pass the exam and go to college.)

My mother would often console me by saying, "Bak, you don't need to go to college or get a degree to be successful in life. You can become a rich man and help others by working hard. Come, we'll work together!" When my mother conceived me, she had a dream in which a full moon came and nestled inside her dress. She told me the moon was so bright its light shone across the fields onto the next village. She considered the dream so fortuitous that she convinced Father to name me Myung (bright) Bak (far-reaching).

Mother worked hard all her life. At the time of the Korean War, Pohang was a small port city, mainly trading and selling fish. This was where my mother would set up her small stall and sell fruit. Her spot was always in the farthest corner of the market, where there was very little traffic. From the age of five, I would hang around the market and do small errands.

When she sold her cakes (more like small muffins, filled with red bean paste) at the market, she had to carry a full load—a metal pail filled with dough, a large bucket full of red bean paste, the metal bread cast used for baking, a water jug, and a kerosene lamp. She stacked them onto a handcart and hauled it every day to her place in the market. She then poured the dough into the metal bread cast;

when the dough turned slightly crispy, she would pour in a bit of red bean paste and then turn it over. It seemed easy enough, but there was a secret—the trick was to bake the cake so that it was crispy on the outside while leaving the red bean paste inside just a little warmer without overcooking it. The consistency of the dough and paste had to be just right; when one took a bite, the red bean paste inside had to ooze out. The dough and filling had to be prepared fresh each day. Each night at home, I would help Mother prepare it. In the morning, I would go to school and Mother would go to the market and bake and sell the cakes.

On our birthdays, Mother would bring home five pieces of her cake and give one to each of us. I remember once on my birthday she brought home these cakes as usual, and I asked Mother why she wasn't having one herself. She replied, "Bak, it's nice of you to ask, but honey, I can't stand the smell of it. You go ahead and enjoy it."

Many years later, when I was mayor of Seoul, I encountered a couple running a stall similar to the one Mother used to have. Out of curiosity, I bought a cake from them and tasted it. It didn't taste right; it wasn't crispy at all, and the inside had none of the richness of the red bean. The couple looked like they'd just started out. I told them I was willing to share my mother's secret recipe. The couple just stared at me. It turned out they were a married couple and both of them were deaf (many such couples own similar businesses because the job doesn't require much dialogue with the customers). So I wrapped an apron over my suit and started to bake the cake. I remember we sold out their entire batch in just two hours. I went back to the couple several more times, showing them how to bake it right, just like Mother did.

Mother was incessantly helping others. She would often tell me to go and help others, too. She also told me to accept absolutely nothing in return for my work. Mother would give me instructions to carry out, such as, "Bak, the eldest daughter over at the oil shop is getting married today. Go over there and help them out, will you?" If I protested, saying that they weren't even our relatives, she would look at me and say, "Didn't I tell you that neighbors are closer than relatives? Now, go!" As I would reluctantly turn around to go, she would always shout at the back of my head, "Bak! Don't accept anything, not even a glass of water, after you help out, you hear! I don't want you taking anything, even if they offer you food, I want you to politely refuse and come straight home!" She would drill these words into me over and over again. I couldn't understand why she was so particular about this. And when she would order me to go and help out a rich neighbor who was throwing a party, I would often complain that rich people didn't need my help. Mother would take none of that, and she would again yell at me not to accept anything.

Years later, I understood why she insisted that I not accept anything. It was because she wanted me to learn the joy of serving. Rich neighbors would hand me leftover delicacies to take home, and I would politely refuse. It was then that I realized that people, whether rich or poor, were grateful for my help. And most importantly, I felt useful. As time went by, I started to feel proud of helping others and expecting nothing in return. Neighbors also began to understand. They said that the kids in our family were proud but not boastful, sincere but not obsequious.

It was difficult at first—not because I didn't want to work, but because I was such a shy boy. I had trouble getting up the courage to say hello or introduce myself. I would usually wade in silently, wander about the kitchen or fetch water, and then leave silently. Later on, I felt comfortable enough to say hello and ask them what they needed.

Another difficulty was fighting the temptation of food. I could have easily picked up whatever food was in front of me when nobody was watching. I would imagine how much my brothers and sisters would like it if I brought them such delicacies. We could all indulge in a feast! But I would remember the words of my mother, and I never did.

Years later, when I was rejected by the military due to my poor health, I came back to the market where Mother worked. I couldn't make myself tell her that I had been rejected for being too weak. When I stood in front of her, Mother was startled to see me. I was supposed to be in the military by then. I told her what had happened. Holding me, she said, "Bak, I'm so sorry. I didn't realize that your health was that bad. Please forgive me." She started to cry. "It's because of all the lees that I gave you when you were little...It's because I didn't take good care of you when you were sick. I'm so sorry." That night, mother prepared dinner for me before the rest of the family came home. On the table was a bowl of steaming white rice and one egg, uncooked. Our family ate white rice perhaps once a year, maybe twice. Egg was normally too expensive for us, so it was an extra-special treat. Mother and I sat together to eat, and we cried a lot that night. That was the first and last time I saw my mother cry.

2 | NOTHING TO HIDE

The entire family was focused on my brother and his future. Meanwhile, I dreamt of going to high school.

Going to High School

As I was about to graduate from junior high school, our family's fortunes became even more difficult. My older brother, Sang-deuk, excelled in academics and was preparing to take the examination to enter college. My oldest brother was already serving out his mandatory military duty by then. Sang-deuk had initially enrolled in the Army Academy because it was free. However, his health deteriorated, and after his first year at the academy, he had to drop out. He then started to prepare for his college entrance exam. He moved to Seoul and was studying there alone. My parents were back home and trying their best to scrape together the tuition Sang-deuk would eventually need. The entire family was focused on my brother and his future. Meanwhile, I dreamt of going to high school.

As junior high school graduation neared, my counselor asked

me about my plans. Back then, students with high scores usually enrolled in the prestigious Kyung-buk High School. Since I was always second in my class, my teacher thought that I would apply for Kyung-buk. He told me he wished to discuss this matter with my parents. Mother was then intent on earning enough for Sang-deuk, and she would sigh whenever the issue of tuition came up. Under these circumstances, I couldn't dare raise the issue of me going to high school because it would just hurt her even more.

One day, though, I decided I had nothing to lose and told my mother that my teacher wished to see her about my high school enrollment. As soon as I said this, she stopped what she was doing and looked away. She told me sadly, "Bak, you know we can't afford to let you enroll in high school, not with your older brother getting ready to go to college. Maybe if your brother failed the exam, then perhaps you could go. If you really want to go to high school, then you could go to the high school run by the National Post Office, which is free. But if you did, then there won't be anybody to help me. I simply can't do this alone, dear."

I expected this, but actually hearing those words was another matter. I was dejected. I had hoped she would at least leave some possibilities. All my life, I had worn hand-me-downs, and now I was prevented from going to high school! For the first time, I resented our family for being poor, and I blamed my brothers. I was too young to fathom the pain Mother went through when she said those words to me. She was being firm because she didn't want me to have any false hopes.

When I told my teacher what my mother had told me, he was perplexed. "I never expected you to go to a school in Seoul, but I thought that your parents would at least send you to Kyung-buk. What a shame. There must be some way. OK, why don't you ask them if you can enroll at Dong-ji Commercial High School in

Pohang? It's a night school but it's a high school. It's better than nothing. You may not realize it now, but in life it's much better to have a high school diploma than a junior high school diploma. Trust me, Myung-bak."

I relayed what my teacher had told me. Mother was still adamant. "Bak, you have to help your brother." This back and forth between my teacher and Mother went on for some time. I was stuck in the middle, and after a while it became tiring for me as well. Mother kept insisting that even if I went to night school, I needed to pay the monthly stipend and tuition, which she could not afford. At the same time, my teacher also dug in his heels, saying it was in my best interest that I should at least be allowed to attend night school. My teacher mentioned to me that the school waived tuition for the student with the highest overall grades. He told me I could get the top grades, and then it would be free. He urged me to try. Mother finally relented and accepted this final proposal. The only reason was because she was told that it would be free. She told me, "Fine. I'll let you go so long as you don't have to pay tuition." With Mother's conditional permission, I started school and was able to graduate. For three straight years, I was at the top of my class.

Business-Boy

In high school, I continued helping Mother. And along with helping her bake cakes, I decided to branch out and start my own business. I sold ice cream or hardened sugar bars or taffy, depending on the weather.

During winter I sold puffed rice, which is made by turning a rice popper. A rice popper was made of scrap metal and resembled a large metal drum turned sideways. Using a crank, one would turn the rice that is poured into a metal mesh. Heat was applied continuously

until the rice popped. When the rice popped, it did so with a deafen-
ing noise. Mother installed such a machine next to her cake stall, and
I would pop the rice and sell it.

It was my first independent business venture. I was always hag-
gard, with sweat pouring down my face, and my clothes were grimy
with dirt and the soot that bellowed out of the rice popper. Because
I had no other clothes than my school uniform, I would work in
them. After a while, with my clothes sullied, I had to head to school.
The problem was that just around the corner from where Mother
and I worked, there was a girls' high school. So every day in the
morning and after school, girls would walk past our stall and look at
the boy in the school uniform popping rice. And whenever girls
looked over in curiosity, I would get flustered and my face would
turn red. I was deeply embarrassed to be seen in such clothes, and I
did whatever I could to avoid being seen by the girls. Unfortunately,
however hard I tried, I remained that lanky boy with the long arms,
dirty face, and dirty clothes, popping rice.

After much deliberation, I came up with a brilliant plan. I scav-
enged around and found a large straw hat. It was tattered and well-
worn, but it served my purpose quite well. And whenever I wore that
straw hat, pulled down low over my head to hide my face, Mother
would make fun of me and say, "Bak! Not the straw hat again! You
have nothing to hide, for goodness' sake! Keep your chin up, boy!"

Later, when I was mayor of Seoul, I saw many homeless men
roaming the streets, and one day I met with them after launching a
city program that encouraged companies to hire such men. The program was supported by the city council, and it sought to help these
homeless men get jobs and start their lives over again. When I
walked into the room where I was supposed to meet them for the
first time, the first thing I noticed was that most of them were wearing hats of some sort. Some wore baseball caps, and others had

tattered hats that they had picked up somewhere. They wore their hats low and kept their heads down—just as I had done years ago. I told them, "Let me see those handsome faces! Keep your chin up!" Mother had been right: there was nothing to hide.

When I became a sophomore, I attempted to gain "independence" from my parents and family. I thought it was better to go out and find a real job and make real money if I was going to continue selling stuff (also, I desperately wanted to avoid being seen by the girls). My plan was to buy fruits from a vendor and resell them for a higher price at night in front of a movie theater. It was a masterful stroke of entrepreneurial genius! All I needed was a handcart and my mother's permission; the latter came swiftly.

With high hopes for my new business venture, I found a carbide lamp to use for light, and I polished the fruits until they sparkled. On the very first day, I was nervous but also excited. When I turned on the carbide lamp, the fruits looked absolutely divine in the light! But I found out what anyone who ever did any business will tell you outright: there is no such thing as easy business.

Selling fruit requires precision timing—I call it "sophisticated arithmetic"—whereby the buyer's price and the seller's price must converge at just the right moment. For instance, if one day I set the price too high in the beginning and failed to sell my portion for the day, I would have no choice but to lower the price to get rid of the remaining fruits. And fruit was a commodity that I couldn't keep indefinitely; it needed to be sold. So for me, each day was about selling the fruit at the highest price, as quickly as possible.

I was fast learning the intricacies of being a fruit vendor when one day it all ended abruptly. I was in front of the theater at my usual spot. It was raining, and this meant that business was excruciatingly slow. As the last group came out of the building, a car that was backing out of its parking space suddenly crashed into my handcart, spilling everything onto the road. All my fruits scattered, and large watermelons burst open. All I had in mind was to try to salvage whatever I could. I crawled along the pavement, trying to stop the fruits from rolling out of reach. It was then that I heard the driver yell at me, "Hey, you dumb bastard! What the hell are you doing selling this shit here?" The driver was an obnoxious man; he continued yelling so violently that I just stood there, drenched and not knowing how to respond. Overwhelmed by the man's fury, I blurted out apologies.

As the man drove away, I became furious. I was tired of being poor. I was sickened at myself for submitting to the man and apologizing. I asked myself, "What am I doing?" I rifled through my pockets to see how much money I had. I had enough to go to Seoul, and I decided to run away there.

First, though, I wiped away my tears and headed toward a tent, a cheap road-side pub that catered to people like me. I walked in and ordered a bottle of *soju* (a liquor that tastes similar to vodka, made by distilling rice or barley) and some food. I wanted to get drunk. The old lady was startled when I ordered the drink. She knew I never drank or slackened at work. She asked me what was wrong, but I was in no mood for small talk. I repeated my order and told her to hurry up. Still the lady fidgeted and took her time. And at that instant, the thought of Mother struck me like a bolt of lightning. I realized for the first time that never once had I offered my own mother a piece of fruit. Whenever I would come home after buying my fruits from the wholesaler, Mother would help me shine the fruits and she would exclaim, "Look how pretty the fruits are! They all look so tasty!" And whenever she said that, I would pretend I hadn't heard her so that I wouldn't have to offer her a piece, which would mean less profit for me. Mother, who always prayed for us in the morning. And I realized how stingy I'd become.

I decided that leaving for Seoul could wait a day. Without drinking, I got up. I collected what remained of the fruits, emptied them into the cart, and headed back home. As soon as I walked in the house I cheerfully shouted, "Mother! Pops! Come have some fruit. I've got lots of leftover today!" When Mother heard this, she took one look at my face and immediately knew something was amiss. And when she saw the broken fruits, the twisted cart, and my unusually wide grin, she turned around and went back to bed without saying a word. I washed up and went to bed, but all I could think about was running away.

Early next morning, Mother woke us up as usual. But that day her prayer for me was longer; it wasn't just a prayer about me growing up strong. Mother prayed in earnest, and it looked like she hadn't gotten any sleep. Listening to Mother's prayer, I was shaken. It dawned on me—"She *does* care about me." My eyes welled up and my heart ached. I postponed my plans—I would run away a month later. Afterward, I postponed my plans several times. In the end, I stayed. As time went by, I returned to my usual self, and my anger and frustration subsided.

If that lady had served me that bottle of *soju* without hesitating, I would have gotten drunk and boarded the train to Seoul that very night. If it hadn't been for Mother's prayer that next morning, I would have left that day. And if I had, my life would have probably turned out completely differently.

Leaving Pohang

During my senior year, Mother made an important decision. She decided to move the entire family—except for myself and my younger sister—to Seoul so that they could better support my older brother, Sang-deuk, who was already there. I was to stay behind so that I could graduate high school.

My parents proceeded to sell almost everything they owned to raise money to move to Seoul. Since they didn't have much to sell, they didn't raise a lot of money. Mother assured me that she would send money to me and my sister every month. With those words, my family packed up all their remaining belongings and left Pohang, and my sister and I stayed behind at the old temple site.

Mother did send us money every month, but it was never enough. My life became even more miserable. My sister and I were always hungry. I would buy rice with the money mother sent me. We had to stick to our daily portion or we would run out of food before the month was over. Using discarded paper, I made thirty small paper bags, and into each bag I poured our daily ration of rice. I gave strict orders to my sister to never exceed the daily portion.

One time, my sister became so hungry that she shouted, "Let's eat as much as we want for twenty days and just starve the rest!" Even today, my sister tells me how mean I was back then. She told me later that she thought about running away many times. I never told her, but I thought of doing the same. I would think how it would all be over if I was dead. The hunger was painful; it literally ached. To make some extra money, I would chop wood and sell it. But whatever I did and no matter how hard I tried, I couldn't escape poverty.

In 1959 I graduated from high school as the class valedictorian, but I had no time to attend the graduation ceremony since I was expected to head to Seoul right away and join the rest of my family. And perhaps I wanted to leave Pohang as fast as I could, to get away from the miserable hunger. I held my little sister's hand as the two of us boarded the train to Seoul. It would be years before I went back to Pohang.

On my way to Seoul, I was filled with worry and trepidation. I didn't expect life to get any better in Seoul. In fact, I worried that it was going to be even more difficult. From what I'd heard, my parents' life in Seoul was more or less the same as it had been back in Pohang. I tried hard to be positive, thinking that a big city like Seoul would have more opportunities and that life could improve. But hope kept eluding me.

When I arrived, I found my parents living in a small shanty in Itaewon, located in central Seoul. They were selling vegetables at a stall. Nothing had changed. My family was still poor. We were still hungry. But now we were poor and hungry in Seoul.

The joy of reunion was short-lived. I found out that the house my parents were living in was too small to accommodate me and my younger sister. The next day, I went and found a tiny room. Our family was still separated, even in Seoul. Mother was always sad to see our family separated. She would tell me to come home twice a day so that the whole family could at least have meals together. But it was too far away for me to walk, which meant I had to take the bus, and I had no money for that.

College Dropout

One good thing about life in Seoul was that for the first time in my life I had lots of free time. Unlike in Pohang, there wasn't much work I was able to do. I would wake up at four in the morning and rush out to the "people's market" where day-laborers stood in line hoping to get picked for a day job. But I was small and lanky, and I would be passed over for the guy next to me, who was usually a head taller. I would straighten my back, puff up my chest, and try to look tough, to no avail. No one cared that I had graduated from high school when I looked like I was going to drop dead lifting a sack of cement.

On days when I wasn't picked (which was quite often), I had nothing to do. During those times, I would hop on the train—without paying—and travel the entire route. Or I would aimlessly wander around Seoul. Many times I found myself near colleges. And whenever I encountered college students in their uniforms, I would think to myself, "What am I doing here?" and turn back. Then I recalled a postcard my older brother had sent me when I was still in high school. He wrote, "Bak, never give up hope about going to college. Although you're in a night school now, if you try real hard you can go to college."

I was intrigued by the idea of going to college, but I had no idea what to do or where to start. And then I remembered my junior high school teacher. Although what he had said about having a high school diploma wasn't helping me find work, I knew he was right overall. And I also figured it would be better if I was a college graduate than a high school graduate.

Since going to college was out of reach for me, I came up with a plan. The next best thing for me was to become a college dropout! People thought more highly of a college dropout than they did of someone who had just a high school degree. All I needed to do was pass the college entrance exam and I would automatically become a college dropout. It seemed like an excellent plan.

The next day I met up with an old friend from Pohang who was also living in Seoul. I moved in with him and we began to study for the exam. The only problem was that I had no clue what kind of books I needed to read or how to study for the exam. My friend was also a country boy who hadn't spent much time in Seoul, so he was no help.

I found another old friend of mine from junior high school. After graduating from Pohang Junior High School, this friend attended one of Korea's most coveted high schools, Kyung-gi. He then got accepted into Seoul National University Law School, which is considered Korea's most prestigious university. When I explained to my friend my ambitious (and loony) plan, he cut me off and said, "*You* want to go to college? Look, Bak, you can't just go to college because you want to. Listen, don't waste your time. I think it'd be much more useful for you to think about doing something else. Besides, graduating from that night school of yours isn't going to help, either."

It was an honest remark and I appreciated his candor. But it still hurt. I didn't blame him, because he knew exactly what my situation was. Still, I asked if he could lend me some books. But my friend kept changing the subject, and I came back empty-handed.

I didn't give up though, and one day a neighbor offered me a solution. He mentioned that I could find all the necessary books at the used-book stores and suggested I go and take a look. After saving 10,000 *hwan* (approximately 30 U.S. dollars) working at the market in Itaewon, I went to a used-book store that traded in "supplementary study guides for college entrance exams." The owner of the shop was a man in his forties. When I told him I came from out of town to buy books to study for the college exam, he asked me what kind of material I was looking for. I answered, "I don't know. I have no idea which books to study."

The man looked at me pityingly and said, "Do you wish to major in liberal arts or the natural sciences?" In Korea, students usually decide during their second year of high school whether they are going to major in liberal arts or natural sciences, and they take different college entrance exams according to this decision. But since I attended a commercial high school, which had no such distinction, I had never thought about this.

So I stood there with a puzzled look. Then I said, "I wish to go to business school," since my older brother was a business major and I had graduated from a commercial high school.

The owner said, "OK, then you mean the liberal arts. Now, which college do you want to go to?"

I said, "It doesn't matter. As long as I get accepted into college, any college is fine."

The owner stared at me curiously, then shuffled to the back shelf and picked out a few books. After placing them on the counter, he began to calculate the price using an abacus. "The total's going to be 30,000 *hwan*. I'm giving you a real discount, kid."

I hesitated, "Um, I only have 10,000 *hwan*..."

The man shot me a furious look and started shouting obscenities. I was startled at his behavior—judging from the man's temperament, I was afraid I wasn't going to be able to leave the store in one piece. But I couldn't back down. I needed books to study.

So I explained my plan to him. When I was finished, the man calmed down somewhat. He returned the books and came back with another set of books. This time, he had selected various reference books and study guides. "Here, if you study these, you'll be able to go to college. Just leave whatever you have and go. Pay back the rest later." I was stunned and wasn't sure what to do. When the man saw me just standing there, he bellowed, "Go, before I change my mind, you idiot bumpkin." Without a moment's hesitation, I scooped up the books and ran as fast as I could. When I was a safe distance away, I let out a sigh of relief and marveled at my good fortune.

Thanks to the bad-tempered and foul-mouthed (but seemingly kind-hearted) store owner, I had the necessary books in hand. But, there wasn't much time before the exam date and I still had to help my parents in the mornings and evenings. The rest of my time I devoted to studying. The more I studied the books, the more I realized how little I knew. I studied like mad.

When it came time to submit applications, I applied to the newly established Business School at Korea University. I looked at other business schools as well, but Korea University was the only college that didn't require a test in foreign language. I figured this would increase my chances. Many people were predicting that competition to enter the Business School at Korea University would be fierce because that year—1960—was its first year.

The exam date drew near, but my workload remained the same. My parents didn't cut me any slack. With one month left, I took a stimulant called *anna-pong* that was popular among students for chasing away sleep. But it took its toll on me, and with three days left, my body gave in and I collapsed into bed.

On the day of the exam, I pulled myself out of bed and hobbled to the exam site. Afterward, I felt I had done pretty well in both English and math, but I had no illusions that I had actually passed the exam. I told myself that taking the exam was worthwhile in itself and that no matter the result I would be satisfied for having tried.

I had no regrets and felt relaxed as I awaited the test results. My wait turned out to be worthwhile. My name was on the list of students who had passed. My dream of becoming a college dropout was realized!

I was happy and my neighbors in Itaewon were even more excited. They all asked me if I had the tuition ready. I smiled and told them, "No, I don't need to come up with the money for the tuition. As long as I passed the exam, I'm a college dropout, so I'm good with that!"

But I was wrong. I soon found out that to become a college dropout I needed to first register and attend at least one semester. So despite my brilliant plan, I had overlooked what was most obvious.

To register, I needed money. Now, an even bigger challenge confronted me, a challenge far more difficult than passing the exam. My parents were pleased that I had passed the exam, but they didn't have any money to spare. The only way for me to come up with that kind of money was to work, and work was scarce.

I was about to give up when the shopkeepers at Itaewon offered me a solution. They decided to hire me as their garbage collector and gave me an advance that was enough to cover my registration fee. Their generosity stemmed from the enormous amount of respect they had for my mother. Mother was always the first one to offer help. She was also the last person to leave the market because she would always stay behind to help others tidy up when the shops closed for the day. By offering to provide me with an advance and a job, the shopkeepers at Itaewon were paying back Mother's generosity. I would round up all the garbage from the night before and dump it at a vacant lot several miles away each morning as soon as the night curfew[3] was lifted. It sounded easy enough. I thanked them for giving me this opportunity and went straight to work. However, I learned that carting garbage was no easy task. In fact, it was one of the hardest and most grueling jobs I did in my life. Each morning I would load my handcart with garbage and carry it several miles. The route was hilly, and going up the hill was treacherous; going down was life-threatening. It took me six round-trips each morning to complete the day's job.

I started this job hoping only to earn the registration fee and my first semester tuition, which would then allow me to become a college dropout. But later, no matter how much I wanted to, I couldn't quit the job. Most of all, I was concerned that quitting would make me seem ungrateful to the shopkeepers. I also did not wish to dishonor my mother in any way. Also, the shop owners wanted me to continue being their garbage collector since my predecessor had been known to skip work whenever he felt like it. When it rained he would go home early; if it snowed, he took a day off. I, on the other hand, never missed a single day. So I continued until I became a sophomore.

By the time I became a junior, I thought the sensible thing to do was to finish school. I didn't realize then how much that would change my life.

3 | A BRAND-NEW PERSON

I began to learn what life was like around me. My eyes had been opened, and my horizon expanded. I started thinking about people and country and what these meant to me.

Student Leader

In spring of 1961, when I entered Korea University, the May 16 Coup took place[4]. Just a year before, Korea University had spearheaded the student demonstrations calling for democratization (dubbed the "April 19 Movement," which led to President Syngman Rhee stepping down) and the mood at the university was subdued when the coup occurred.

My life, however, remained the same. Each morning I hauled garbage, and in the evenings I helped my parents. Naturally, I had no time for studying; all I managed to do was write term papers in the middle of the night, always dead-tired and half asleep.

At college, the only time I had to myself was between classes. I would sit by myself and read as many books as I could. I often daydreamed. Other freshmen students were busy enjoying their freedom and life as college students. They went out to party and meet girls. But my college life had none of that.

During my sophomore year, Mother finally attained her life-long dream. She managed to rent a small shop located inside the market. To us, this was a huge step. When I was little, I remember Mother having to constantly move from one spot in the market to another. This was because shop owners would usually shoo her away, telling her to go find some other place to sell her stuff, annoyed that she was blocking customers. There was one particularly nasty shop owner who was always badgering my mother and me, telling us to get lost. I hated the man so bitterly that my biggest dream was to earn enough money to buy up his entire lot. Many years later, when I became president of Hyundai Construction, I visited the market where this man used to have his store, but the place had already been demolished as part of an urban redevelopment program.

Although our family attained the dream of having a permanent shop to call our own, our lives followed the same grueling schedule. For me, getting up every morning at 4:00 a.m. to make those six round-trips hauling garbage was pure torture. My body was wasting away, and I was exhausted. It was then that I decided to seek a way out of this misery. And the way out was to enlist in the military.

All able-bodied Korean males perform obligatory military service. Almost all Korean males, to this day, dread serving in the military. Unless you were a cadet at one of the military academies or seeking a career in the military, the military was regarded as a place where regular beatings took place (now prohibited), and enlisting was a major event in one's life. Parents worried for their sons' safety; the boys went through an elaborate ritual of saying good-byes and end-less bouts of drinking and melancholy, as if they were actually going to war. To a certain extent, such sentiment was understandable, since South Korea was situated alongside a belligerent neighbor, North

Korea, which had invaded the country before. There was no guarantee that it wouldn't do so again. The threat of war was always real, and military training was hard.

But to me, enlisting in the military seemed like the perfect solution. I expected life in the military to be challenging, but I didn't think it was going to be nearly as hard as my civilian life. The military would feed me and clothe me; I wouldn't have to worry about money or tuition. Most importantly, I wouldn't have to haul garbage. I figured that once I had endured the first few months of training, I would be able to enjoy some free time.

After finishing my first semester as a junior, I volunteered. I was sent to basic training camp in a city called Non-san. After spending a night, we were summoned to undergo a medical checkup to see if we were fit enough to serve. We all stood in line and went through the standard procedures. The checkup was a formality. Barring a life-threatening illness or severe disability, everyone was accepted.

I stood in line for the checkup, and when my turn came, I expected to be checked perfunctorily and waved through. Instead, the military doctor poked around with his stethoscope a bit and said, "Son, do you know what condition your body is in right now? The military can't accept conscripts like you." The doctor seriously suggested I go back and undergo some additional tests.

The doctor was right; it turned out that my body was in terrible condition. My bronchial tubes had stretched, and this was causing inflammation of the throat, a condition known as bronchiectasis. I recalled that I would cough and run a high fever frequently, another symptom of my condition. They also determined that I was suffering from empyema. These conditions were all related, and the doctors said that there was no fundamental cure. In particular, the bronchiectasis would worsen with fatigue. After a formal evaluation, I was rejected by the military. Later, I was visited by the military's investigative police, since they thought I had employed illegal means to avoid conscription. They found out pretty quickly that that was not the case.

Afterward, with help from my friends, I was able to check into an infirmary that didn't require me to pay huge sums. One day when the doctor was on his regular rounds, he came to my bed and looked at my charts. He instructed one of his resident doctors to administer a certain type of drug (the doctor said the name in English, so I assume it was a rather expensive drug). But when he was told that I was classified as a "patient unable to pay," the doctor said nothing and moved on. After spending a month at the infirmary, I had regained some strength and was discharged. Luckily, the cheap medicine I was given instead of the one prescribed by the doctor had worked.

Once I was out of the hospital, I returned to my life as a college student, supporting myself by hauling garbage. A small yet meaningful change did happen, though. My older brother Sang-deuk graduated from Seoul National University and got a job at the Kolon Company, a well-established Korean company that specialized in textiles. With my brother now working at a well-paid job, our family's fortunes improved somewhat.

But politically, things were turning more and more ominous. The newly established military government of President Park Chung-hee was exercising its authority aggressively, and college campuses around the country were on the brink of exploding. Students began to call for democracy. And when the Park administration began formal negotiations with the Japanese government to normalize relations, the students erupted.

Many considered the negotiations premature and humiliating, considering Japan's history of occupying Korea. Massive student demonstrations began to take place. What started out as a demonstration opposing the government's normalization talks with Japan turned into an antigovernment demonstration condemning the authoritarian rule of President Park.

The April 19 Student Movement the year before had lacked a coherent strategy and was disorganized and spontaneous in nature. By comparison, the students this time had a clear goal and a strategy. They knew what they wanted and they had clear targets. The student movement began to gain tremendous momentum. It led to the creation of the so-called June 3 Generation, which refers to those who came together to oppose the government's normalization talks with Japan. The June 3 Generation later evolved and, along with the April 19 Generation, laid the foundation for democracy in Korea.

Solidarity among students was at its peak, and universities around the country held elections to select student council presidents for each department. I decided to run for the Business School student council.

My decision seemed rash. Since I never had time to attend extracurricular activities or join clubs, I didn't have many friends. I also didn't have any alumni associations to depend on, which is crucial in Korea. I was the first student from Dong-ji Commercial High School to attend a university in Seoul. I was virtually unknown. My chances of getting elected were slim at best. All I had were a few friends from Pohang. Plus, I was still that shy boy. I never stood in front of people, and I rarely, if ever, shared my thoughts with others. Public speaking was something I never did.

But I had a reason for running. Until my sophomore year, my life had been a long series of struggles. My mind was occupied with survival and how to make ends meet. Nevertheless, I had begun to learn what life was like around me. My eyes had been opened, and my horizon expanded. I started thinking about people and country and what these meant to me. As I watched the student demonstrations, I contemplated what was really important. Korea was still a poor, developing country, and even the best universities were hanging placards advertising how many of their alumni got into which companies. I knew that there was much more to life. I realized that freedom, democracy, and prosperity were far more important and that I had a part to play, albeit a small one. The vendors in Itaewon had taught me what life was really like. They also taught me about compassion, responsibility, and what it means to help others in need. If it wasn't for them, I wouldn't have been able to earn my tuition. And they were the people who needed to be represented. Many of them were the outcasts and the voiceless; our family was one of them. I knew hardship. And I knew that life was about much more than simply making money.

But what I observed also disturbed me. Apart from a handful of student activists, many of those who took part in the demonstrations seemed to lack any sense of purpose. When asked, many of them admitted that they had no clear idea why they were taking part, or that they had no interest at all. Some seemed to simply enjoy wreaking havoc and skipping school. They had never worked a day in their lives. To them, life was about getting a decent job and making money. They were ignorant of how brutal life was for millions of others.

Unlike them, I knew how harsh life could be and how prevalent injustice was in society. I was disheartened to see that the students' tuition was not being used to enhance or promote the interest of the students. I was appalled that the students didn't care. I was angry when demonstrations were used as an outlet for venting rage and nothing more. Each had different reasons, and all sounded plausible, but in truth it was chaos with no discernible purpose. I was becoming more and more disillusioned.

On a more personal level, I wanted to change myself. I noticed I was becoming more introverted. I hoped that running for the

student council would make me a different person, one who was
more active and engaged. I was realistic. If I was elected, it would be
a victory worth savoring, but even if I lost, I figured I would at least
have let others know about who I was. I continued to tell myself that
this was a chance for me to become a brand-new person, a different
Lee Myung-bak. I became convinced that this election would be an
important turning point in my life.

Although the election was relatively minor in terms of importance, it had all the elements of any big-time election. The candidates
fought for votes just as in any other race. Each told the student voters what he did for the department and what he intended to do if
elected. The other candidates were all well-known and had the necessary funding and organization to mount an effective campaign. I
had none of these. After registering as a candidate, I went out and
had a drink with few friends from back home. When I told them
what I intended to do, all of them looked at me in disbelief. They
thought I was drunk.

Regardless, I started campaigning. Since I had rarely taken part
in student activities before, my classmates were unenthusiastic about
my bid. But slowly I started to gain some supporters among the
freshmen and sophomores. My opponent rented out buses to take
students on a sight-seeing tour of the DMZ near the South-North
Korea border. I readily admitted to the students that I had no money
to do such a thing, but told them I was committed to improving the
lives of students and to making our department a place of academic
achievement where such pursuits would be fully supported by the
university. It was my sincerity that started to win students over. I
wasn't a great public speaker, and my speeches lacked flamboyance,
but I made up for this by being honest and forthright.

At first, my opponent didn't regard me as a worthy challenger.
But with only two days to go before the election, he realized I was

going to be a problem. Panicked, my opponent's camp sent over a few friends of mine to convince me to withdraw. The opponent also had a deal ready: cash payment. He was trying to buy me out. A few of my friends pointed out the futility of my bid. They said I should quietly accept the "gift" and withdraw.

I told them no. For one thing, I had spent close to nothing campaigning since all I did was give speeches. Therefore, I had no money to be reimbursed. Besides, why should my opponent reimburse me? That was absurd. Second, my conscience wouldn't allow it.

My friends and I talked for hours, and I told them that it would be a humiliation to accept that money and withdraw. Again, my friends told me I was bound to lose. "Why do you want to continue with this when you can get your hands on some money? And you've already made your point!" they said. But I wasn't convinced. Some of my friends left angrily, but many more stayed and finally relented. And a lot of them decided to help me. All I could offer them was cigarettes, but they helped me.

On the day of the election, I went to cast my vote. I felt I had run a good, solid, and decent campaign. I was most pleased with myself for spurning that disgraceful offer, and I was feeling quite pleased that I had stood up to my opponent. I felt I had won the moral battle. I was no longer the shy country boy from Pohang.

When the ballots were counted, I won by a margin of forty votes. It was a slim victory, but a sweet one. A new Lee Myung-bak was born. But meanwhile, the country was reeling toward chaos.

4 | ALWAYS BE HONEST AND NEVER LOSE COURAGE

At 8 p.m.... the police announced their most-wanted list. I was on that list, along with my colleague Lee Kyung-woo and several others from different universities. I became a fugitive.

The June 3 Student Movement

The Park Chung-hee administration trudged ahead with its plan to normalize relations with Japan. Public sentiment turned against the government; the people believed that Japan, as the perpetrator, should apologize before any talks of normalization were carried out. The Park administration tried to argue that it was now time for normalization and that this was necessary for Korea to launch its much-needed industrialization efforts. Such assertions fell on deaf ears. The people were not buying it. While the government was approaching the issue from a purely economic point of view, the people were demanding that the government take a more historical approach, heeding the people's sentiment and ethos. Moreover, such an important matter needed to be conducted in an open and transparent manner, but the Park administration had been engaged in secret negotiations from the very beginning. The people were outraged.

When Kim Jong-pil[5], who was head of the ruling party, went to Japan to finalize the deal, students in Seoul immediately reacted. Five thousand of them gathered on March 24 to demand that the government refrain from further negotiations with Japan. The student demonstration quickly spread to other parts of the country, and it turned bloody as riot police fired on the students. Eighty-one students were severely injured, and 288 students were arrested and taken into custody. At Korea University, one thousand students gathered at 3 p.m., adopted a statement titled "Student Declaration Opposing the Government's Humiliating Diplomatic Policy Towards Japan," and took to the streets. The government fought back fiercely, and it seemed the situation was coming under control. But that was only temporary. Anger and resentment were simmering just beneath the surface. And the demonstration that began as a protest against the government's stance toward Japan slowly began to shift. Demonstrators were now calling for the removal of the authoritarian regime.

At Korea University, the president of the student council was noticeably absent from and unenthusiastic about these developments. He was calling for a more passive approach. When a meeting of all department presidents was held, it was decided that he would be replaced by a two-man interim council, which would include a student named Lee Kyung-woo, who was president of the Law School's student council, and me.

I thought the public display of the students' anger wasn't such a bad thing. For one thing, since it was too late to scuttle the talks, I figured our demonstrations would apply pressure on our negotiators, which would in turn help them win concessions from Japan by citing political opposition back home. In particular, we were aware that our negotiators were inexperienced military officers, and we figured we might as well give them some leverage. So, I jumped enthusiastically into my new role and we prepared large-scale demonstrations.

On June 3, 1964, at exactly noon, 12,000 students took part in a massive public demonstration. It was a well-organized event. Preparatory work for the protest was done secretly, as the police and intelligence agents were prowling the streets, especially within the college campuses. We knew that plainclothes undercover agents had already infiltrated many schools. Later, I would find out that Korea University was no exception.

The government was badly spooked by the demonstrations, and immediately declared a state of emergency. At 8 p.m. the same day, the police announced their most-wanted list. I was on the list, along with my colleague Lee Kyung-woo and several others from different universities. I became a fugitive. That night, I managed to sneak out of campus and, with Lee Kyung-woo, made my way to my mother's house. In my possession were documents outlining our discussions and plans, as well as the names of all who had participated in preparing the demonstration. I also had a written pledge stating that we would all swear to keep our discussions secret. If I were caught with these documents on me, everything would be revealed.

Quickly, I explained the situation to Mother and handed her the documents; she was the only person I could trust. I thought that even if the agents found the papers, Mother would not be harmed. Later, I found out that Mother had stashed the papers inside one of the walls after ripping away the wallpaper. She then pasted back the wallpaper to hide any traces. Although she didn't understand what those papers were, she knew that her son's life depended on hiding them.

After telling Mother not to worry, I closed my eyes to get some sleep. I slept with my shoes on. As I had expected, right before the daily curfew was lifted, the police raided our home. We narrowly escaped. Promising to meet up afterward at a safe location, Lee Kyung-woo and I went our separate ways.

I went into hiding inside the city and managed to call my brother. He told me to call one of his friends, a newlywed who worked with my brother at the same company. I felt uncomfortable staying with him, but I had nowhere else to go. After spending one night, I decided I needed to find another place. The government made sure to let everyone know that anyone aiding and abetting fugitives would be punished as well, and I worried for my brother.

After thanking the newlyweds, I walked across one of the bridges over the Han River. My brother suggested I go to Busan because he knew someone there who would be able to help me. But getting there was not easy. Normally it would take a little less than four hours by train; but any time I began to feel suspicious I would get off the train and take the bus instead. It took me four *days* to get to Busan.

I couldn't stay long in Busan, either. One day, the man who was hiding me came in and showed me a newspaper that said the government was going to punish those who were hiding fugitives like me. He said, "Look, I don't want to be the one to say this to you, but you've got to make a decision. I can't risk everything for you, I'm sorry. Someday you're going to get caught, and the authorities are going to find out you were staying with me. I hope you'll make the right decision, son." He was right. But I had nowhere else to go. I didn't have any money on me, either. Most of all, I felt depressed because I knew I hadn't done anything wrong.

I thanked the man for his kindness and left. As I was walking, I noticed a most-wanted poster with pictures of hardened criminals. I was shocked when I found my face staring back at me. I was lumped together with murderers and rapists.

I called my brother in Seoul again. He was very worried and asked me what I intended to do. I told him that turning myself in was out of the question. My brother told me, "They say if you turn yourself in they might reduce your sentence. I know a guy in the metropolitan police department who's from our hometown. Go see him."

"I didn't commit any crime!" I protested. However, I knew I couldn't hold out much longer. There were no more options left. "OK, well I can't turn myself in since I'm not guilty of anything, but I will show up and walk in there myself."

My brother said, "Fine. Just don't get caught coming back to Seoul, you hear me?"

It turned out that going back to Seoul was even more danger-ous than going to Busan. There were many checkpoints. I suc-ceeded in returning to Seoul undetected and met up with the man my brother had mentioned. We met at a coffee shop in front of the metropolitan police department. I "showed up" at the police depart-ment, as I said I would. However, I was told that that man was later rewarded for "apprehending" me. He was even given a special award. I was surprised when I later found out that the police had known all along of our plans, down to the most minor details. They knew where we had our meetings, what we discussed, and who took part. It turned out that one of the student council leaders was an informant working for the Korean Central Intelligence Agency (KCIA). Years later, I learned that he got a job working as one of their agents.

I was taken to the Capital Defense Command headquarters for interrogations. The country was under martial law at the time, and interrogations conducted by the military were intimidating affairs. Torture and threat of torture were widespread, and human rights were summarily ignored. When I refused to volunteer information, they began to threaten me. Sleep deprivation was standard. The interrogators would say, "Hey asshole, there are so many ways we can make you disappear. We can either stuff you inside a freezer or we can just tie a rock around you and throw you in the water. Getting rid of you is really nothing. If you don't want to accidentally disappear, you'd better answer our questions. Remember, I'm being very nice right now." The terrifying part was that everything they said was true.

Despite such threats, I kept my mouth shut. I pledged that no matter what happened to me, I would never divulge information about my comrades. This was an oath we all took together.

The interrogator didn't want to waste any time, so he began to lay out the documents that outlined when and where we had our discussions and what we talked about. It was information he had received from the informant. The interrogation dragged on for days. Martial law was eventually lifted, so my final trial took place in a civil court. This didn't mean, though, that I could expect a lighter sentence or a fairer trial. The state requested I be given a five-year sentence and that the others receive similar sentences. We were all sent to Seodaemun Prison[6]. We were jailed in ordinary cells along with the petty thieves.

Our cellmates accorded us respect since they knew we were student activists. Whenever we appeared in court, opposition lawmakers, religious leaders, writers, and various activists were there to offer us support and encouragement. We were treated like heroes. Although I didn't quite feel like a hero, I understood their need to make us into heroes; these opposition leaders wanted to use us as the public face of resistance. Many of them sought to overthrow Park Chung-hee's dictatorial regime. Big-shot politicians and prominent figures came to the prison, including former president Yoon Bo-sun and others. Some of the student activists started to take public adulation for granted. Some of them seemed to bask in the glory, perhaps a little too much.

But I knew that what I had done was minor and inconsequential compared to those who had occupied the same cells before me, many years before. The famous as well as the nameless independence fighters and activists who perished at Seodaemun Prison are the real heroes. All I did was oppose the government's humiliating stance toward Japan. I knew this didn't make me a hero. I had simply done what I believed was right. Of course, it took a bit of courage and gumption, but I wasn't about to turn myself into a full-fledged hero.

Once I reached this conclusion, it became abundantly clear what I needed to do from then on. Ever since becoming one of the interim presidents of the student council, I had had no time to study. So in prison I began reading books. I would read any book I could get my hands on. Prison was a good place to read and think without being disturbed. I also thought about life and what happiness is. For me, being able to sit quietly and to read and think without all the planning, the hiding, the hard work, and the hunger was OK. In fact, it was a time of renewal, both physical and spiritual.

Life in prison also allowed me to experience the awesome power of human adaptation. At first, I was unable to even wash my hands with the water they provided us, since they gave us so little. However, after a while I had no trouble washing my hands and my face, with a bit left to spare. The food they gave us was barley rice mixed with a few beans. When I first saw the beans, I didn't think much of it. But when the rice came without any beans in it, I found to my astonishment that my body reacted very sensitively; I became noticeably lethargic and listless. When I did my ten-minute daily exercise, I would come back to my cell exhausted if I hadn't had those beans. After that, I came to appreciate even the smallest things in life. I learned that it doesn't take much water or food to keep one alive. Ever since then, I have never indulged in "good food" or sought out "stamina food" that so many people swear by (especially Asian men).

My experience as a student organizer taught me a lot about state governance, social responsibility, and the role and scope of each actor. For instance, I learned to set clear parameters for each. The students had an obligation to raise an issue, to point out the problems, and, if need be, to demonstrate their point in a way that makes the authorities take note and do something about it. On the other hand, relevant authorities were the ones with the mandate and responsibility to resolve these issues. If these roles were reversed or neglected, that's when trouble began. I believed that my role as a student representative was to raise the issue, not to solve it. I also came to the conclusion that being a student representative must not be a stepping stone for something else, such as a political career. Student activism is not a job. And a student activist mustn't consider his role a way to fatten his résumé. But many of my fellow student leaders considered it this way. I ended up being the only one from that bunch who entered the private sector; the rest became politicians.

I entered Seodaemun Prison in June of 1964, and I was out by October of that same year. In the end, the court sentenced me to two years in jail, the term being suspended for three years. I was set free[7]. When I was out of prison, I found myself a famous man. Apparently, the newspapers had recounted in detail all that was happening to me, including my arrest, imprisonment, trial, and release. Relatives from my mother's side who had lost contact years before saw an article in the newspaper and, out of sympathy, sent us a box of apples grown in their orchard. On the box, the address simply said, "Lee Myung-bak, Yong-san gu, Seoul." This is like writing "John Smith, Los Angeles, California" and expecting it to be delivered. But I had become so well-known that the box of apples arrived at our home anyway.

Death

Mother visited me just once while I was in prison, just prior to my release. I didn't want her to see me in prison garb, so I asked one of the kinder guards for a pair of pants and a shirt and went out to see her in the visitor's lounge. Mother came wearing a traditional white dress which is usually worn during mourning. I thought it odd that she would come wearing those clothes. Then I knew. I could tell just by looking at her that the years were finally catching up. Her frail body was shriveled, and I could tell she was sick. She seemed to sense that her time was near.

We sat down, and I was unable to say anything. I knew that Mother was worried sick; she had become ill soon after I was caught and imprisoned. Being a strong person, she was trying hard not to break down in front of her son. After a while, she looked at me. "Are you studying? Are you praying? Are you reading your bible?" That's all she said. My mother soon got up to leave. The puzzled guard told her that she still had five more minutes left, but she just said, "That's OK, I saw his face. Thank you."

When I was released from prison and went home, my mother was lying in bed, unable to get up. Her heart was failing, and her condition was getting worse. Knowing that her youngest son was safely out of prison, she seemed to have finally let go of all the worrying and the heartache. Her entire life, she had lived and worked for her family.

My mother never had a house to call her home. By then, my older brother had enough to purchase a small apartment for the family, but Mother would not live to enjoy what she had always dreamed of. When the rest of the family moved into the new apartment, after she had passed away, we all cried.

Some time after my mother died, Father handed me a letter she had written. It was handwritten and addressed to me. I found out she had written that letter on her sickbed before she saw me in jail, worried she might die without seeing her youngest son. It read, "My dearest Myung-bak, I hope you'll continue to live standing up for what you believe in. Always be honest and never lose courage. I've always believed in you. Remember, I'm always praying for you. I always will."

When Mother passed away, Father was deeply shaken. Decades later, Sang-deuk bought my father a small farm on the outskirts of Seoul, and as soon as he moved in, my father relocated my mother's grave to his backyard. There, my father made a tombstone for my mother with an inscription that read, "Here lies my dear wife, who passed away before being able to enjoy the happiness of life. Forgive me for enjoying them all alone." We told Father that the engraving was a bit out of the ordinary, but he insisted. He carved it into the tombstone himself. He would spend the rest of his life taking care of Mother's grave. It was Father's way of telling her how much he loved and missed her.

My father passed away in 1981, when I was president of Hyundai Construction. He died in December, just like Mother.

5 | CONSTRUCTION IS CREATION

I was pinned to the wall, completely surrounded. I was helpless and afraid. It was the first time in my life that I was afraid of dying.

Hyundai

Once I was out of prison, I suddenly found myself a college graduate. Korea University offered to give me free credits for all my missed classes. The reason was that they wanted me out of their school, as quickly as possible. They didn't want me causing anymore trouble or embarrassment. My criminal record stated that I had been imprisoned for "inciting rebellion against the state" and therefore, whenever I wanted to go beyond a 2-kilometer radius from where I lived, I was obligated to report to the local police station.

My interest in business and economics amplified. While in prison, I read a lot on both subjects because I thought this was where Korea needed the most focus and improvement. Back then Korea was a developing country with a per capita income of roughly one hundred U.S. dollars. Unemployment was rampant, and society was teeming with disgruntled, highly skilled, but penniless adults; even those with college degrees from the best schools were unable to find decent jobs. My friends from the student activist days entered politics, and many of them encouraged me to do so as well. But I figured I could always enter politics later. First, I wanted to experience business. I believed this was where I could really get involved and make a difference.

I proceeded to submit applications to various companies. Interviews normally came next, but I could never get that far, as they would always first run a background check. Whenever the company ran a background check, my criminal record would pop up and my application would immediately be revoked. I could feel an invisible hand, a master puppeteer checking my every move. The state was always there, in every corner, preventing me from getting a job and pursuing my dream.

After I repeatedly failed to get an interview, the extent of the state's grip on my life began to frighten me. As I struggled to find a job, the university stepped up and offered me an interview opportunity with a small textile company down south. I knew it wasn't a lifetime employment opportunity, but it was better than nothing. I could earn a living and also get away from the prying eyes of the police, at least for a bit. I accepted.

The company was smaller than I had expected, and they were lost as to what kind of job I should be doing. It turned out that no one from Korea's top universities had ever applied to the company. I soon found out why I was hired. One day the company boss came to me and asked if I would help prepare his son for his college entrance exam. In short, I was hired to become a private tutor for the boss's son. I thought for a minute and cordially refused. If my aim was to earn a living and lead a quiet life, I would probably have accepted the offer. However, I didn't spend months in prison and go to college to end up being a tutor in a remote city. I also had ambitions and visions about business; this company was far removed from what I had in mind. I returned to Seoul, again unemployed.

One day as I was reading the newspaper, I noticed a small advertisement. The ad had been placed by an up-and-coming construction company called Hyundai. The ad stated that Hyundai was hiring employees to work in construction abroad. Hyundai was looking for people to work at one of its sites in Thailand.

The reason I was intrigued by the ad was not that the company was Hyundai. All I knew about Hyundai was that it was a fairly new company that was doing quite well. It was the chance to go overseas that caught my interest. During the 1960s and '70s and even into the 1980s, the only Koreans who were permitted to travel abroad were government-sponsored students studying on state scholarships, high-ranking government officials, diplomats, and a handful of businessmen. Even applying for a passport was considered a momentous event, and those who went abroad were sent off by a throng of well-wishers who came to the airport with flowers and confetti. But with such a high unemployment rate, young people like me were seeking a way out of Korea.

In May 1965 I submitted my application to Hyundai Construction. I was not alone. Scores of other college graduates also submitted applications. I could clearly see that it wasn't going to be easy to get the job. Although the company was relatively small, with only ninety or so employees at the time, many college graduates were interested, since jobs were so scarce. I took the written application test and did pretty well. After taking the exam, I went home and waited. All sorts of thoughts went through my mind. Did I pass? Would I be able to get a passport even if I did pass? Would the police let me go?

A few weeks later, I received a cable that simply said, "Please report for an interview with head of personnel division. Hyundai

Construction." I didn't know what to think. I knew that companies usually invited applicants to report for one-on-one interviews with hiring personnel if they passed the written exam. But the cable stated that the *head* of the personnel division wished to see me. I could sense that invisible hand once again.

When I sat across from the head of personnel, he took out my documents and sighed. He said that my written test scores were excellent but that my record as a student activist was going to be a problem. It turned out that he was also from Korea University and wished to help me, thus this unusual interview request. He said that the matter hadn't been reported yet to his superiors. He asked me if there was anything I could do to help my case, and I assured him that I would try my best. However, in the moment, I couldn't think of anything I could do.

I explained to my brother, and he managed to get me a reference letter from a chairman of a state-owned company who vouched for me. But I knew that the letter wasn't going to make much difference. Running out of options and desperate, I decided to tackle this issue head on. I sat down and started writing a letter. It was addressed to President Park Chung-hee. In my letter, I explained the reason I had become a student council president and why I led the demonstrations. I pointed out that I was facing many hurdles in finding a job. I closed the letter by harshly criticizing the state's behavior in using my past to prevent me from pursuing my dreams.

A few days later, I got a call from Mr. Lee Nak-sun, who was then working as the president's senior secretary for internal and civil affairs, and we agreed to meet. He seemed reasonable enough, but my plea had no effect on him. He was adamant. He said that anyone who fought against the state must be held accountable and should be prepared to face any and all consequences. He also went on to say that as a warning to students wishing to take part in similar activities, I should be made into an example. He finished by saying there was nothing he or the president could do. However, he did offer me an alternative. He asked whether I would be interested in studying abroad on a state scholarship or working at a state-owned company.

I told him no. In my mind, I couldn't accept the carrot the government, which had been my enemy so recently, was holding out to me. I also considered it a disgrace. Before we parted, I told him, "If the state prevents one of its citizens from merely trying to make a living on his own, then I must say that the state owes the man a great deal. I hope you remember that."

After that day, I forgot uttering those words. But years later, when I became president of Hyundai Construction, Mr. Lee was head of the National Tax Service, and we bumped into each other at a social function. Mr. Lee reminded me then of what I had said years earlier. He went on to tell me that he had been absolutely shocked when he heard me say those words. So when he got back to his office that day, he convened a meeting and agreed to allow Hyundai to hire me, on the condition that I would only work and not do anything else. I was grateful, and also pleased that he had taken my words so seriously.

In June 1965 I was granted an interview with Hyundai Construction. Several people from Hyundai were present. One of them was Chung Ju-yung[8] himself, who was wearing a workman's jacket with the emblem of Hyundai stitched on the chest. He seemed a cheery man, robust and full of energy. He reminded me of an army field general rather than the owner of a fledgling construction company. With my fateful encounter with Chung Ju-yung, my life would enter a new beginning, but of course I wasn't aware of this back then.

Chung looked at my résumé and asked me, "Young man, what do you think construction is?"

I replied without hesitation, "I think construction is creation."

Chung said, "Why?"

I replied, "It's because you're creating something out of nothing."

Chung cracked a smile and said, "Well, you're certainly a smooth talker." He then turned to his executives, who were sitting by his side, and said with a bemused look, "There are lots of these smooth-talking, good-for-nothing idiots these days."

There were few questions about my background. I could sense that they were aware of my past as a student activist. But none of them mentioned anything about it or asked me questions.

After the interview was over, I went back and waited. Chung, the man who smiled when I said "construction is creation," had a peculiar appeal. His relaxed manner and smile had a mysterious pull. I kept getting the notion that I could achieve a lot if I worked for him. I became more excited the more I thought about it. But my encounter with the senior secretary from the president's office kept bothering me; I didn't know whether that had helped my chances or scuttled them. I had no idea whether I would be freed from that "invisible hand" for good.

One week later, I was told to report to work on July 1.

The next time I was able to see Chung up close was during the company training camp held annually for new employees, at a seaside resort about four hours from Seoul. It was an occasion for new employees to get together and everybody took part, including the chairman. It became a company tradition for the chairman to sit down with the new recruits and get to know them over beer and barbecue. And there was lots of beer. Once everyone was settled in, we would all come out to the beach, where at night a huge bonfire would be erected. Chung would let out a hearty laugh and declare, "I want everyone to enjoy tonight! We're going to drink all night. A man's got to be good at what he does, but he also needs to be a romantic! Now, we're going to drink until that moon disappears!" With those words, he would raise his glass. Those who couldn't drink would soon drop out and the circle of people would become smaller and smaller. In the end, it was just me and three others, including Chung. At around 5 a.m., Chung finally said, "Boys, I think I've had enough. But I want the rest of you to continue drinking!" When he left, the three of us stopped and fell sideways. I've never been a drinker, and I didn't enjoy it, either. However, that day I was tense and nervous, and when that happens, I rarely get drunk no matter how much I drink. This would help me later on in life, especially when I was negotiating business deals.

The next day, we were told that Chung had to go to Seoul to receive treatment for a minor injury. Apparently, as he was heading back to his room he tripped and fell, cutting his upper lip. Years later, I was still able to detect a faint trace of that injury.

I quickly learned how large companies operated. I spent time in management then worked as an accountant at a construction site. Several months after I joined Hyundai, Chung informed me that he was sending me to the highway construction site in Thailand. In Thailand, I would go through a near-death experience, turn into something of a company legend, and become the youngest site manager in the company's history.

The Thai Safe Incident

The Pattani-Narathiwat Highway construction was Hyundai's very first overseas project. In fact, it was the first overseas project for any Korean company. The two-lane, 98-kilometer highway connected the cities of Pattani and Narathiwat, which were located in southern Thailand near the border with Malaysia. The Thai government was undertaking this project through a grant provided by the International Bank for Reconstruction and Development (IBRD). International bidding commenced in 1965, and Hyundai won the contract, beating twenty-nine companies from sixteen countries, including West Germany, Japan, France, Italy, and the Netherlands. The bid was for $5.2 million dollars, the equivalent of Hyundai's yearly revenue at the time.

Hyundai put a tremendous amount of resources and care into the project. At one point, the office in Thailand was far bigger than the headquarters in Seoul. In his welcoming remark, the mayor of Narathiwat said that while Japanese soldiers during the Second World War invaded Thailand armed with bayonets, today Korean workers were in Thailand with shovels in hand, ready to help the Thai people rebuild their country. A commemorative plaque was set up, which is still there.

All of this made us proud, but inside we were concerned. Hyundai had very little experience building highways. For one thing, there weren't any highways in Korea! The heavy equipment we brought over from Korea was so outdated and broken down that the American engineers derisively said they would bet anything we couldn't get it done on time. The machinery was constantly under repair, and many machines sat idle, waiting to be fixed.

It wasn't any better on the management side. No one had any prior experience managing a project of such scale. There were no manuals to follow. As a way to lessen costs, Hyundai hired local Thais, but the language barrier and cultural differences meant there was always trouble and misunderstanding. As a result, during the first year alone, Hyundai ended up spending more than 70 percent of its total budget, while making only minimal progress. The company was in danger of becoming an international joke; more importantly, the company's future hung in the balance.

Then one day, all the latent trouble that had been brewing beneath the surface exploded. Disgruntled workers revolted. These were not the Thai locals, but the Korean workers. Many of them had been lured from Korea by the benefits we were providing. But what happened was that back in Korea during the hiring process, local thugs had managed to get themselves hired. So now, armed with knives, two-by-fours, and whatever weapons they could get their hands on, they were wreaking havoc on the construction site. Soon they were headed to the management office, and in particular the accounting office, where the money was kept. I was in charge of the safe.

As drunken thugs started turning over anything in their path and demolishing everything in sight, other Korean managers fled the scene. Thai workers also left. I was at my office with two Thai associates. They told me to leave immediately. I looked out the window and saw the mob; they were headed my way. But I couldn't leave my office and the safe. My Thai colleagues fled, leaving me alone. The mob moved closer, knocking over equipment. Some of them had taken their shirts off and were shouting obscenities, becoming more agitated and wild. Soon my office was surrounded. There was a back entrance, but I knew I wouldn't get too far before I was caught. I had no choice but to remain in my office.

The mob knocked down the door. There were about fifteen of them. One of them slammed his military-issued dagger into the desk next to me, and the dagger sank in. He growled, "Hey asshole, give me the keys to the safe." I said, "No." As soon as I said that, I saw the blade of a knife coming toward my neck. I instinctively turned my head the other way. Again, a blade came toward me, so this time I turned the other way. I was pinned to the wall, completely surrounded. I was helpless and afraid. It was the first time in my life that I was afraid of dying. They say that when something like this happens, the human mind thinks of the most important thing. I thought of my mother.

I was tempted to hand over the keys to the safe. The safe didn't contain much cash, and no one would blame me for handing over the keys. Instead, I felt the urge to hold on. I couldn't give in to these thugs. Then my mind went blank. I closed my eyes. One of them shouted at me, "Open your goddamn eyes! It's no fun if you close your eyes!" Sensing that I wouldn't give them the keys, they changed tactics and told me to get up. They then pushed me toward the safe so I could open it for them. I got up and slowly walked over. I was shaking. When I reached the safe, I suddenly grabbed it with both my arms and closed my eyes again. Instantly, they began shouting, and all fifteen of them knocked me down and started kicking and punching me. I felt the dull thud of a boot against my buttocks and back. Some of them tried to kick my head, so I curled myself up as tightly as I could. My entire body was on fire; I was gasping for air. I grabbed the safe even harder. But the blows kept coming at me. Pain shot through my entire body like a razor. Luckily, none of them thought of using the dagger or any other weapon.

Then I heard the sirens. It was the police. The mob started running away. My co-workers who came in with the local police saw me bloodied and sprawled on the floor. I was still holding on to the safe.

The story of the "courageous accountant" soon spread to Bangkok, our regional office, and Seoul headquarters. People started to exaggerate the story, and as more people talked about it, the account became more and more colorful. I was lauded as a hero. But it wasn't because I'm a courageous person by nature that I clung to that safe. It was simpler than that—I didn't want to give in.

First Promotion

The so-called Thai safe incident made me famous in the company, but my work as an accountant continued as before. And the highway project continued to encounter many difficulties. As the project stumbled along, I became increasingly worried that the company was losing money. A *lot* of money. When Chung came to Thailand one day to inspect the site, I gently raised the issue with him. He said there wasn't anything to worry about; he was getting daily reports from the managers, and he was confident that Hyundai would make money once the project was complete. I explained to him that according to my numbers, the project was bleeding heavily and that something needed to be done quickly. I admitted that I wasn't in a position to look at the big picture, but common sense and the daily operations at the site indicated that the situation warranted closer examination. Chung assured me that everything was fine and that I should concentrate on my job.

However, I couldn't let it go. So I began gathering all the relevant information I could and wrote up a report. I gave it to my superior, and he told me he would read it and take care of it. I found out later that he reported it to Seoul as if he had written the report.

Six months later, Chung was back in Thailand. I normally got up at 4 a.m. It was a habit that I inherited from Mother. Chung was also an early riser, and one day he saw me reading a book and came over to my desk. I thought this was my chance to raise the issue once again. He listened closely, but again, he reassured me.

Chung returned to Korea. But when the report from my superior reached headquarters some time later, Chung came back to Thailand immediately, and this time he brought along people from the audit division. He had been fully informed of the extent of the problem. He was worried and mad. He believed employees at the

Thailand office were skimming money, and he intended to find out who it was.

The first employees to be investigated were the ones in charge of accounting and those responsible for signing off on expenditures. I was one of them. My section chief and the administrative chief were called in for questioning by the audit inspectors. Chung was closely monitoring the questioning in an adjacent room.

When my turn came, I was summoned alone. This time, Chung was in the room. He said, "Lee, I've been through a lot in my life. I've been tricked and swindled before. And I know from experience that someone's been dipping their hands into the cookie jar. I want to know who that person is. I just spoke to your superiors, and each of them is blaming the other, plus you. Who is it?"

I told him, "Mr. Chairman, as you know, I'm in charge of the daily expenditure account and I'm responsible for signing off on all spending requests. Therefore, there is no way anyone could have stolen any money without me knowing about it." I then continued, "This isn't about someone skimming money for personal profit. This is a systemic failure. It's about lack of efficiency. It's about bidding at a level that was far too low. Also, costs have been rising because we miscalculated from the very beginning. This is a problem that's been festering for a long time."

Chung looked at me and said, "So, did you do it alone?"

I looked him straight in the eye, "Mr. Chairman, with all due respect, I'm not in a position to do such a thing. Remember a couple of months ago, I asked you whether this project was making money, right? You told me there was nothing to worry about. But I wrote up a report about it and gave it to my superiors, not once but several times."

Chung became furious; he thought it was the administrative chief who had written the report. Chung said, "OK, so you think neither your chief nor the administrative chief were in on it? It's funny because both of them seem to think it was you and the other guy who did it. How can you be so sure it was none of them?"

I wasn't sure, and I didn't have anything to add.

Chung was staying at a hotel with the audit team, and I was given a room for the night. I was told to go back to my room. The section chief and the administrative chief came to me later that night and asked me how the questioning had gone. I told them what I told Chung, and both of them just nodded and went away.

The next morning I was summoned to the hotel restaurant downstairs. I told Chung that I'd better wait for my chiefs; he told me to forget about them, since they were going to have breakfast by themselves in their rooms. He asked me what I wanted for breakfast. He proceeded to order in his broken English. After we finished breakfast, the table was cleared, and he spoke. "Lee, what do you say you take charge of the site as manager?"

I was dumbstruck. "Excuse me? Then what about the administrative chief and my boss?"

Chung waved his hand and simply said, "They're going back on the first flight to Seoul."

I didn't understand what he meant but said, "Then I assume their replacements will be here." Chung took a sip of his coffee. "No need. I'm confident you can handle all this alone. Those guys let me down. The bastards pointed fingers at each other and you. They failed to do their jobs. I want you to go back to Seoul, personally pick the people who will work for you, and come back."

I realized what I was being offered. This was unprecedented. I cordially thanked him but refused. I wasn't experienced enough, and I was afraid of making mistakes. Besides, I was too young. I was also fearful that such an appointment would disrupt the organization and affect overall morale, especially since Korea valued hierarchy and seniority more than anything else.

All of these thoughts raced through my mind at lightning speed. Chung sat there, waiting for me to accept. It wasn't an offer; it was an order. Despite my pleas, Chung didn't budge. He had already made up his mind. His philosophy, when it came to personnel decisions, favored skill and talent. Age and seniority didn't matter to him. Later, when I was promoted to manager, executive, and finally CEO, Chung's practice remained the same. This was a reflection of his personal style—he was a man of action, he was never restricted by precedent, and he was bold and quick in his decisions.

Immediately, his orders were carried out. I flew back to Seoul to handpick my own people. I chose three new recruits. My previous bosses also flew back to Seoul. They soon quit the company. Since Chung thought it was awkward for a junior employee to supervise his peers, I was given a promotion and made deputy section chief. It was barely two years since I had joined the company.

6 | FOR THE COMPANY

"He's a young manager who sticks to his principles no matter what. Please, I hope you'll excuse him, he doesn't know yet how things work in the world."

Kyung-bu Expressway[9]

As I predicted, Hyundai suffered incredible losses building the Pattani-Narathiwat Highway. The cost was much larger than initially expected. Fortunately, Hyundai was able to win additional contracts from Thailand and some from Vietnam. And finally, the completion of the Kyung-bu Expressway was our fantastic comeback.

The Kyung-bu Expressway was not a regular construction project; it was like war. The commanding general was President Park Chung-hee, and the field general was Chung Ju-yung. Initially, the Korean government requested an IBRD loan to finance the project, but the IBRD team concluded that Korea didn't need an expressway for at least another few years. (To determine this, the IBRD team picked a point midway between Seoul and Busan and counted the number of cars that passed by daily, which wasn't many.) Unconvinced, President

Park devised an ambitious plan on his own. He was determined, and he was not about to give up. And Hyundai, with its overseas experience, was the ideal company to take up that challenge. Needless to say, Chung Ju-yung was enthusiastic about the plan and ready. A fearless team was born.

Then, in 1968, a group of North Korean elite commandos crossed the border area and infiltrated deep into Seoul. Their aim was to assassinate President Park, and they had almost succeeded when they were stopped by the local police near the presidential compound. This was a shocking event and a stark reminder of the vulnerability that the country faced. It led President Park to put the country on high alert. The mood of the country turned dreadful. Nevertheless, construction on the Kyung-bu Expressway began according to schedule. Hyundai was put in charge of two-thirds of the project, including the symbolic section between Seoul and the city of Suwon. (It was considered symbolic because this route connected the capital, Seoul, with Suwon, which is the first city on the southern-bound highway.)

After returning from Thailand, I was posted at one of Hyundai's offices, in charge of the heavy equipment. It was an unexpected assignment, and many thought it odd that Chung had sent me there. Some said I had fallen out of favor and that my career at Hyundai was finished. I, however, used my new assignment as an opportunity to learn about the operation of heavy machinery. I also experienced the pleasure of working with engineers and mechanics. As it happened, this office would play a pivotal role in supporting the Kyung-bu Expressway construction.

By the time I was assigned to this post, preparations were underway for the building of the expressway. Bulldozers and other heavy machines were laying the foundation. Chung was busy traveling back and forth in his custom Jeep, supervising the work and barking out orders. He would spend many nights sleeping in tents and staying out in the field. President Park would also personally inspect progress once a week by flying over in his helicopter. Thanks to such dedication, the project was completed in record time. Total cost was also unbelievably low. Of course, sacrificing quality for speed had its price; we were obliged to carry out extensive repair work for many years after that. But symbolically, it was an admirable feat worthy of praise. It instilled in the Korean people the belief that nothing is impossible. And it also had tangible economic benefits, fundamentally altering the essence of the Korean economy for good.

Some critics point out that the Kyung-bu Expressway was way too shoddy, especially when compared to expressways in countries like Germany or Japan. But building an expressway similar to the ones found in Germany or Japan would have taken us at least a decade. Based on our technological capacity and our finances at the time, we did our best.

Another change that happened as a result of the Kyung-bu Expressway project was that Korean construction began to rely more on heavy equipment and machinery instead of shovels, pick-axes, and manual labor. My job—taking care of the machines, repairing them, and supplying them to the site on time—became integral. But with no background in mechanics and little knowledge of engineering or repair, I was always a step behind.

Chung, whose first business had been running an auto-repair shop, knew all the intricate details of machines. He was familiar with the terminology and expected me to be thoroughly prepared. And he was famous for being impatient. He would barge in unexpectedly and demand to know where the machines were and why they were late. To him, workers were out there literally risking their lives to get this project completed and I was stuck in my office unable to provide timely support. He would shout obscenities and curse and shout some more before leaving abruptly. When he didn't show up in person, Chung would call me regularly and scream into the phone and ask me what the problems were. Many times, I couldn't provide an answer since I didn't know what he was referring to. When this happened, he would shout, "You freaking idiot! No wonder work is being delayed! It's because you don't know what the hell's going on over there!" then hang up.

One day after getting shouted at again, I decided to do something about it. I ordered the complete dismantling of a bulldozer that was awaiting repair. This particular bulldozer was needed on-site; when I took it apart, the mechanics were appalled and started panicking. I was unfazed. I took out a manual and started putting the pieces back together, carefully taking note and memorizing the name and purpose of each part. I also familiarized myself with the mechanical movements. It took me hours. When I was done, I became quite confident and proceeded to take apart other machines as well. When Chung was told that supply would be delayed by a few more hours because I was dismantling the machines, he threw a fit but said no more. Chung knew I wouldn't stop until I was satisfied. He also seemed pleased that I was getting my hands dirty. (Chung told me years later that he always thought I came from a relatively well-to-do family and that I would find it hard to survive in the rough world of construction; he was greatly surprised when he found out how poor I was growing up).

Next to my office there was a company called Kong-young-sa, which at the time was Korea's largest producer of aggregate. They had a contract to supply Hyundai Construction, which was the largest consumer of that material. Naturally, our two companies were closely linked.

A problem, however, was the tremendous amount of dust that was being emitted from this plant. Enormous dust clouds would constantly blow our way, causing all sorts of damage to our heavy machinery. Kong-young-sa was fully aware of what was happening; they promised many times that they would take measures, such as installing dust containment facilities, to alleviate the situation. But they never kept their promise.

I called the manager in charge at Kong-young-sa and demanded that they immediately install the containment facilities. I gave the manager a specific date as an ultimatum. When that day came, I didn't receive any word that Kong-young-sa had installed those facilities. In fact, workers over at Kong-young-sa were seen working extended shifts that day, late into the night.

I picked up the phone and called the manager again. I shouted, "You promised me that you would stop operating your plant if you failed to keep your promise. Well, it looks like your guys are planning on working through the night, and as a result we can't get any work done over here!"

The manager was unperturbed. "We received orders from the Blue House for ready-mix. I have no choice but to operate the plant throughout the night in order to make that delivery."

I told the manager, "That's between you and the Blue House. We had an agreement."

The manager smugly replied, "I said we are carrying out orders from the Blue House! So, I'm afraid this makes our promise with you a little less important."

I gave him a final warning, "I'll give you two hours. After that I have no choice but to use force."

The manager replied, "Fine, do whatever you want, but let me just remind you that I'm carrying out orders from the Blue House," and he hung up.

Two hours went by, and it was 8 p.m. We saw no sign that they were about to install anything. This time I walked over to Kong-young-sa.

I said, "I'll wait until midnight tonight. If you fail to honor our promise by then, your factory will not be able to operate tomorrow morning."

Morning came and nothing happened, not even a phone call. I walked over to one of our bulldozers and started the engine. I shifted it into gear and drove it slowly toward Kong-young-sa. Once I reached the driveway, I started making deep ruts; trucks were now unable to move in or out of the factory.

Panicked, Kong-young-sa informed the Blue House. They also told our general manager to restore the driveway at once. I told them that was out of the question.

An official from the Blue House called me. I told him, "Restoring the driveway depends on whether Kong-young-sa is willing to keep their part of the promise. So I suggest you call them. The reason I did what I did was because they failed to keep their promise. This is not something the Blue House should get involved in. I don't know how important your contract with Kong-young-sa is, but if our heavy machinery doesn't work properly, then the highway construction will no doubt be adversely affected." The official from the Blue House realized I had a point.

Around noon, police officers from the local precinct came to our office and issued threats and warnings, but I wasn't about to give in to them, either. Finally, when evening came, we got a call from Kong-young-sa. "OK, we'll install some temporary containment facilities for now, and afterward we'll make sure to put in place proper facilities." We proceeded to restore their driveway.

When this was done, I got a call from our head office reprimanding me for what I had done. "How in the world could you do such a thing without consulting us?" they demanded.

I told them, "Listen, I'm the one in charge here when it comes to repairing and maintaining our machineries. I also want you to know that I spared you the awkwardness of dealing directly with the Blue

House." Headquarters knew I had a valid point. I was glad the official from the Blue House had called me instead of our head office; if he had called our head office, I'm sure things would have gotten a lot more complicated.

Once this issue was resolved, a high-ranking official from the Blue House called one of my superiors at the head office and asked him, "Who is this guy at the plant? What the hell is he up to?"

My superior, trying to mollify the official, answered sheepishly, "He's a young manager who sticks to his principles no matter what. Please, I hope you'll excuse him, he doesn't know yet how things work in the world."

Life at Hyundai

Chung developed a habit of calling me whenever there was a problem that needed fixing. He would always yell, "Call Lee!" Sometimes he would call me when, in fact, he was trying to reach someone else. When I answered the phone, he would start talking about something I knew nothing about. When I told him, "Boss, this is Lee Myung-bak" he would say, "Huh?" and hang up the phone.

My promotions continued to happen without my input. First, Chung would give me an assignment that was above my rank; he would then promote me so that I could finish that job. When that job was done, he would find me other assignments, also above my rank. In this way, I was promoted in record speed. Aside from direct Chung family members, I set a record for the fastest promotion of all the employees who entered Hyundai.

I was also gaining a reputation as a person who was a bit too inflexible. Some said that I was becoming arrogant, thanks to all the promotions. When Mrs. Chung came to me one day asking me to hire someone from her hometown as a personal favor, I refused, citing company regulations. Young people were hard-pressed for jobs, and Mrs. Chung was probably bombarded with such requests, some of them hard to turn down. She was, after all, the wife of the founder of Hyundai. I felt bad for turning her away, but I felt I needed to stick to principles and refrain from giving out favors. I was just another employee working for the company.

Even my older brother heard about my reputation. Over dinner, he advised me that it was good that I stuck to principles, but that if I wanted to go far in life I should be more cautious and learn when to grant favors. Especially if that favor was for the wife of the boss. I told him I appreciated his concern but that my aim wasn't to become an executive, but to do my job properly. Perhaps I was a bit too stiff, but I couldn't help it.

Around this time, Hyundai began pursuing a new venture: apartments. Today, there are rows and rows of high-end apartments lining the Han River. You will find some of Seoul's most expensive real estate along the river. But in the 1960s and '70s, this was where Hyundai and other companies had their factories. Being close to the river, they were ideal sites for industrial factories. However, these factories bellowed smoke and caused a lot of complaints from the people living nearby.

As more and more people came to live and work in Seoul, housing underwent many transformations. The city had to come up with ways to cope with and accommodate the burgeoning population. One result was the advent of modern apartment complexes. They were still in their nascent stage. These so-called first-generation apartments all looked the same, as if stamped out of a mold. But with their modern amenities, such as heat and gas burners, they were fast becoming the preferred choice of housing. And they were also a status symbol for the newly affluent. Some of them were tailored solely for the purpose of housing as many people as possible into cramped areas, but others were more luxurious, equipped with the latest fixtures.

These apartments were being built mainly by second-tier construction companies, and Hyundai wasn't yet involved. But when I noticed the enthusiasm these apartments were generating among the housewives, I thought Hyundai should get into the business.

Chung at first was reluctant. More than anything, he thought apartments were "below" Hyundai. He always prided himself in thinking that Hyundai was about making history. He said that Hyundai should be seen as a pioneer, building factories and shipyards and laying highways through the jungles. But I continued trying to convince him. I told him that apartments were the trend and that it would only continue. Consumers wanted reliable apartments with a recognizable brand name, and demand for such was only going to get higher. Plus, the Hyundai factory where I was working at the time was receiving a lot of complaints from nearby residents about the noise and pollution we were emitting every day. If we relocated the factory and instead built apartments at the site, which offered marvelous river views, it would be perfect.

In the end, Chung reluctantly agreed. I told him if he was worried about Hyundai having an image problem, all he had to do was establish a separate company to deal solely with building apartments. That is how the Korea Urban Development Company was founded. It grew into a company with an annual revenue of nearly $1 billion. And today, Hyundai Apartment is one of the most expensive and sought-after apartment brands in Korea.

However, a few years after we began, Hyundai Apartment was forced into the center of a huge controversy that would be remembered as one of the most embarrassing moments in Hyundai's history.

Promotions

In the early 1970s, Hyundai was gearing itself up for another big transformation. The business environment was changing rapidly, and so was Hyundai. It had become a conglomerate with thousands of employees. Now Hyundai owned many subsidiaries, and its business empire included shipbuilding as well as automobiles[10]. It continued to grow, and change was happening quickly. In order to stay ahead, it had to change.

Corporate transformation depends on the people. This is especially true when a mid-size corporation begins transforming itself into a conglomerate, both in size and scope. Hyundai was no exception. Hyundai was beginning to change its people, recruiting young, creative minds to replace the first generation of "Hyundai-men" (and women). Inevitably, such transformation is met with resistance, a period marked by growing pains. Nonetheless, Hyundai could no longer remain content being simply a construction company with secondary subsidiaries.

In 1971 I was appointed director, and my first task was to revamp Hyundai Construction, the mother company of Hyundai, so that it would become more competitive. As director, my priority was streamlining management in all aspects. This meant focusing on quality and profitability over outward expansion, solidifying our strengths and increasing productivity. I adopted various schemes to help achieve these goals, such as transparent accounting mechanisms, better human resource management, and the setting of mid- to long-term goals. It was about putting in place the system and the structure that would enable the group to become globally competitive.

As expected, there was resistance from within. Some accused me of overstepping my boundaries. Some said I was becoming more arrogant. I wouldn't say that I was arrogant, but I did consider the company's money my own—the earnings belonged to the company, and as one of its executives, I considered the company mine. I wasn't working for Chung Ju-yung or for his family or just for my own sake. I was working for the company called Hyundai.

In 1974 I was promoted to executive director, and in 1975 I was promoted once again to vice president. In just ten years, I'd risen to the top levels. Again, many questioned my meteoric rise; many were envious, and rumors circulated. One rumor had it that I was related to Chung Ju-yung. Another was that I had something incriminating against Chung and so he had no choice but to promote me to keep me quiet. Another rumor said that I was being supported by President Park Chung-hee. It wasn't just those who worked at Hyundai; regular folks were also spreading the gossip. The press always had a field day when I was promoted, and I was fodder for the millions of salarymen and women who talked about me over drinks. Chung was aware of the rumors, and he would say, "Look, Lee. I didn't promote you. You promoted yourself! All those out there who talk about you and spread rumors about you don't know what they're talking about. So, don't listen to them." And he would laugh it off. When I was interviewed by the press, I was asked how I managed to get promoted so fast. I replied, "Let me just say that I deeply admire Chung Ju-yung for having the discernment to find the right people and the courage to appoint those people to the right place, at the right time."

The joy and excitement of getting a promotion tends to wear off when you get promoted once every year. But in 1975, when I was promoted to vice president, I was truly excited. The night I was promoted, I bought a bottle of wine and went to see an old friend. It was my good friend Chang-dae, with whom I had shared a room when I was trying to study so I could become a college dropout. It had been years since I had last seen him. Chang-dae ended up majoring in engineering and by then was working. We hugged each other warmly. Chang-dae said, "I saw the article today. Congratulations on your promotion!"

"Thanks," I said.

Chang-dae was beaming, "This is great! C'mon, let's have a drink and celebrate."

The two of us drank through the night. After finishing the bottle I had brought, we ordered another. We talked for hours. For the first time in many years, I was able to let down my guard. I realized I had a lot stored up. As I pulled back the layers one by one, I realized I was crying. Pretty soon, I couldn't stop. It was the first time since becoming an adult and starting work that I had cried in front of someone else. I thought of Mother and how proud she would have been to see me as vice president of such a large company. And I couldn't stop crying, thinking of her.

Chang-dae told me, "Go on, Myung-bak. Cry all you want. It's OK. I can only imagine what you had to go through, what you had to endure. I know you. I know you have a good heart. You're a good, honest, decent person. And I know how hard it must've been for you all these years! So it's OK, you can let it all out tonight. Go ahead, my friend, cry all you want."

And I did cry a lot that cold January night in 1975.

The Middle East

Korean construction companies began to tap into the Middle Eastern market beginning in 1974. Hyundai's experience in Thailand and Vietnam allowed it to become one of the front-runners in exploring new markets, including the Middle East. There was a desperate need as well. Many construction companies working in Vietnam were

pulling out as the Vietnam War intensified; they needed new markets, and they turned their eyes toward the Middle East. Also, the oil
shock of the previous year was devastating to the fledgling economy
and a stark reminder of its weakness and vulnerability. Nationalism
led to a spike in oil prices. Countries like Korea that imported almost
all of their energy from abroad were forced to make painful adjust-
ments. Foreign exchange reserves were depleted, and Korea was on
the brink of bankruptcy.

It was during these times that Hyundai and others stepped up.
The money these companies earned in the Middle East and the
remittance sent back home sustained Korea. Hundreds of thousands
of young Korean men weathered the desert heat and scorching sun,
working for their families, their companies, and their country. These
engineers, welders, and mechanics were true heroes. The companies
had a sense of mission, and they were all singular in their pursuit of
new markets. They were modern-day explorers and adventurers.

However, many were opposed when companies sought to enter
the Middle Eastern market, and Hyundai had its dissenters as well.
Chung Ju-yung and I were enthusiastic about this new venture, while
Chung In-yung[11] (younger brother of Chung Ju-yung) was vehemently
opposed. The younger Chung was skeptical, saying that Hyundai was
biting off more than it could chew. As our projects in the Middle East
got bigger, his opposition became stronger. He was concerned that
Hyundai would ultimately fail, just like the other Korean companies
that were continuously losing money in the Middle East.

When we decided to enter the bidding for the $150 million Arab
Shipbuilding and Repair Yard in Basra, Iraq, Chung In-yung came
down hard. He was then chairman of the Hyundai Construction
overseas division. This difference of opinion soon escalated into
internal discord, and each side squared off against the other. The
stand-off continued for a long time. Finally, when the bidding

proposal was completed, Chung Ju-yung urged the team to fly out immediately, while Chung In-yung ordered them to stay put. In the end, we won the contract, beating other world-renowned construction companies, and we successfully completed the project ahead of schedule. This marked the pinnacle of Korean overseas construction. Combined annual revenue of Korean construction companies at that time exceeded $10 billion.

The Jubail Industrial Harbor project became our crowning achievement and a testament to Korean industriousness and determination. This was a project of historic proportions, not only for Hyundai but for the future of the Korean economy. It marked a turning point for us. We were always trying to be creative. One idea that stunned the world was when we manufactured the steel structure of the harbor facilities at the Ulsan shipyard in Korea (later renamed Hyundai Heavy Industries) and then shipped it by barge all the way to the Arabian Peninsula. This cut costs, increased efficiency, and shortened delivery time.

Becoming CEO

With the completion of the Jubail project, morale was high at Hyundai and Hyundai Construction was on a roll. The company was growing and the country was expanding; it was a time of phenomenal growth, and the future was filled with promise and hope.

There was, however, a cloud over the jubilation. Chung In-yung decided to step aside. The brothers decided it was best to go their separate ways. The feud between the brothers, which became evident and intensified over the Arab shipyard project, took its toll. Chung In-yung left to head a separate subsidiary. This was no small shift in personnel; it was a disagreement at the highest level, which had reverberations throughout the company. Many who were loyal to Chung In-yung announced their intention to leave Hyundai to join him. There were rumors that Cho Sung-keun, who was president of the domestic division of Hyundai Construction, was also about to submit his resignation. The mood within the company was skittish.

One evening, Chung Ju-yung called me to his room. His face was grim. "It looks like we're going to have to make some personnel decisions at the top. I'm thinking of moving Chun and Kim to be senior executives and sending Kim as the site manager. What do you think?" He wasn't asking for my opinion; he had already made up his mind, I could tell. "And by the way, did you hear anything about Cho Sung-keun? What's he thinking?"

I pretended I hadn't heard anything worth reporting. This was because Cho was keeping quiet about what he intended to do, and I wasn't about to jump to conclusions.

Chung seemed about to say something else, but then he said, "Never mind. I'll see you tomorrow."

A couple of months later, when the new personnel decisions were about to be announced, I found out what Chung had wanted to say that night. As usual, Chung asked to see me in his office. After sharing some tea and talking about company matters, he said, "Well, now that Cho has left the company, who should I name as his successor?" I could tell he was feigning indecision, a habit of his that usually presages an important announcement. A second later, I found out what that important announcement was: he asked me to be the next president of Hyundai Construction.

I was, by then, quite used to getting promoted early (and some would say prematurely). However, this time I was really surprised. "Boss, I'm not experienced enough to assume such an important position," I said.

Chung replied, "There isn't anybody suitable. Vice President Kwon is an engineer, so he doesn't know anything about management. Sae-young and Soon-young [Chung Ju-yung's younger brothers] are involved in autos and cement, so both of them are out, and as for..."

I interrupted him, saying, "Sir, there are lots of people who have more experience than I do."

Chung shouted, "Well, damn it, then offer some alternatives! Don't you have any ambitions? You're a young man, what's wrong with you?" he grumbled.

Chung was determined. And I knew he hadn't made that decision overnight. I understood better than anyone how difficult that decision must have been. And that was why I refused. This wasn't just about enjoying the trust of the founder and being able to get any job done. It was about taking the helm of a world-class company that was also one of Korea's most lucrative and influential conglomerates.

Chung continued. "Look, Lee. What do you think a construction company is? Construction is a sophisticated industry. It involves all aspects of business, and so whoever succeeds in construction can do anything. But what's most important is recruiting and managing good people. I admit I overlooked that part. I thought all I needed to do was get the job done and make money. But that's not all. Now I know."

There had been recent labor disputes, intense strikes, and riots at overseas plants seemed to have had an effect on him. He was humbled and realized that he had underestimated the importance of having good people around.

He continued, "Lee, I know you. You know how to manage people. I'm asking you to take this job, if not for me, then for the company. Think about it."

This was the first time that Chung had actually asked for my opinion regarding my promotion. It was an offer that was

different from any previous promotions; he was asking me to take
on something that was completely different from what I had been
used to, Chung also understood very clearly that this decision
could affect the future of the group itself. I sensed his intensity
and felt his anguish.

Several days later, at the board of directors meeting, I was
appointed as president of Hyundai Construction domestic division. I
was thirty-five years old.

The hoopla following my appointment was more than I
expected. I'd been through this before, especially when I was
appointed vice president; now that I'd become president and CEO, I
knew what people would be saying about me. All sorts of rumors
started flying again. Some derisively dismissed my appointment, and
some were plainly disturbed. Older employees lamented that they
would have to work for a man many years younger than themselves.
And others were outright furious. Some gossiped that President Park
Chung-hee was the one who had pressured Chung to promote me.
The same thing was happening all over again, but this time it was
far more intense. The press was fueling it, and interview requests
poured in.

I was embarrassed and didn't know what to do. I couldn't get
myself to go to work. Some reporters staked out my home to get an
interview. I was unable to quietly sort things through. So my wife
and I decided to visit my hometown of Pohang to take some time off
and get away from all the commotion.

It was my first visit to Pohang in fifteen years, since I left in a
hurry without even attending my own high school graduation. I was
reminded of my life back then—the destitution, the uncertainty, the
pain, and most of all, the hunger. I decided then that I would relish
this opportunity and tackle the challenge head-on. I vowed that I
wasn't going to be just another CEO, comfortably ensconced in

luxury and simply approving whatever was brought to me. Instead, I was determined to make the best of it. But I was unaware of what lay ahead of me—it was beyond my imagination.

7 | MY MAY QUEEN

That night, I felt happy. I vowed to myself that I would make this woman happy. I also promised myself that I would do my best to make my mother proud. And I was thankful to Yoon-ok for trusting me.

In college, I had no time for any sort of leisure activities, and my circle of friends was very small. Of course, dating was something that I couldn't afford. Even after joining Hyundai, I still didn't have much money, so marriage was out of the question.

But when I became an executive at twenty-eight, people started asking me if I had a girlfriend and whether I was interested in getting married. I became a so-called catch in the marriage market, and matchmakers started calling me with prospective brides. They wanted to introduce me to young women from wealthy families and daughters of powerful politicians. Some even tried to introduce me to famous actresses. But I didn't feel rich or successful; on the contrary, I was somewhat intimidated by these women, who seemed to have lived a life completely different from mine.

Once, a woman in her early twenties called my office and asked to speak with me. She sounded desperate, so my secretary put her

through. When I answered the phone, the first thing she asked me
was, "Are you the real Lee Myung-bak?"

I said, "Yes, as a matter of fact I am."

She began sobbing and said, "I was swindled by a man who
said he was Lee Myung-bak. I would like to see you so I can find
out the truth."

I was worried; if what she said was true, that meant there was
someone who was pretending to be me. I agreed to meet her at the
lobby coffee shop.

She was an attractive twenty-something. She told me, "I met a
man who claimed he was you, Lee Myung-bak of Hyundai
Construction. I gave him everything I had, and even my parents bor-
rowed money when he told us he needed quick cash for his business. You *are* the real Lee Myung-bak, right?"

I told her, "Unfortunately, yes, I am the real Lee Myung-bak."

She kept sobbing. "Then you don't know that man?"

Unless an impostor asked for permission from the person he
impersonated, how could I possibly know who that guy was? I told
her, "Miss, I wish I could find out who he is. I'm sorry, I don't know.
Did he look anything like me?" She didn't say anything.

My wife, Kim Yoon-ok, and I were introduced by my high school
English teacher, who was particularly fond of me. He was friends
with Yoon-ok's older brother. What I liked most about Yoon-ok was
that she wasn't just someone from a rich family. Her father had been
a public servant with a reputation for being upright. She graduated
from Ewha Womans University in 1970—the year we got married—
and I later found out that she was once voted the school's May
Queen. She was pretty, but more importantly, she seemed like a
good person with a kind heart.

We weren't able to go out on too many dates. This was because
I was never able to make it on time because of work. Sometimes I

would have to call the coffee shop where we were supposed to meet and ask her to wait for me at a restaurant, but then I would be late for the dinner appointment as well. She ended up having dinner all by herself. This happened many times. There were days when I was unable to go at all, in which case I would ask my chauffeur to pick her up and drive her home.

When I finally decided that I wanted to marry her, I asked her to accompany me to my mother's grave. I wasn't sure if she would agree to go with me; it would be dark by the time we arrived. We hadn't gone out on many dates and we hadn't even talked about setting an engagement date. Luckily, she agreed.

When we arrived in front of my mother's grave, I bowed my head. I prayed. "Mom, it's me, your youngest son Myung-bak. I'm doing fine. I'm working at Hyundai, and I also worked in Thailand. Father's doing well. I wanted to introduce you to your youngest daughter-in-law. I hope you like her. If I hadn't gone to jail, you'd be alive today, and you'd be taken care of by her." I laid there in front of my mother's grave for quite a long time.

That night, I felt happy. I vowed to myself that I would make this woman happy. I also promised myself that I would do my best to make my mother proud. And I was thankful to Yoon-ok for trusting me. Yoon-ok never met my mother, but since that day, she has always been aware of my mother's presence. She would have been a terrific daughter-in-law. After we got married, Yoon-ok became a devout Christian, just like my mother.

Yoon-ok admitted to me long after we got married that when her friends saw me for the first time, they all exclaimed, "Yoon-ok! What's wrong with you? What are you doing marrying a man who looks like *that*!" Her friends were appalled that Yoon-ok, who was once voted one of the prettiest girls in school, ended up with a guy who looked like me. I fully understood their dismay. I had suffered from an "ugly face" complex since I was a young kid. Even my family readily admitted that I wasn't such a good-looking kid.

When I was a young accountant in Thailand, I became infatuated with a local Chinese maiden whose name was Chen Ling. She was the daughter of a Chinese merchant who lived near our office, and I was allowed to go and fetch water from his well. The only reason he allowed me entry was because he considered me trustworthy and safe.

After seeing Chen Ling from afar and becoming instantly smitten with her, I would go and fetch water all the time. I couldn't speak Chinese, and she couldn't speak Korean, so we communicated using broken English and hand signals. But we quickly became close friends, dating at the nearby tea house until her father found out and forbade us to see each other. (My water-drawing privilege was instantly revoked as well). I used to tell Chen Ling that I was too ugly for her. I told her seriously how I wished to go and get my eyes done so they would look bigger. She became upset whenever I confessed my complex, telling me that my eyes were perfectly fine and that I was a good-looking man. She was the first person who told me I was good-looking.

Compared to other bachelors I wasn't such a good catch in terms of my background either. After Yoon-ok agreed to marry me, she told me I had fooled her in two things. One was my education, and the other was my family background. On the former, she told me she never imagined a Korea University graduate could have graduated from a night-school high school. Regarding my family background, she told me that she knew my family was not well-off, but she had no idea we were *that poor*. My father was not able to offer any financial help when we got married.

But, with the cash gifts given to us at our wedding, we managed to find a tiny apartment. We had only the bare minimum of household appliances and furniture. We rented the apartment on a monthly basis. Hyundai laid carpet in that small apartment as a wedding gift. The carpet looked out of place, but we couldn't complain. Our sole source of income was my salary.

Every six months, our landlord would raise the rent, so we ended up moving eight times in three years. Until our second move, we would unpack, but after that we decided to unpack only what was necessary. By our seventh move, we only unpacked our spoons and chopsticks. I remember one time forgetting that we had moved, when I went to our previous home after work.

The first apartment we actually purchased was a small apartment built by the National Housing Corporation. It didn't have any premiums attached (Premiums are attached to apartments as they become popular. This is how apartments, properties, and villas are dealt with in Korea. In this case, the house was cheap so there was no premium attached), and we paid a down payment. The remainder was paid in installments over a period of fifteen years. Years later, we moved into a Hyundai apartment provided to us by the company.

One day I was told that there was a rumor in the area that "Lee Myung-bak of Hyundai Construction is living with a young mistress." When I first heard it, I brushed it aside. But when the rumor persisted for weeks, I felt the need to find out why such a rumor was spreading. I asked our company's administrative department to find out.

It turned out that since I went to work early in the morning, came home late, and was often overseas, my neighbors rarely got to see the president of Hyundai Construction in person. And many of them assumed that the president would be in his mid-fifties at least and that his wife would be in her mid-forties or thereabouts. So when some people discovered that my wife was only twenty-nine, they found it hard to believe. Whenever my wife would go outside holding our daughter's hand, people would say, "Is she really the wife of Lee?" This led some people to speculate that she wasn't my real wife, but my mistress. The rumors finally stopped after people became aware of my age and saw my photo in the newspapers.

Another time, I became "involved" with a fictional woman on television. A television drama loosely based on my life, called *Ambition*, was on the air. My character in the drama was a married man who was still seeing his girlfriend from college. This led many viewers to confuse fiction with reality. My wife was often approached by these concerned viewers, who asked her why she was letting her husband see his old girlfriend. My wife told them it was not true and had to explain that it was just a television show.

Still, Yoon-ok was often confused herself. When I arrived home one night, she asked me coldly where I'd been. I didn't understand why she would all of a sudden ask me such an obvious question. I told her, "Where do you think? I was at work, of course." Later on I found out why—that night's episode had my character coming home after seeing his old girlfriend at a hotel. Just by sheer coincidence, I came home at exactly the same time the television character came home (on the program), and Yoon-ok was momentarily confused.

The "college girlfriend" in the drama was not entirely fictional. The character was based on a real person, but the last time I'd seen her was years before I got married. She was a girl I met right after I was rejected by the military. We went to the same church. Since I had no money, she would be the one to buy noodles or movie tickets whenever we met. (I later found out that she was the daughter of a high-ranking public official.)

On Sundays, she would often come over to my house and ask that we go and watch a movie. She was able to afford a taxi, but she always took the bus and ate cheap noodles, for my sake. She expected me to ask her out when my school had what they called a "couple's party"; I had no intention of attending the party and so I never asked her out. She was quite angry at me for some time.

On her birthday, she asked me to take her out to dinner. It was her attempt at making up. I agreed, and we went to a fancy restaurant downtown. It was a Japanese restaurant. We were taken to a private room upstairs. I assumed it was a restaurant that she and her family went to often. But to me everything was unfamiliar, nothing more so than the menu. I'd never heard of *sukiyaki* in my life, but that's what she ordered. The waiter brought a small bowl with raw egg in it and placed it in front of me. I looked at it then gulped it down. The waiter brought another one and again placed it in front of me. Without thinking, I gulped it down (I always liked eggs). Realizing that I had no clue how to eat *sukiyaki*, she demonstrated by mixing the egg in the bowl and explained that I was supposed to dip the food into the bowl.

I was embarrassed, but what disturbed me more was the bill. I kept worrying how I was going to pay it. I was nervous throughout the meal. When we were done, she waited for me outside. I looked at the bill; there was no way I was going to be able to pay it. I handed the cashier my wristwatch as collateral (a practice that was readily accepted in cheap restaurants and bars near colleges where there were other students like me who had no money). The cashier gave me a crooked smile and handed back my watch, which was full of scratches and green with mold.

Feeling miserable, I went out to her and told her the truth; I told her I would pay her back if she would pay for the meal. She was more than happy to do so, but after that I felt more uncomfortable seeing her. I paid her back later by giving the money to a mutual friend.

When I was jailed for leading the student demonstrations during the June 3 Movement, she would leave her house early in the morning to come visit me in prison. When her father found out that his daughter was seeing one of the student leaders jailed for inciting rebellion, he was furious. She was soon forced into engagement and prohibited from seeing me. When I was released from jail, I looked around to see if she was among those who were waiting to welcome me. She wasn't there. Later, I ran into her in a coffee shop. As soon as she saw me, she started to cry. "I got engaged because I couldn't disobey my parents. But if you tell me to, I'll run away." I couldn't. We never met again after that.

Yoon-ok took care of our four children by herself. My three daughters and youngest son rarely saw me when they were growing up. I was never there for my wife when she gave birth to them. When I became president of Hyundai Construction, I stayed overseas most of the time or was busy at the office working. Our family never went on a family vacation. One time I went to visit my hometown with my wife, but this was to give myself some time to think about work; another time our family went to an island resort, but this was so that I could think about what to do next after leaving Hyundai. Both instances ended up being respites for me, but not true family vacations.

Nonetheless, all my children tell others that I'm an attentive father. Their teachers, who never got to see me, found that odd. I never went to parent-teacher meetings or attended their recitals or gave them rides to school. I never brought them any gifts when I came back from overseas business trips. (I did give them the toiletry bags that airlines provide to their first- and business-class passengers. Until they realized that the toiletry bag was free, my kids thought I bought those for them as presents.)

The secret to being called a considerate dad was knowing my children's schedules at all times. Before going on long overseas trips, I would ask my wife for the detailed schedules of all the kids. The list contained all the important details; for example, the dates of exams and school outings, who their friends were and what their parents did, and so on. I would call them from abroad and ask them how they had done on their tests; I would ask them specifically how they had done on certain tests, since I knew which tests they took. The children would be astonished that their father knew everything. I would ask them about their friends as well. But I would only ask them about friends I knew were good kids. I would ask them if their friends' parents were doing OK.

I would never tell my children what kinds of friends to hang out with; I would only ask them continuously about the good kids and show interest in them. Over time, my children would know that I was interested only in their decent friends, and they ended up hanging out with them only.

I never told my children to be friends with parents who were rich or influential. As all parents, I wanted them to be friends with those who came from honest, hard-working, decent families.

I also never told Yoon-ok to do this or that for the children. I know what my wife had to endure raising four kids on her own. I know I didn't earn any right to dictate how to raise our children. My only duty was to support my wife and to try to be a caring, loving dad to my children whenever I could. I'm grateful to all my children for understanding my not being there for them. Most of all, I'm deeply thankful to Yoon-ok—my May Queen—for bearing it all.

Yoon-ok and I married on December 19, 1970. My birthday is December 19, so I proposed to Yoon-ok that we get married on that day so I would never forget our wedding anniversary. It was a clever idea. I never once forgot to send her flowers and a handwritten note on our wedding anniversary.

8 | A NEW ERA

Now, I was really ready to dive into my new job. There was nothing I could do about the rumors except prove them wrong.

CEO

If the public was surprised by my appointment as CEO, the Korean business community greeted the news with concern. Many of them knew what I was capable of, but they were nonetheless concerned that Hyundai Construction was too big for me to handle. Some were predicting that Chung Ju-yung had gone too far this time and that my appointment would be the beginning of the company's slow but certain decline.

After being appointed CEO, I was invited to speak at a seminar hosted by the national association for human resource management. Those in charge of personnel at private companies were also invited. Many of the participants that day were intrigued by the newly appointed thirty-five-year-old CEO and were keen to hear what I had to say. I thought it was a good opportunity for me to explain the reason behind my "sudden" rise and to offer my own business philosophy and vision for the future.

"I am fully aware that many of you are surprised at my appointment as president," I began. "As you know, I am only thirty-five years old. I know that I have a lot to learn. But I've dedicated my life to making my company successful and I am proud that I was able to take part in the development of my country. As for my appointment as the president of Hyundai Construction, I assure you that the decision by Mr. Chung Ju-yung was not an impromptu decision nor one made in haste."

I looked at the participants. "It was a decision that reflected the changing times that we live in today. Our economy was one that relied on foreign aid and outside assistance; it was all about development. But now, we are living in a new era, one where innovation and entrepreneurship is called for. The world is moving toward globalization and improving the quality of life; we must be prepared and answer these calls. And the first thing to do is to hire specialists. If we wish to change the way we do business, we must first put the right people in place. No longer is the founder or the CEO alone able to make the necessary decisions on time and implement them. We need specialized and highly structured organizations that can efficiently adapt to the current trends and predict the future."

I closed my remarks with, "I believe this is the reason Mr. Chung Ju-yung appointed me as president of Hyundai Construction. Like I said, I am fully aware of the concerns about my appointment and the rumors circulating about me, saying that I will soon be kicked out or that Hyundai will go under. Well, I intend to prove them wrong. I intend to show that unfounded rumors are just that: unfounded rumors." The crowd applauded, and I felt a bit of relief to have gotten this off my chest. Now, I was really ready to dive into my new job. There was nothing I could do about the rumors except prove them wrong.

Competition

Coinciding with my appointment as the youngest-ever president of Hyundai Construction, that year the Hyundai Group overtook Samsung[12] as Korea's number one conglomerate. This was a significant achievement, since Samsung had reigned as the indisputable leader of Korean industry for many years. Until then, it was unimaginable to think that Samsung would fall to second place. But it was our venture into the Middle East that altered the business landscape and our standing within it. Hyundai was already established in the Middle East, while Samsung was never quite able to get involved. As a result, Samsung was finally overtaken by Hyundai. It was humiliating for Samsung and a significant victory for Hyundai.

However, Hyundai becoming number one and Samsung falling into second place was more than just switching places. The country was reeling in the aftershock of the first Arab oil embargo. To overcome this crisis, Hyundai went out and brought back much-needed revenue that helped the country weather the storm. At one point during the height of the crisis, Korea's foreign exchange reserve fell to less than $30 million. Samsung was noticeably absent throughout the ordeal. As such, the rivalry between Hyundai and Samsung took on a new meaning and became far more intense. For Samsung, Hyundai was now a formidable foe. And sometimes the rivalry got personal. As a way to dampen the winning streak, Samsung declared war against Hyundai using its daily newspaper, the *Joong-ang Ilbo*[13]. They opened fire. Hyundai responded. It turned out to be an embarrassing public spat between the top two conglomerates in Korea. It was a story of abuse of power, corporate responsibility, business ethics, and of course, personal egos.

In February 1980, *Joong-ang Ilbo* ran a front-page story with the headline, "Hyundai Construction Blamed for Shoddy Construction; Underground Tunnel at Gimpo International Airport Riddled with Faulty Work." Soon after it ran another story under the banner: "Full Story Behind Hyundai Construction's Poor Work at the Petroleum Storage Tank at Onsan Industrial Complex." Both articles were blatant and biased attacks against Hyundai, making it seem as if Hyundai Construction was second-rate and, worse, lacking expertise and integrity. We filed an official complaint to the newspaper, but we received no response. We were denied any opportunity to explain our position or refute the stories.

So we fought back by running a massive newspaper ad campaign. Our ads raised questions about the integrity of the publisher of *Joong-ang Ilbo*, Hong Jin-ki: what he did as a high-ranking cabinet member during the Syngman Rhee era, and his ties to Samsung and its founder Lee Byung-chull, as well as his questionable and shady conduct as a businessman. The ads ran in almost all the major newspapers except *Joong-ang Ilbo*.

In return, Samsung retaliated with full force. It circulated a memo to all its employees titled, "Why Samsung Is Fighting Hyundai," and carried out a PR offensive.

We fought back, but only Chung Ju-yung, Song Yoon-jae of our Strategic Management Office, and I were involved. Everyone else was prohibited from taking part in what was turning out to be a nasty fight. While running our ad campaign, we made our position clear: we will stop only if Lee Byung-chull issues a formal and public apology. But we knew Lee Byung-chull wasn't going to give in so easily; this was now a war between two gigantic egos.

Our fight generated so much public debate that the National

Council for State Security got involved (this council was created to ensure social stability; in other words, its main job was monitoring anti-state activities). The chief of the National Council, Kwon Jung-dal, summoned me and suggested that we find an amicable solution and end this public spectacle. He also went on to assure me that Samsung would no longer attack Hyundai. I said to Kwon, "Why are *you* telling me that Samsung will no longer slander Hyundai? We want Lee Byung-chull to apologize. We don't need the government to apologize to us."

Kwon replied, "As long as somebody takes responsibility and apologizes, then it's over. Why are you demanding that Lee Byung-chull apologize?"

I replied, "It's because even if everyone over at Samsung agrees to never slander Hyundai again, Lee Byung-chull can overrule them just like that. You know that, and we know that. There is no one at Samsung who can assume responsibility other than Lee Byung-chull himself. *That's* why we're demanding an apology from him."

Kwon became irritated, and he raised his voice. "Stop it! You guys have fought enough. It's no good for either of you to keep on fighting like this!"

It was my turn to raise my voice. "No, you listen to me. Think of what this means for the country. If we let this pass, what kind of message are you sending the people? And what about the role of the press? You can't let the press off the hook like that! You can't continue to let companies like Samsung use their own newspapers to attack their competitors to settle scores and make profits. Look, the articles about Hyundai are factually incorrect and blown out of proportion; they don't warrant front-page headlines. Think also about the future of the Korean press. What do you think the journalists are saying about all this?"

I continued to vent my frustrations at Kwon. While I was arguing, my colleague who had accompanied me—Song Yoon-jae from the Strategic Management Office—stepped hard on my foot beneath the desk to tell me to stop. Back then, the National Council was one of the most feared state institutions around; when you were summoned, you made very sure to answer questions cordially and tried to be as docile as possible. So as I vented, he stepped on my foot repeatedly to get me to stop, and it hurt. I turned to Song and said, "Stop stepping on my foot! What's wrong with you? I'm going to say what needs to be said." I continued, "Unless Lee Byung-chull agrees to meet with Chung Ju-yung and apologizes, we're going to run the ads as planned."

Kwon said, "Look, Lee Byung-chull isn't even in Korea, so how do you expect him to meet Chung and apologize?"

I was surprised. "What do you mean? We know he's in Korea."

"He's in Japan. He took the noon flight."

I checked my watch; it was not yet noon. "It's not even noon yet! How is it possible he's already in Japan?"

Kwon said, "He's in Japan. Look, that's not important. We don't want this to continue. So put a stop to it. I *mean* it. I trust you'll make the right decision and act responsibly."

"That's up to them."

With this, we left the Council and went back to the office. Once we got back, Lee Kun-hee (son of Lee Byung-chull and current chairman of Samsung) was on the phone. He wished to speak with me. Lee Kun-hee said, "Mr. Kim Deok-bo of Dongyang Broadcasting Company will be there to see you. I'd appreciate it if you would talk with him and settle this matter."

I told Lee Kun-hee, "I don't know who Kim Deok-bo is, and this doesn't concern him."

Lee said, "Kim Deok-bo represents the interest of Samsung, and he is in a position to make the necessary decisions."

It was becoming obvious that it was futile to keep insisting on a direct apology from Lee Byung-chull. We found out that Lee Byung-chull was already in Japan. We couldn't force him to come back. We reluctantly accepted their offer for a meeting.

At 5 a.m. the next day, we went to the Chosun Hotel in central Seoul. We wanted to keep the meeting a secret. Kim Deok-bo and Hong Jin-kee, the publisher of *Joong-ang Ilbo*, were representing Samsung. From our side, it was just me and Chung Ju-yung.

As soon as he sat down, Chung started to fume. His ire was primarily directed at Hong Jin-kee. He pointed out the nature of the construction business and explained that projects of such scale inevitably had cracks and that such mistakes were common and always fixable. Chung thought it outrageous that journalists who didn't know a thing about construction were writing articles accusing Hyundai of negligence; to him this was degrading.

As Chung continued, Hong Jin-kee stopped him and said, "Chairman Chung, I am not familiar with the technicalities of the construction business, so I'm afraid your explanations aren't quite necessary at this point. And besides, we're not here to talk about construction, right?"

The mood turned awkward, and the four of us sat there without saying a word. After a while, I decided to speak. Chung didn't say anything, which was his way of telling me to go on. "First of all, many people are critical of large companies owning and operating newspapers. However, I disagree. In fact, I think it's a good thing. If a company like Samsung owns a newspaper, there is a high probability that that newspaper will have a better understanding of and appreciation for business. But, the problem is that the newspaper you own is giving business a bad name and hurting the entire business community by writing articles that are false and misleading. It's giving us a bad reputation for all the wrong reasons, and all of us are suffering as a result. What's more disturbing is that your newspaper has turned into a mouthpiece for Samsung. That's disgraceful for any reputable news organization! Chairman Chung just talked about the difficulties and nature of the construction industry, and I must add that we can offer convincing evidence to refute your claims, if given a fair chance. If you, as a newspaper publisher, signed off on the story knowing that the article contained facts that were questionable, then I'm afraid you've let down the entire profession and sacrificed your journalistic integrity. For this alone, I think you should apologize, Chairman Hong."

As soon as I finished, Chairman Hong straightened in his seat and bowed to me with utmost courtesy. I was taken aback. "Mr. Lee, I have heard a lot about you. I'm glad that we finally met." Hong then said, "What you just said is quite true. As a publisher, I must thank you for enlightening me. Thank you."

I was mindful that what Hong Jin-kee said could be taken the wrong way by Chung—he might feel insulted. I told him the reason I talked about journalistic integrity was only because Chung Ju-yung had already pointed out the technical aspects.

Hong Jin-kee admitted that things could have been handled differently, and he bowed again, which made me uneasy. Then Kim Deok-bo said, "The country's facing a lot of challenges. It's important that our two companies get along and work with each other so that we can help our country. The government and the people are unhappy to see us fighting like this. Let's stop this and move on."

Chung remained quiet. There was nothing more to talk about. Chung and I shook hands with them and left.

The feud between Hyundai and Samsung came to an end. Two of Korea's leading conglomerates mended fences and went back to business. As for Chung Ju-yung and Lee Byung-chull, the two towering tycoons of Korean business, they didn't exactly become friends, but they weren't enemies either. They met occasionally to talk about business and other matters. The sense of rivalry didn't disappear, though. Every year, both companies would await the annual announcements regarding company performance and revenues and then compare the other's to their own. Later on, Hyundai would start its own business in semiconductors and electronics while Samsung invested in construction and shipbuilding. (Samsung also started its own automobile business, manufacturing its SM line of vehicles, which it later sold to Nissan-Renault.) Competition between the two groups continued, and at times it led to ugly public disputes. But overall, competition spurred innovation and led to positive growth.

Founder's Son and the Salaryman CEO

In early 1980, Chung Mong-pil, who was head of our London branch and the eldest son of Chung Ju-yung, was appointed executive director of the overseas division at Hyundai Construction, a position that reported to me. It was an odd pairing; one the eldest son of the founder and presumptive heir to the throne, the other a salaryman[14] who rose to become CEO. Since Hyundai had many subsidiaries, it would have been easy to prevent such an uncomfortable union. Chung Mong-pil could have been given charge of a smaller subsidiary. I sensed Chung Ju-yung had something else in mind, but I didn't ask.

Whatever Chung Ju-yung's intentions were, I'm sure Mong-pil had a hard time. His younger brothers were already in charge of other companies by then. He was "just" an executive director. I found out later that mid-level managers also were going through some tough times, stuck between me and Mong-pil. I wasn't surprised, but I was annoyed that it took so long for the managers to confess their troubles.

When one of the managers cautiously told me about the

situation, he said he was doing so out of loyalty to the company. I could immediately tell he was deeply uncomfortable even talking about it. I could imagine how hard it must've been for him to bring it to me. The manager explained that ever since Mong-pil had been appointed executive director, he had given the mid-level managers a hard time by holding up memos that needed my approval or questioning decisions that I had already approved. When Mong-pil was told of my decisions, he would either ignore my directives or tell the managers to carry out his decisions instead. This behavior was causing a lot of confusion among the managers, dampening morale, and slowing down business. It was also a direct challenge to my authority, which I wasn't about to condone. I thanked the manager and told him that I wouldn't tell anyone, including Mong-pil, what he had told me.

The next day, I asked Mong-pil to come to my office. He came, but only after taking his time; he was clearly not pleased at being told what to do. As soon as he sat down, I got straight to the point. "Mr. Chung, what I am about to say isn't personal; it's official business between the president and his executive director. I hope you understand this very clearly." We sat across from each other, and I went on, "I recently found out, to my dismay, that you have been questioning my decisions, thereby causing a lot of confusion among the staff. I can easily imagine the staff, especially the managers, trying to please both of us at the same time, which in my opinion is both unnecessary and wrong. This can't go on. This is no way to run a company as big as ours. I know that you are slated to move on to bigger, more important positions. One day, you're going to be chairman of the Hyundai Group, and before that, you're most likely to become chairman of one of the subsidiaries. But right now, you work for me. Your job is to be truthful, to give me good advice, and in the end, to follow whatever decisions I make as president. If you don't want to, then I suggest you take it up with Chung Ju-yung and ask that you be transferred to a different company."

Mong-pil was listening intently. I continued. "I'm younger than you, but I have far more experience than you. Just look at the number of years and the effort that I have put into this company. I'm one of the founding members belonging to your father's generation, not yours. When you assume chairmanship one day, I'll be one of those retiring along with your father and his generation. So, I hope you will grant me the respect I deserve and understand where I am coming from. How you wish to proceed from now on is entirely up to you."

Mong-pil said, "Thank you, I understand."

After some time, I summoned the manager who had first informed me of the uneasy situation. I asked him how things were going. The manager told me that everybody was perplexed by how much Mong-pil had changed. He asked me if something had happened between us. I told the manager, "No, nothing happened."

After his time at Hyundai Construction, Mong-pil was promoted to chairman of the Incheon Steel Company. Soon thereafter, Mong-pil began to blossom as a businessman. Sadly, he was killed in a car accident while driving back to Seoul from Ulsan after inspecting one of the company factories. We found out that he wanted to come back during the night so he could attend to other business early in the morning. It was a devastating loss, for Hyundai and especially for Chung Ju-yung. News of the tragic accident reached Chung while he was in the United States on business. Chung decided he couldn't attend the funeral of his eldest son; the unflappable leader was shattered. In his absence, I was designated to represent Chung Ju-yung and was put in charge of the funeral arrangements.

Shadows

A company can't win all the time. As they say in Korea, "Big trees cast big shadows." On July 6, 1978, President Park Chung-hee was elected to his third term under the Yushin constitution[15]. But instead of this ignominious event making the top news, another headline was on the front page of all the major newspapers: "Hyundai Apartment Caught Giving Special Favors to Select Would-Be Owners." This was the "Hyundai Apartment scandal" that rocked Korean society; it became emblematic of the relationship that conglomerates, government, and special interests have had and which the ordinary people came to detest.

Normally, such a situation would not be considered scandalous enough to be treated as front-page news (and the facts were bent way out of shape as well). But public mood regarding President Park's reelection was extremely hostile. People were seething. Many were fed up with his increasingly dictatorial style of rule and wanted change. So when the Hyundai scandal broke out, the government had found the perfect diversion. The press was told to fuel the flames, and soon the people had shifted their anger and frustration toward those "greedy and corrupt" businessmen.

The government made sure the people stayed angry. They immediately began investigations into the incident and indicted scores of people: High-ranking officials and bank executives were either indicted or jailed; several prominent journalists were publically harangued and many had to quit their jobs; famous artists were named in the inquiry and their reputations sullied as they were dragged through the mud. As for Hyundai, Chung Ju-yung's son, Chung Mong-koo[16], who was then chairman of the Korea Urban Development Company, was jailed along with one of his associates. Soon the government ordered the shutdown of the Korea Urban Development Company.

The incident had its origins back in 1976, when I was running the machinery plant. The Hyundai apartment complex today lines the southern side of the Han River, which traverses Seoul from west to east. Today, it is considered one of the prime real estate areas in Seoul, with many luxurious apartments, condos, and villas situated there. But when Hyundai first started to develop this area, it was nothing but barren, windy land dotted with small plots for growing vegetables. Hyundai purchased this land and, beginning in the mid-1970s, started to build apartments there. Apartments until then were considered mass-housing projects and a way for the government to alleviate the housing shortage. Koreans have always been traditional house dwellers, and so apartments did not appeal to them. Plus, these apartments were simple and crude; they had almost no modern amenities or comforts and were considered impersonal. They resembled giant matchboxes stacked one on top of the other. People called them ugly. And they were.

However, based on my idea, Hyundai tried to turn that perception around by building modern, comfortable, and aesthetically pleasant apartments. Hyundai's subsidiary—Korea Urban Development Company—was to oversee the operation, and Hyundai Construction was in charge of the construction work. I thought that it would be the trend of the future. We sought to attract would-be homeowners to invest in these apartments by constructing desirable homes. And we were confident that we would succeed and that people would appreciate this new culture.

We were wrong. When we began advertising our apartments to prospective buyers, the application rate was absolutely dismal. No one seemed interested. Now, today, buying a home is a cumbersome process with financial background checks, requirements that call for guarantors, and so on. However, back then the process was fairly simple. Yet the boom never caught on. Also, the apartments were the only things standing on what seemed like barren land; the location was considered monstrous and an eyesore. People were saying, "What *is* that? How do you expect us to live *there?*"

As applications dwindled to almost nothing, the company had to do something to attract buyers. So we changed the payment scheme to allow for deferred payments. When this didn't have much effect, we offered extraordinary incentives to make the units more accessible and affordable. But still prospective buyers did not appear.

We then changed our plans; we started courting the wealthiest individuals and encouraged them to invest. These people with money to spare started showing interest. Many of them approached us seeking more favorable conditions. Initially, Chung and I rejected such approaches, but then we figured it wouldn't be bad to have well-known and prominent figures investing in the apartments. Having such individuals residing in our apartments would increase the property's value and showcase our new model of modern living. We took our new strategy a step further by reaching out to public officials and journalists we knew through our business and encouraging them to invest. Artists who were close with Chung were also asked whether they would be interested. All of this was perfectly legal, and there were no problems. Only when the apartment boom started a year or two later did the troubles begin.

With apartments springing up all across Seoul, investors and buyers started to realize that apartments were attractive investments. And word began spreading that apartments were not only good investments, but much more comfortable to live in than traditional homes. Demand exploded. Premiums were added to the original price.

Then something unexpected happened: people started to question the fairness of the Hyundai apartment sales that had taken place the year before. People started calling it "unfair practice" and accused us of being unethical. Our promotional efforts suddenly became "special favors." The government was more than willing to stoke the fire, and that was how it became a scandal.

After the scandal broke, the Minister for Construction, Shin Hyung-shik, summoned Chung to his office, and he ordered Chung to bring me with him. I had an uneasy relationship with Shin Hyung-shik, dating back to 1976, when Hyundai Construction beat out Yulsan Construction, a small and inexperienced construction company, to win the contract to build houses in Jubail, Saudi Arabia.

When Korean companies first started to enter the Middle East market, Kim Jae-kyu (the same person who later shot and killed President Park Chung-hee) was Minister for Construction. He feared that allowing too many Korean companies to participate in the Middle East market could backfire, so he gave orders limiting the number of construction companies to ten. Only these select ten were given the right to participate in the bidding for overseas construction projects. When Kim Jae-kyu became Chief of Intelligence, Shin Hyung-shik was appointed the new Minister for Construction. Shin was a politician with considerable clout, and he enjoyed flaunting it. The first thing Shin did was increase the number of allowed companies to thirty.

Now, it wouldn't matter if the number was increased to three hundred as long as all of them had the necessary skills and the capacity to undertake overseas projects. More Korean companies meant more revenues, and that was good for everyone. Unfortunately, many construction companies in the expanded group were far from capable of building factories and plants in the middle of the Arabian desert. Yulsan was one of them.

During a meeting held at the Ministry of Construction where representatives of companies operating overseas were gathered, I raised this issue. Shin Hyung-shik was running the meeting. When I took the floor, I said, "First of all, please don't think that I'm trying to restrict my colleagues from doing business overseas. What I wanted to mention is that some of these companies that earned the license to go abroad do not possess what it takes. With all due respect, some of these companies aren't capable of winning contracts here in Korea!" I was being honest. "Now, if we are to send such companies abroad and let them take part in the bidding process, I'm afraid we will undermine our own efforts, bring disgrace to our country, and make fools out of ourselves."

Minister Shin scowled at me and said angrily, "Mr. Lee, the Middle East market is going through a tremendous boom. The government believes it is in the country's best interest to fully utilize this golden opportunity by allowing as many companies as possible to go out there and win contracts." Then he added menacingly, "Watch what you say, Mr. Lee. I think you've become a bit too arrogant for being lucky."

I wasn't bothered by what he said, but I felt the need to make myself clear. I again emphasized that my intention was not to limit companies from earning these rights.

As I got up to leave, I told the director general at the Ministry of Construction to record everything I said in the meeting. "Write down everything I said today, because this is going to be a huge headache for you when countries start filing complaints against you and these so-called construction companies. Remember that."

My concerns proved correct. When Hyundai Construction was preparing to submit its bid for the housing project at Jubail, Saudi Arabia, Yulsan decided to compete against us. The project was a turnkey order, and it was awarded to Hyundai. Yulsan came in second. But the Ministry of Construction determined that Hyundai's price was too low and feared that it might bring charges of dumping (selling your products or submitting a bidding price that is abnormally cheaper than your competitors in order to "dump" your products or win the bid). On this reasoning, the Ministry tried to impose restrictions. I had no choice but to prove that everything was done by the book and that our price was adequate. If Hyundai lost the contract because of dumping accusations, then Yulsan, as runner-up, would be the winner.

I could tell that Minister Shin had a favorable disposition toward this company Yulsan. I had no idea why, though. As I was contemplating what to do next, I was shocked when I got a chance to review Yulsan's bidding documents. Yulsan's paper listed Hyundai's achievements as if *they* had accomplished them. The list contained the Gori Nuclear Power Plant and the Soyang River Dam project, which were enormous projects that Hyundai carried out to much acclaim. It was preposterous that Yulsan would be so bold as to falsify their documents. I immediately went to Minister Shin and objected, but his answer was even more appalling. "Mr. Lee, it's already done, so let's not make such a big fuss out of it. If you keep raising this issue, it's just going to reflect badly on all of us. Drop it."

While our own Ministry of Construction was obfuscating the facts, the Saudi government hired outside consultants from the IBRD to look into the matter. As the experts from the IBRD were checking the documents, they noticed that many of Hyundai's and Yulsan's projects overlapped, and that some of them were even identical. The IBRD was already familiar with Hyundai, since we had carried out many projects together in Southeast Asia. In the end, Yulsan was disqualified for falsifying legal documents and dropped from the bidding altogether. Minister Shin then accused Hyundai of telling the Saudis about Yulsan. And he thought I was the one who had done it. Shin met with Chung and threatened him. "Get rid of Lee Myung-bak or send him to another subsidiary. As long as I'm the minister in charge of construction, don't even think about keeping him on as president. If Lee Myung-bak is president, I assure you, Hyundai's going to pay for it." When Chung told me about this little incident, he laughed. Obviously, Minister Shin's out-rage didn't work on Chung.

So when Chung and I met with Minister Shin following the Hyundai Apartment scandal, he was sitting in his office and seemed extremely agitated. As soon as we sat down, he rattled off a list of what we had done wrong and how we had made mistakes. I realized I had been mistaken before about Shin's mood—he wasn't agitated, he was enjoying himself. Then he gave us an ultimatum: "Dismantle the Korean Urban Development Company voluntarily. And do it today. I expect you to announce your decision by holding a press conference at five o'clock this afternoon." He then had one of his staff bring him a prepared statement that he had "kindly" written up, and handed it to Chung.

Chung, with our "statement" in hand, asked, "Mr. Minister, are these orders coming from you or are they coming from the president?"

Shin pointed his right index finger toward the ceiling and said, "This is the president's wish. So make sure you carry it out." As we got up to leave, Minister Shin said to me, "Hey, Mr. Lee. What do you think of all this?"

I knew that Shin wanted me to be there just so that he could tell me the news to my face. I answered him, "You already made the decision, and my boss already accepted. Why do you want to know what I think? It doesn't really matter what I think. And besides, I'm not even in charge of the Korea Urban Development Company."

Shin smirked. "That's *precisely* why I'm asking you, since what-ever you say isn't going to change anything." He was thoroughly enjoying this.

"Well," I said, "since you asked, let me tell you how I feel about all this. I'm against dismantling the company. A company is a legal entity. If a company erred, then the one in charge should be held accountable, not the entire company. If we were to get rid of a company for every

mistake, then I'm afraid we wouldn't have many companies left standing." Chung was standing next to me with his hands folded behind his
back. I continued, "Take a look at those foreign companies whose histories go back one hundred, two hundred years. They've been around
that long because the rules were abided by. They were allowed to make
mistakes, take responsibility, and improve. I thought we were living in a
free-market economy. But if the government keeps doing this, I don't
think there'll be any company that could last ten years."

Even before I was finished, Shin said, "Young man, you don't
know what you're talking about. People like you will sacrifice the
big fish so that you can save the small stuff."

I let out a sigh and said, "Mr. Minister, I didn't intend to say anything. It's only because you asked me for my opinion. Like I said,
you've already made up your mind, and my boss agreed. What's
there to lose? I don't have any big fish or small stuff to lose."

Minister Shin abruptly got up and said, "I expect you to give
that press conference at five p.m. today at the Ministry." Then he
dismissed us.

As we were getting in our car, I told Chung that something was
not right; the order didn't look like it was coming directly from the
president. I suggested we go see the president's secretary for audit
and inspection, Kim Young-joon (he later became head of the
Board of Audit and Inspection). We were able to see him at the
Blue House, the president's office. At first, Kim Young-joon thought
the matter was closed. But as we continued talking, he nodded and
said that it was worth looking into. He assured us that he would
take a closer look. He promised to let us know if there were any
new developments.

We returned to our office and reluctantly began getting ready for
the press conference. After an hour, Kim Young-joon called back to
inform us that the matter had been reported to the president and

that the president's instruction was to not dismantle the company. Kim Young-joon told me that my argument had worked. He told me that the Ministry of Construction would also be informed of the president's decision.

It was now Minister Shin who called me. He wished to see me immediately, and this time Shin wanted me to come alone. So I went to his office. When I entered, Shin seemed a wreck. His smugness was gone. He was distraught and asked me what had happened. I told him everything. Minister Shin was resigned. "You shouldn't have done that." But it was all over. Chung Mong-koo, who had been jailed over the scandal, was found not guilty and released.

In the end, we didn't have anyone to blame but the unexpected boom that instigated all this drama. But the government accusing us of fraud—for whatever reason—was difficult to swallow. The scandal remained a permanent scar for the company.

9 | THE RULES OF THE GAME

"No one, absolutely no one, knows you're here with us. And remember: until you tell us what we want to know, you're not leaving this room."

Last Meeting with President Park Chung-hee

My "relationship" with President Park Chung-hee was, to be honest, exaggerated. One reason for this was my rapid rise within Hyundai. My promotions at Hyundai always caused a sensation, which led many people to speculate. Not finding any convincing explanation for my success, people started saying that the president was my backer. This seemed to satisfy everyone, and to many people, it seemed like the only plausible answer. So the rumors continued. Besides, who was going to verify such a rumor?

Another reason rumors linking me with President Park abounded had to do with our looks. During my early twenties, my friends called me "Little Park" since I resembled him so much. Whenever my friends called me that, I would say, "Guys, I'm taller than he is, so stop calling me 'Little Park.'" As I grew older, I became famous for my long work hours, as was President Park. People found us to be similar, so the rumors about President Park being my backer persisted.

But Park Chung-hee was the one responsible for my time in jail, and he (or his policies, to be more precise) was the one who made it so hard for me to find a job after graduation. So for people to assume that he was supporting me seemed ironic.

The last time I saw President Park Chung-hee was exactly six days before he was assassinated[17]. On that day, I was told to present myself at the president's office. It was completely unexpected, and I didn't know why I was being called. All I was told was that the meeting was scheduled for four in the afternoon. I was told to arrive at Sejong Cultural Center (located ten minutes from the president's office) by ten a.m. I found out I wasn't the only one summoned. About twenty people were gathered at the Sejong Center. I noticed newspaper publishers and civic leaders, among others. I was the only one from the business sector. So I figured we were all there to represent the various segments of society.

The idea of the meeting came from Cha Chi-chul, President Park's notorious chief of security[18].

The purpose of the meeting was to reassure and console the president by forcing figures from various fields to say good things about the state of affairs and the president. It was, in short, an infantile attempt by Cha Chi-chul to win points with the president. When all of us were gathered, people from the president's office handed out sealed envelopes to some of us. I opened my envelope, which contained "talking points" that I was required to recite word for word in front of the president. My talking points were that I used to be a student activist and that the president shouldn't worry about what was going on among the students. (At that time, students were engaged in vehement protests against President Park.) My talking points ended by saying that these "immature" students were "too young" to realize what they were doing and that they would soon understand.

Publishers and civic leaders who had also received envelopes were busy memorizing their talking points. They were having a hard time, since the sheets were quite long. I started getting very worried. First of all, I was worried because I didn't believe anything that was written on my sheet of paper. Second, if I said what was really on my mind, I would risk putting my company in jeopardy. I was stuck.

All of us were then given lunch, so I quietly slipped out and found a pay phone. I called one of my friends and asked for his advice. He said that it would be best if I didn't say anything at all. He added that if I said anything that offended them or even slightly annoyed them, my company—as well as myself—would get into deep trouble. What he said frightened me: "Myung-bak, those guys are *crazy*." After lunch, the others continued to memorize their sheets. The order of speakers was also decided. The publisher would speak first, followed by the civic leader, and then it was my turn. Once all of this was settled, we were all ushered into a bus and taken to the president's office.

I noticed that the president seemed to have lost a lot of weight. He looked gaunt and tired. His face betrayed his inner thoughts—he seemed distressed and distracted. We were led into the meeting room. Behind the president was Cha Chi-chul, staring at us. He was motioning with his eyes and telling the participants to speak, according to the pre-arranged order. The publisher spoke first, as agreed. I was sweating, and my mouth was dry. I still didn't know what to do. I was determined not to recite what had been given to me. But then again, I didn't know what else to say that wouldn't offend the president (and Cha), and that at the same time would be of some value to him.

As the publisher spoke, Cha looked more and more threatening.

His black hair glistened under the chandelier. His eyes were darting, never still. The publisher performed without a hitch, and now it was the civic leader's turn. He was an old man, a grandfather. Soon after he began, he turned pale and started to stammer. He spoke like a first-grader reading from a textbook. He was straining to remember what he had managed to memorize. He started off well enough, but after saying one sentence, he got stuck. A minute went by, and then three. The man was completely frozen with fear and began trembling. He was in no condition to improvise. It seemed as if all his senses stopped operating. Cha Chi-chul turned pale.

After a while, President Park broke the silence. "Did you forget what you were supposed to say?" The rest of us, who were frozen still, let out a sigh and managed to chuckle. President Park then said, "Why don't we stop now?" He knew all along that we had been told to read whatever was given to us. With that, the president rose from his seat and quietly left the room. As I watched him leave, I felt relief as well as sadness.

A few days later, President Park was assassinated. Many thoughts went through my mind that day, but one thing that stood out was the importance of having good people around you. I thought sadly that if only President Park had had good, decent people around him, his life would have never ended in such a way.

Tumultuous Times

Since I became the president of Hyundai Construction in 1977 at the age of thirty-five, my life has been exposed to the fickle and often dangerous political winds. Two years after I was appointed president of Hyundai Construction, President Park Chung-hee was assassinated; the following year, another army general, Chun Doo-hwan, took over the country, and months later he became the next president. Later on, the Fifth and Sixth Republics[19] continued the stifling political climate that permeated the entire country. Korea eventually blossomed into a real democracy with the election of its first civilian president through democratic elections, but that path was fraught with dangers at every turn.

Tremendous sacrifices were made along the way, and for me, as president of one of Korea's largest conglomerates, life was always perilous. Following the assassination of President Park, the "Seoul Spring" began, but it was far from the pleasant spring we were yearning for.

It was during this time that I was visited by two strangers at my office in central Seoul. They barged in without warning and said, "Come with us." No explanations were given. When I asked them, they simply said, "You'll find out soon. We just want to talk to you outside."

I followed them down to the first-floor lobby, and as soon as we got there, each man took one of my arms. I told them I would call my driver. They said, "We don't need your car. We have our own car." It was a nondescript black sedan. They told me to sit in the backseat, and they sat on either side of me.

I asked them where I was going. I got no reply. I asked again, and one of them answered, "We're going to the Jongno Police Station."

Once we were inside the Jongno Police Station, they began to treat me roughly. Without saying a word, they threw me into a solitary cell. I was being treated as a criminal. I was prevented from contacting my office or my family.

I was left in the cell for maybe two or three hours; they gave me a bowl of Korean stew. A sympathetic police officer who seemed to belong to the Jongno Station came and told me in a hushed voice that the men were going to take me to another place for questioning.

He advised me that I should get rid of all the documents in my office. While he stood watch, I quickly phoned my assistant and told him, "I don't know which agency they work for, but I'm here for some questioning."

As I waited, I figured the incident wouldn't take that long. I knew I hadn't done anything wrong. They couldn't possibly keep me locked up indefinitely. Or so I thought.

Soon, I was once again shoved into the back seat of another black sedan and taken to a different location. As we headed up Namsan (a mountain located in the center of Seoul), the car stopped and I was told to get out. I was transferred to a different sedan. The ones who had brought me signed some papers and handed me over to a set of different men. The men didn't seem all that professional.

I was taken to the basement of the Namsan branch office of the KCIA (parts of it were later demolished, and the remaining buildings are now used by private companies). It felt like a dungeon. Here, many men and women were questioned for demonstrating against the state, for criticizing the president, and for colluding with ene- mies—most of them on trumped-up charges. Many who came here were beaten, imprisoned, and severely tortured; some died or were left with permanent physical and psychological scars. No one was spared—democracy activists, opposition politicians, artists, writers, students, and even priests were taken and interrogated.

Agents came in and started asking me questions about Chung Ju-yung's political contributions to the Three Kims (Kim Dae-jung, Kim Young-sam, and Kim Jong-pil), who were the leading opposition leaders at the time. They demanded that I confess to being aware that Chung Ju-yung was giving contributions to the Three Kims. It became obvious that their aim was to arrest and imprison all three Kims, who they considered the ringleaders behind the series of demonstrations that were taking place. This was the essence of the Seoul Spring.

I straightened up and said, "I never met the Three Kims in my life. Why are you asking me about them?"

One of them looked at me with an absolutely blank face. He was wearing a shirt with no tie. The windowless room was small and there was a wooden table in the middle of the room and above it, a single light bulb with a shade. The bulb was tilted toward me and the heat was quite unbearable. "Well, we've looked into your activities, and we weren't able to find anything to suggest that you gave them any political funds. But we do know that your boss, Chung Ju-yung, has been funneling money to them. We have reliable intelligence. But we have a slight problem. We know that old man's doing something we don't approve of, but even we can't tell an old man to come in for questioning. However, we think you know how much Chung Ju-yung has been giving to whom, and when. That's what we want to know. And let me remind you, my friend. No one, absolutely no one, knows you're here with us. And remember: until you tell us what we want to know, you're not leaving this room."

I felt a chill, but I couldn't confess to something I didn't know anything about. "I never heard of Chung Ju-yung giving political funds to any of the Three Kims. I know the man—he would never do such a thing. I think you made a mistake."

Next, I spoke with a different interrogator, who said, "I hope you realize where you are right now. My colleague told you already— unless you tell us all that you know, you are not leaving this room." This interrogator spoke slowly. My answer was the same. I noticed them hesitate for a moment. "Fine. Let's make a deal then," one of them said. "Let's assume that you never saw Chung Ju-yung give any of the Kims any money. Let's assume that you don't know anything and never heard anything. But the *possibility* of Chung giving them

money is still there. All we want you to do is to admit that. We all
know that Chung may very well have given them money. He did it
before, so even a kid knows that he may still be doing it right now.
If the Three Kims aren't receiving any money from people like
Chung, how do you think they're able to prance around like that? So,
just admit that the possibility is there. That's all we ask." Then the
man looked at me and said, "If you can't even do that, then we're
going to have to take you to another room." It was clear what he
was implying: torture.

It was a clever ploy, trying to force me to admit to the possibility of Chung providing political funds to the Three Kims. They
weren't concerned with the facts and were even less interested in
the truth. All they wanted was an excuse to pressure the chairman,
who was heading one of the largest businesses in Korea, and to
arrest and imprison the three leading opposition politicians. They
wanted to kill the Seoul Spring. The notion that the state could be
so bold—and so reckless—was frightening. I said, "I don't know
anything about politics. I don't know what went on between him
and President Park, but I do know that Chung never gave any political funds to any of the Three Kims. And neither did any of the subsidiaries of Hyundai."

The men were becoming impatient now. I was thinking fast and
hard. I could have easily said, "I'm president of Hyundai Construction;
maybe Chung and some other president of one of the subsidiaries
gave those guys some money, who knows? But I don't know anything
about it." If I had, however, it was clear that these men would have
just hauled in someone else and questioned them, and who knows
what would have happened then. Some of them could very well have
fabricated stories or distorted the truth; that would have led to more
lies. So I felt the need to stop it there and then.

But then it was time for them to do what they did best—break a person's spirit through force and fear. "You son of a bitch! All you have to do is tell us what you know, and as for what you don't know, you just have to say that it's always possible. Is that so hard to understand? You think we're a bunch of idiots?" They took turns. They didn't torture me, but the fear was enough to scare anybody.

I pleaded, "Look, I'm in a position to know if such things really did happen. But I'm telling you that neither Chung Ju-yung nor any of the subsidiaries gave money to any of them."

The interrogation went on for hours. It was past midnight. The interrogators stepped outside to smoke. Then they came back in. This time, they tried to cajole me. One of them actually smiled at me. It was unnerving. "President Lee, listen to me. Chung Ju-yung's an old man, and even if we find something on him, there's not much we can do. But you're different. If something happened to you here, no one would know." The man continued, "And everybody has something to hide, right? If we just peek into your life and see how you did business, I'm sure we're going to find some interesting stuff. So as long as you're here with us, I suggest you cooperate, because if you don't, then things are going to get a lot more complicated."

Another agent stepped in. "We're not making up something so that we can put away Chung or hurt Hyundai. All we're trying to do is to find out where these goddamn politicians are getting their pocket money. We're not asking you to rat on your boss or your friends, and we're sure as hell not telling you to betray anyone, either. Just admit that there is the *possibility* that Chung or Hyundai could have given money to these politicians. That's all we ask. Don't make it any harder for yourself." He was waving a piece of paper that seemed like a prepared statement ready for me to sign.

I was tired, but I told them, "Please, I'll say it again: Hyundai never gave any political funds to any of the Three Kims, and there isn't any possibility that they could have done so."

Everyone was getting tired and irritated. The interrogators stepped outside again, and they were gone for a long time. When they came back, they told me to straighten my tie. I was allowed to go to the bathroom. I was disheveled.

We all then went outside. They shoved me into the backseat of a car. I could tell it was early morning.

We arrived at the Pacific Hotel in central Seoul, just a few miles away, and entered a large hall with an adjacent meeting room. I noticed a man sitting there who appeared to be of higher rank than the interrogators. This man said, "I hope you didn't go through too much trouble last night. I hope the boys weren't too rough on you and didn't cause you too much distress." His voice was monotonous and dry. His face betrayed nothing, and his words rang hollow. I knew this was going to be my last hurdle. I mustered my remaining will so that I wouldn't lose concentration. I listened intently. "Other businessmen came to this room, and they were most cooperative. I hope you will do the same, Mr. Lee. If you don't, I'm sure you can imagine that things will get difficult for you. It's an open secret that Hyundai's been providing political funds to many opposition politicians, including the Three Kims. Like I said, other businessmen have confessed already, so we have the necessary information and evidence to prove it. What we need is final confirmation from the culprits themselves, and that's what we're doing right now. So, please tell us."

My voice was cracked from fatigue. "I told your people that that is not true. Hyundai could not have given funds to those politicians. Chung Ju-yung could have provided money to the ruling party politicians, but he would never give money to opposition leaders."

"How are you so sure?"

"I'm senior enough to know such things."

This irritated the man, and he raised his voice, "If you don't know something, just say you don't know. Don't be coy and try to make cute comments about why we're conducting this investigation, you understand?"

I said calmly, "I have no idea why you're conducting this investigation; I'm just telling you what I know for a fact."

The man muttered to himself, "This guy's hopeless..." It looked like he had made up his mind. "Fine. If that's the way you're going to be. Just make sure you initial these papers." It was a record of everything that I had said. I dipped my right thumb into red ink and stamped the papers. As I was wiping away the ink with tissue paper, the man said, "Thank you for going through all this trouble." He was back to his calm and dry self. It didn't look like he meant what he said, but I wasn't concerned with that. We stepped out of the hotel, and soon I was dropped off by the road near my office.

As expected, the office was in sheer panic. I had been missing for more than a day, and no one had any clue as to where I was. My assistants worriedly asked me where I had been and if something bad had happened. I didn't tell anyone what happened. It was not because the agents had made me promise to keep quiet; it was because I knew what would happen if people knew. It would only cause a lot of concern, and I knew no one was able to do anything about it.

Even to Chung, I made sure to be brief, telling him that some people had asked me about his political donations. I told Chung what I had told the agents. Chung listened and simply nodded. He didn't ask any questions.

During the early days of the Fifth Republic, the relationship between Hyundai and the government was less than cordial. In fact, it was one of mutual distrust. The government's hatred of Hyundai was obvious. Their tactics were calculated and brutal. Hyundai was able to develop a working relationship with the government later on, but it was tenuous and uneasy. However, as the Fifth Republic was nearing its end, the relationship turned sour once again, instilling in Chung Ju-yung a deep hatred for the government, and at the same, a desperate yearning to attain power. And our run-ins with the government continued.

Tears of Blood

The Fifth Republic hoped to realign the entire business sector. This was so that it could get what it most desperately needed—legitimacy. It also needed something it could claim as its own. Discontent was high. People's demand for political and social reform was becoming more impassioned. The government needed to do something to turn the tide.

The only problem was that the government didn't have a good plan. In fact, its plan to consolidate similar industries was one of its worst policies. It was an attempt to shake up big business to get what the government wanted. The plan was misguided and ill conceived. But the government was determined. As they say, a stupid man who works hard is the most dangerous.

Korean scholars who studied abroad and those in the government's economic department were saying that the Korean industrial sector, especially the heavy industries and chemical industries, were inundated with companies competing for the same market. The government saw redundant investments as stumbling blocks and asserted that these sectors needed to be consolidated. Getting rid of competition was not the solution. And that the state ordered companies to oblige was outrageous.

For example, no one would say that Korea's automobile industry today has too many companies. A professor or government official calling for consolidation of the car industry, saying there were too many auto manufacturers, would be laughable. We all know that competition spurs innovation and entrepreneurship, which then leads to growth and jobs. We also know that allowing for competition and abiding by established rules is vital for growth. This is the difference between an advanced and a developing economy.

However, during the 1980s in Korea, so-called experts, economic professors, and high-level government officials were insisting that, to strengthen competitiveness, we needed just one company for each major industry—cars, heavy industries, chemical plants, and so on. It was an absurd idea. The policy could have reverberations throughout the economy for decades, but the military government wasn't concerned. It was hopelessly bound by short-term gains and quick fixes. And the government was determined to push the plan through.

The government's plan was made to look elaborate and sophisticated, but the gist of the plan was simply to consolidate the auto and heavy chemical industries. Specifically, the plan was to consolidate Hyundai Motors, Daewoo Auto, and Asia Motors into one group. The other part of the plan was to create a single entity by combining the Daewoo Okpo shipyard, Hyundai Heavy Industries, and Hyundai Yang-haeng (later renamed Korea Heavy Industry).

For Hyundai, which had been investing continuously in both autos and the heavy industries for many decades, it was painful to be forced to choose one industry. In particular, Hyundai had been developing its nascent auto division and was on the brink of major breakthroughs; we envisioned Hyundai Motors being able to compete in the global market, if only it were given more time. It had already made inroads into new overseas markets, and the potential for growth was incredible. Forcing us to abandon this now was unthinkable. The power plant facilities were the same. By then, Hyundai had managed to accumulate valuable expertise and experience in building power plants, including nuclear power plants. If Hyundai were to forfeit its advantage in this field, it would mean forever giving up the chance to take part in the vast thermal and nuclear power plant market. Both the auto and the power plant industries were prized assets that were precious to us.

The military government's plan seemed like a trap to ensnare the Hyundai Group and prevent us from making any more progress as a business. It was madness. However, the government had already made up its mind. The only thing left was for us to choose.

We held numerous internal meetings and discussed what to do. In the end, Chung made the final decision. He chose to retain Hyundai Motors. Chung's decision was based on his prediction that the auto industry had limitless potential; the power plant industry was also attractive, but production was sporadic. At the same time, Chung thought that Hyundai could always jump into the power plant market later on. He reasoned that Hyundai's expertise would be invaluable when the country inevitably decided to start building thermal and/or nuclear power plants. He was betting that Hyundai would be invited back. Chung's decision was prescient.

After a series of exhaustive meetings among the Hyundai executives, I was designated to represent Hyundai to the government. My job was to inform and, if possible, negotiate with the government. My counterparts were two military officers who belonged to the National Council for State Security (the same Council that had called me in during Hyundai's public dispute with Samsung and *Joong-ang Ilbo*). It was this council that was carrying out the orders to consolidate the industrial sector. It may seem odd that military officers were put in charge of such an important project. But back then the military was in charge of practically everything; there was nothing we could do.

We took our seats. I was seated opposite the two officers. One of them asked me what industry Hyundai wished to retain. But before I answered that question, I needed to explain what many of us were feeling regarding this new policy. I began by saying, "I really cannot understand why we are being asked to choose. To you, it may seem like there are redundant investments in the heavy industries. But believe me, pretty soon there will come a time when we don't have enough of these companies."

I went on. "Let's say we consolidate all these companies into one, like you suggest. What's going to happen is that companies will lose all incentive to innovate and competition will of course go out the window. Once that happens in a market economy, you can bet your house that the industry will never grow."

The officers didn't say anything. One of them scribbled notes while the other was fiddling with his pen. Both of them were trying to look stern.

I continued. "It's not just that Hyundai doesn't want to give up either its auto or its heavy industries. All I'm saying is that your plan to consolidate the industry is just plain wrong. And bad for the future of the country."

When I was done one of them said, "Well, thank you for that little lecture. Unfortunately, there's no need for debate or to make any arguments against it. It's already been decided. All you have to do is tell us what Hyundai wants to keep—autos or heavy industries."

Our first meeting went nowhere. It was over after half an hour. I left without telling them our decision.

The next day we met again, but there was no progress. I was becoming increasingly suspicious that the National Council had already made up its mind how to partition the industry. I began to get the feeling that the council had been conspiring with our competitors. My hunch was that the council and our competitors wanted Hyundai to take the power plant facilities. They were trying to lure us into doing so. They needed Hyundai's consent, and that's what they were trying to get out of me.

During our third meeting, they finally showed their true colors. "President Lee, we know that Hyundai's been investing heavily in heavy industries for quite some time and that your group is built around Hyundai Construction. As such, we believe your company should choose the power plant facility industry. I think this is the right decision for your company and for ensuring the success of our policy."

I had suspected that something like this was coming, so I wasn't surprised. As soon as he finished I informed them, "Hyundai will choose the auto."

Both officers looked up at me, then at each other. They were clearly surprised, both at what I had said and how I had said it. Then they tried to force me to accept their proposal. They began to explain their reasoning in great detail; I told them again that Hyundai believed that the plan itself was dangerously flawed but that if it was inevitable, Hyundai would choose the auto industry. I told them there was no room for compromise. They continued to try to convince me, but I was firm.

Soon they began to threaten me. When I still wouldn't budge, they began to attack me personally. One of them asked me where I lived. I simply said "Gang-nam" (an area south of the Han River known as an affluent neighborhood).

They then asked me, "You live in an apartment?"

I said, "No, in fact, I live in a fairly large house."

"Oh, really?" one of them snorted. "I live in a shitty house the size of your closet on top of a hill. While people like you are living in fancy houses, enjoying good food and living carefree lives, people like us are thinking about the future of this country. The government made a decision for the sake of the country. Don't you think the least you could do is to cooperate?" He looked at me contemptuously. I shot back. "Look officers, let me tell you something. When the two of you were attending the military academy, which by the way was paid for by the state, I went to college, but I had to haul garbage every single morning so I could pay for my tuition. When your parents sent the two of you to high school, I almost didn't make it to high school, because we had no money. When the two of you didn't have to worry about what to eat, I never had enough to eat, and my younger sister and I almost starved to death many times."

I continued, "After graduating college, I got a job and I worked day and night. I went overseas and had to endure a lot of trouble. I don't know if the two of you are aware of this, but in 1974 this country was on the brink of bankruptcy. You know what saved it? It was people like me who went overseas to bring back hard-earned foreign currency, sweating and working like dogs in the deserts and jungles. When the two of you graduated from the academy and started work, was there any war? I know what it's like out there. It's a jungle. It's a war. I worked eighteen hours a day trying to survive. I never slept more than five hours a day in my life."

One of the officers cut in, saying, "We also took part in a war. The Vietnam War."

I suppressed a bitter smile and continued. "Gentlemen, just because you are officers doesn't mean that you're patriots. Likewise, just because I'm a businessman, don't think that I'm a scoundrel. Companies can and should be criticized if they do something wrong. However, belittling the positive role of business is wrong." I looked at the officer who had told me he lived in a hill-top apartment. "You said you live in a shitty apartment on a hilltop. You know what? I used to live in a hill-top shanty, but I bet your apartment is a luxury condo compared to the shanty I used to live in. And let me ask you. What's so wrong with the president of Hyundai Construction living in a large house? That house was built for me by the company so that I would be able to entertain foreign guests."

The officer who lived on a hilltop just looked at me. I said, "If my living in such a house is wrong, then should I lower my standard of living and go live next to you in a dilapidated apartment on a hill-top? Is that what you people want? If I were you, I would aim to raise the standard so that officers like you and public servants and others like them can live in large, comfortable apartments! That should be the aim of politics. Don't try to pull down people who work hard to better their lives. Don't patronize them."

One officer sheepishly said, "That's not what we meant. It's just that some businessmen seem only to be concerned with making money for their own good." With that, our meeting came to an end, again with no results.

After I got back, I sat down with Chung to try to come up with a strategy. But as time went by, I knew I was being driven to the brink; they were the ones holding all the cards.

One day, someone I knew who worked for the government came to see me. He was an official helping the military's "reform" efforts. He told me that it was futile for me to keep resisting. He gently reminded me that the country was in a state of emergency and that it was advisable for me to just quietly accept their proposal. He also warned me that this was something that could determine the very survival of the Hyundai Group. After he left, I wasn't quite sure whether he was genuinely worried for me and the company or if he had been sent by the military men to try to persuade me. Nonetheless, I went to Chung and told him about our meeting and what the man had said. I also told Chung that it seemed like the time had come for us to make the final decision.

"What should we do?" I asked him. Chung didn't say anything. He seemed very tired. Ever since President Park Chung-hee was assassinated and the new military government came to power, Chung had had to endure one too many beatings. Being determined and stoic wasn't always enough to weather these storms that were often so brutal and unforgiving.

"Go over there and try once more. If the tide is already against us, then there's nothing we can do but to agree." With that, Chung gave me his personal seal, which was used to initial important documents and contracts (documents initialed with personal seals are considered legal documents).

I asked him, "Mr. Chairman, what do you want me to do with this?"

Chung shrugged. "You don't have to blame yourself. Just go along with the tide."

I protested, "Mr. Chairman, if you want me to use this seal, then I think you should go over there and do it yourself. There are others who can represent the company."

Chung said, "Look, you're the one who's been dealing with those people, so you should be the one who wraps it up."

I got up, put Chung's personal seal in my pocket, and headed toward the National Council for a final meeting. At the meeting, as usual, we fiercely debated back and forth. All that I had, however, was my principled and consistent objections to the decision itself. I also tried to help my two military counterparts understand the nature of the auto industry and what it meant for the future of the country. I didn't have anything to lose. Besides, I didn't want to hand over what meant so much to me and the company too easily. I became deeply upset, knowing that the end was near. I hated to see them gloat.

I pleaded, "Officers, the auto industry is one of the most sophisticated industries around. If you combine them all into one, competitiveness is bound to drop, negatively affecting growth and exports. It's only going to become a burden to you and to the people. Take a look at India. India has only one motor company that is wholly owned and operated by the state. Did you ever see their cars? They didn't invest in research, so over the years the industry has turned into a gigantic sucking hole where money has been poured in with no output whatsoever. Their cars perform dismally, and their models are hopelessly outdated. But they are expensive, and since they don't produce that many cars, I would have to wait for months to get delivery. This is because there is no competition in India. Unless you see for yourself, you will never be able to fully appreciate the gravity of the situation."

I stressed, "Our auto industry may seem like it has too many companies, but trust me, once the economy bounces back and people start buying again and our industries get stronger, all of them are going to contribute to overall growth. You *have* to reconsider consolidating the auto industry."

One of the officers jeered, "Mr. Lee, please. Spare us your lessons in economics. Our policy is based on objective reports written by scholars who earned degrees abroad and who know a lot more about economics than you. So enough with the lecturing."

I ignored his snide remark and said, "I don't know on what basis these so-called scholars are advocating for consolidation, but let me tell you that people like me are far more knowledgeable about what goes on in the real world of business. We know what works and what doesn't."

I went on: "I also never heard of getting rid of competition in a market economy as a way to make profits. Monopolizing industries will only lead to stagnation. Of course, at first it may seem as if all's working well and everyone's happy. But in a competitive world, that's where companies really flourish. Their potential becomes limitless! And such companies make the economy healthy and competitive. If you try to force consolidation of industries, then you may achieve some short-term gains, but in the long run, the country's going to suffer. We will never be able to compete in the global market. And when that day comes, you'll regret your decision and know how stupid it was."

The officers had had enough of my lecturing. I also didn't feel like talking anymore. I was wasting my time. They kept insisting that I choose. They told me, "Mr. Lee, we're not here to listen to your lectures. Just tell us what you want. We're out of time now. Do whatever you want, that's up to you."

Our discussion by now had been going on for hours. It was already late in the evening. I then thought that no matter how long I stayed, I wouldn't be able to change a thing. The mood was turning more tense.

I took out Chung's personal seal and placed it on the table. "OK, here's Chung's personal seal. I'll accept whatever you decide." There was no way I was going to use that seal with my own hands.

A junior officer came over and picked up the seal. As he was about to stamp it, one of the officers suddenly shouted, "Stop! Don't!" He realized that if one of their men used the stamp and not me, I could always claim that I was coerced and that I never sealed it myself. The officer then ordered his junior officer, "Put that down." He stared at me with distaste.

I said, "Can I go back now?"

He let out a great sigh. "What the...get the hell out of here!"

"Will you be needing this seal? Should I leave it with you?" I asked.

The officer shot back angrily, "No! Take that useless seal with you, damn it."

When I walked out of the National Council, it was already dark. When I got back, only Chung's office was lit. I walked in and Chung looked at me. "What happened? Did you stamp it?"

"No," I said.

Chung was surprised. "Really? What happened?"

"I'll brief you in detail tomorrow." I was suddenly exhausted.

Chung looked at my face again. "Hey, your eyes are bleeding."

"Huh? My eyes are fine."

"No, go and take a look. It's bleeding."

I went into the washroom and looked in the mirror. My right eye was filled with red liquid. I took out my handkerchief and wiped at it; it was stained reddish-black. *Tears of blood.* For the first time in my life I experienced what I had only read about in cheap novels. I never thought it possible that humans could actually shed tears of blood. Now I knew it was true.

My confrontations with the feared National Council did yield results in the end. Following our discussions, the National Council was unable to finalize the consolidation of the auto industry, since Hyundai never consented. It ended up transferring the issue to the Ministry of Industry, where the discussion became public. It was then Chung Ju-yung's turn; he stepped forward to strongly argue against consolidation, using his considerable influence to win over the public. In the end, the auto industry was spared.

Unfortunately, the power plant industry was not. And the repercussions of that fateful decision lingered for many years afterward. This matter was something that could, and did, have a tremendous impact on the Korean economy and the country's future.

On a more private level, the uneasy relationship between Hyundai and the Fifth Republic continued. This time, it was regarding Chung Ju-yung's presidency of the Federation of Korean Industries (FKI).

FKI President

The newly inaugurated Chun Doo-hwan administration never stopped in its quest to gain legitimacy. The surest and fastest way to do so was to attack business. And one way to send a strong signal to the business community was to change the FKI president. This would also send a message to the public that the government was on top of matters.

The FKI represents the interests of the major conglomerates in Korea. Its chair is elected by the members, and it is a private organization. It is funded by contributions given by its members. The president of FKI is considered the face of the Korean business community, and the position carries much symbolism and gravitas. And now, the Chun administration wanted Chung Ju-yung to step down.

During the Fifth Republic, the FKI was under the auspices of the Ministry of Industry. This meant that it was the minister of industry's responsibility to oversee its activities and to offer various recommendations. One day, Minister Seo Seok-jun sent a message that he urgently wished to see me. Minister Seo informed me that President Chun wished Chung Ju-yung to resign from his FKI presidency, effective immediately. Minister Seo told me that we would be given four days. In four days, Chung was expected to resign in a way that would seem natural. There could be no delay, since this was the president's order.

I protested and said that such an issue should be dealt with by the FKI and not me. However, Minister Seo explained that the reason I was called in was because they felt that I was the only person who was straightforward enough to tell Chung what he should do. I asked why the administration wished to see Chung go, but I got no clear answer.

There were rumors that Park Tae-joon, the chairman of POSCO (Pohang Steel Company), was already slated to become the next president of FKI, so I asked Minister Seo point-blank, "Who's the next president?" The minister didn't answer. I went on, "As you know, Mr. Minister, the FKI is a private organization. If the government decides to change the president at its whim, that would send the wrong message to the people. What kind of a new government are you trying to become?"

I was customarily blunt, but this time I went a bit far. Minister Seo was insulted by my response; it was the early days of the new military government, and no one dared question the intentions of the government, and especially those of the president himself. Minister Seo just repeated that this was coming from the highest authority and that I should go and tell Chung Ju-yung.

I did tell Chung, but I also told him to hold out as long as he could. I reasoned that it would be wise to sit on the order and not let anyone know about it. We should wait it out and see what happens, I told him. I also pointed out that although they said this was the president's wish, it might not have been. Someone other than the president could very well have been using the president's name. If it was the president's wish, we had to find out who was giving the president such advice. Chung was duly concerned that if he didn't follow their wish, Hyundai could be targeted again. That would mean another round of confrontations with the military government, a prospect that was less than appealing to both of us. Besides, Chung had assumed the presidency of the FKI reluctantly. It was a job that he initially refused. In 1977, the president of FKI asked Chung several times before Chung accepted, but once he assumed the presidency, Chung dove in with his usual intensity and zeal. He had no qualms about leaving the FKI presidency.

However, leaving after finishing his term and being forced out prematurely without any acceptable reason were inherently different. I argued strongly for him to stay put for the time being.

The next day, Minister Seo called me in again and asked me what Chung had said. He was fully expecting to hear that Chung intended to step down in the next three days. I told him, however, that Chung seemed to be in deep thought, contemplating what to do. I told him Chung had said nothing. Minister Seo became troubled. He kept repeating that this was the president's wish.

Once I got back, I repeated to Chung that he must hold on. It was wrong to step down when the government was still not giving us a good reason. Plus, we feared that Chung stepping down now would be a disgrace for Chung personally and a severe blow to Hyundai. It would make it seem that Hyundai had been reduced to a spineless coward and a pushover.

Chung agreed. "You're damn right. I'm not just going to fold. I'll leave when my term is over. No way are they going to force me to leave." This was not Chung's first time butting heads with the new military government. He seemed to relish the chance to make them sweat, and he was spiteful. As I stood in front of him he started cleaning out his desk, shredding his personal memos and locking away sensitive papers. He knew what the military government was capable of. He knew that they would find another excuse to lock him up. "If they put me in jail, that's fine. I'll finally have some time to study English!" he joked.

On the fourth day, Minister Seo called me in for the last time. He was now visibly nervous. He wanted an answer. I told him, "Mr. Minister, Chairman Chung is still having trouble making up his mind. He's being very cautious." I searched the minister's face and continued. "If Chairman Chung were to submit his resignation voluntarily, the business community and the people will wonder why, especially since he has only a year left until the end of his term. Naturally, everybody's going to think the new government forced him out. That's not going to look good for the government, meddling in the personnel matters of a private organization like the FKI. That's not going to reflect well on Chung, the business community, or the government. Why not let him finish his term? It's only one more year. Perhaps you could make that suggestion to the president?"

Minister Seo turned pale; that was not the answer he was hoping for. It was outrageous that I would make a suggestion that required him to question the president's decision. "Do you realize where this order is coming from, Mr. Lee?" he asked.

At that time, Chung was having a meeting with Deputy Prime Minister Nam Deok-woo, who was conveying the same message to Chung that Minister Seo was delivering to me. Soon rumors started flying. Some were saying that the next FKI president had already been selected. Specific names were appearing. As the rumors spread, we were forced into a delicate position. I told Chung that we had no choice now but to dig our heels in further.

Fortunately, Chung was given an opportunity to express his position directly to the president. Chung proceeded to write a letter, and I personally delivered it to a man who was considered one of the president's right-hand men (he was a military officer but was known to be reasonable). As I handed him the letter, I explained the unfairness of the government's decision. I watched him nod in consent. I realized that all of this might not be coming directly from the president's office. The man said, "Something doesn't seem right."

Eventually, Chung was able to finish his term. His relationship with the government markedly improved during this time. At the end of his term, he was reelected by members of the FKI, thereby becoming one of the longest-serving FKI presidents in history.

Being a businessman, and especially the chairman of a large corporation, during the Fifth Republic was fraught with danger. I was constantly exposed to threats and abuse. I was taken in for questioning and denied my basic rights and privileges. The government would make outrageous demands, would implement polices based on dubious theories, and wouldn't hesitate to undermine a company that had taken years of hard work to get where it was. For example, when Hyundai won the contract to build liquefied natural gas (LNG) storage facilities following the new government policy to diversify energy imports, we formed a joint venture with a French company called Technigaz and

All Korean schools—from elementary to college—required their students to wear uniforms (a practice which continued until the late 1980s). The uniforms were normally black with a matching cap and the students wore a pin on their lapels to show which school they belonged to. Since I did not own any other clothing, I used to wear this school uniform all the time.

A portrait of my mother was done decades after she passed away. My family could never afford to take photos; this portrait of Mother was rendered by an artist who painted it not by looking at a photo but by listening to descriptions from family members and relatives.

With some of my class-
mates at Korea University
during the early 1960s.
Back then, college students
were also required to wear
school uniforms and I wore
them while hauling gar-
bage every morning.

Newspapers carefully detailed the trials of the
student leaders implicated in the June 3
Movement; as a result, many of us became
celebrities, including myself. A long-lost distant
relative of the family who read about me in
the newspapers sent me a box of apples with
just my name and city on it; it arrived at our
home nonetheless.

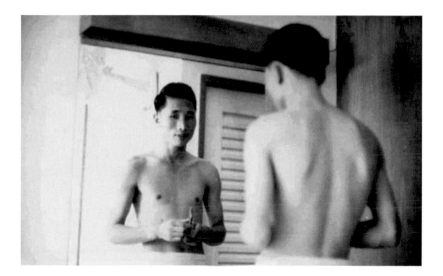

This photo was taken by a friend when I was working as an accountant in Hyundai's Thailand regional office. My father and elder brothers are all taller than me; Mother used to say that I could have been taller only if I had eaten better as a child.

My first overseas posting for Hyundai Construction was to our regional office in Thailand as an accountant when Hyundai was building the Pattani-Narathiwat highway. It was at this office that I was attacked by an angry mob of workers who demanded I hand over the company safe; I didn't and I was severely beaten. The "Thai safe incident" made me into a fearless hero but at that time all I could think about was my mother.

I used to move around on a motorcycle while I was working at our regional office in Thailand during the early 1960s. I always enjoyed sports and outdoor activities so riding the motorcycle was my way of relieving stress after a hard day's work.

Yoon-ok and I got married on December 19, 1970 at the Sejong Hotel in down-town Seoul. I proposed to Yoon-ok that we get married on December 19th since this was also my birthday (this way, I figured I would never forget our wedding anniversary). Thirty-seven years later on December 19, 2007, I was elected president of the Republic of Korea, making December 19th a "Triple Crown Day."

Photo taken during our honeymoon in 1970.

Yoon-ok holding our eldest daughter, Joo-yeon, in 1971. Many say that Joo-yeon resembles me the most in temperament and her outlook on life. Behind them to the right is a Sansui speaker that I bought after receiving my first bonus as an executive; the photo was taken with a Leica camera that I bought from a bonus after finishing my first stint overseas. Both the speaker and the camera were my most prized possessions for many years, apart from my family. It was during this time rumors that "Lee Myung-bak is living with a mistress" persisted since many thought Yoon-ok was too young to be the wife of the president of Hyundai Construction.

At the Al-Jubail SNOS opening ceremony in Saudi Arabia in November 1980.

With Chairman Chung Ju-yung at Hyundai's traditional annual welcoming party for new employees held at a seaside resort. It was during one of these parties in the 1960s when I was a young recruit that Chung Ju-yung fell and cut his lip after an all-night drinking session; the scar was visible years later.

A company outing in 1981 for new employees. Chung always enjoyed hosting parties for company employees, whether it was for new recruits as shown here or for site managers braving the war in Iraq.

A delegation from Taiwan visiting my office at Hyundai Construction in April 1987 to discuss building a subway in Taiwan.

Standing in front of a Hyundai Construction regional office overseas.

With former prime minister Mahathir of Malaysia when Penang bridge was built by Hyundai Construction.

Chairman Chung Ju-yung and I posed in front of the Kremlin in Moscow's famous Red Square during one of our numerous visits to the former Soviet Union. Our meeting with President Gorbachev was a historic moment for South Korea and our foray into the former Soviet Union paved the way for eventual diplomatic ties between South Korea and the Soviet Union.

As a member of the National Assembly (parliament) of Korea.

Campaigning for mayor of Seoul in 2002.

Campaigning for mayor of Seoul.

Before the restoration of the Cheonggyecheon stream.

After the restoration of the Cheonggyecheon stream.

This photo was taken when I lived in a traditional Korean house, *hanok*, from 2006 to 2007.

entered the bid. (Since LNG storage facilities required transporting and storing liquefied natural gas at extremely low temperatures, the government required Korean companies to enter the bidding process in conjunction with foreign firms that possessed the necessary technology.) Hyundai and Technigaz eventually won the contract, beating out a rival Korean company called Hanyang that had formed an alliance with the Japanese firm Marubeni. Later, the government cancelled the contract altogether, citing technical reasons.

Despite our repeated complaints and meetings with top officials, the contract was finally given to Hanyang, which formed a joint venture with our French partner, Technigaz. The government was the matchmaker that put Hanyang and Technigaz together.

Technigaz came to us to apologize. We could have raised an issue with Technigaz and demanded compensation according to the clause in our original contract prohibiting both parties from reneging on the deal. However, we decided that Technigaz wasn't to blame. It was our own government that had decided to terminate our bid.

It was another instance where the rules of the game and sheer common sense were thrown out the window. This was how business was conducted under the military government during the 1980s in Korea. It was a brave (and dangerous) new world. I was a businessman, and we all needed to be brave in order to survive.

10 | NUCLEAR POWER

With mounting public concerns about the safety of nuclear power plants, the Korean government was in a bind. It knew that Hyundai was the only one capable of satisfying the new safety standards. However, it still didn't want to give the project to Hyundai.

An announcement came over the loudspeakers—"Would President Lee Myung-bak of Hyundai Construction please come to the office located near the boarding area."

I was in the lounge at Changi International Airport in Singapore waiting for my 11 p.m. flight to Thailand. I hurriedly ran to the office (this was before cell phones and beepers). Chung was calling me from Seoul. When I picked up the receiver, Chung yelled, "Lee, you'd better come back to Seoul right away. Our private contract for the nuclear power plant project has just been annulled."

I was stunned. "How can that be?"

Chung said, "It's true. The Deputy Prime Minister just had a press conference and announced it. This is bullshit! Anyway, return immediately. I need you here."

This was December 1987, near the end of the Fifth Republic. The country was caught up in the fever of the upcoming presidential elections. During this time, Korean Electric Power Corporation (KEPCO) issued a bidding process for the construction of units 3 and 4 of the Young-kwang Nuclear Power Plant. There were six companies in Korea at the time that had experience building power plants. Of the six, only Hyundai and Dong-a Construction had experience building nuclear power plants; the remaining four had built only thermal plants.

Construction of nuclear power plants involves building the nuclear reactor that produces energy through nuclear fusion and the power plant facility that uses the heat energy generated by the reactor to produce electricity. The nuclear reactors in Gori and Wolseong were built by Hyundai; the power plant facility was completed by Dong-a. Later on, Hyundai built all the reactors as well as the power facilities at the Young-kwang plant, thereby becoming the first company in Korea to build an entire nuclear power plant on its own.

Hyundai's quest to build nuclear reactors was not easy. In the early 1970s, Hyundai started off as a minor subcontractor for Westinghouse. It was a smart decision to invest in nuclear power, but at the time Korea didn't know anything about nuclear energy or how to build a nuclear power plant. Naturally, we had to learn from others, and Westinghouse became our partner. In the beginning, all we did was assemble parts and do as we were told. But all the while we learned valuable lessons.

By the late 1970s, Korea had emerged as an attractive market for other nuclear power companies. The near-monopoly Westinghouse enjoyed, as well as the one-sided relationship between Hyundai and Westinghouse, came to an end. As Hyundai became an attractive joint partner for foreign firms wishing to win contracts in Korea, Westinghouse started to treat us with more respect. I recall that in the early 1970s, when I traveled to Pittsburgh to meet with the executives at Westinghouse, my counterpart was a director, even though I was president. Later on, I was met by the senior vice president and treated lavishly, which I didn't mind at all.

During one of my numerous face-offs with these Westinghouse executives, I tried to win as many concessions as I could. And it wasn't easy. One time, the same senior vice president came to Seoul, and we started our negotiations regarding the renewal of the specific terms of our partnership (for instance, how much in technological transfers we would receive from Westinghouse). We were now demanding to be treated as more of an equal partner. Of course, Westinghouse thought otherwise.

As we sat down in my Seoul office, we started what turned out to be a fourteen-hour marathon negotiation. It took so long because the senior vice president would often get up to consult with his boss back home; however, knowing that our intelligence agents were eavesdropping on all international calls—especially his—he would cleverly call the Tokyo office to relay a message and ask for instructions. The senior vice president also kept asking for more coffee, which seemed to invigorate him, so I told my secretary to stop bringing coffee and bring tea instead (this seemed to sap his energy considerably and ultimately do the trick).

The senior vice president was also aware of the statewide curfew, which began at midnight and lasted until 4 a.m. He knew that I would be bound by this curfew, but he wouldn't[20]. When I realized that he was using this against me, thinking that I would fold so that I could finish the negotiations before midnight and go home, I ordered my secretary to bring a military-style folding bed into my office. When the senior vice president realized, to his astonishment, that I was willing to sleep in the office if necessary, he finally gave up and signed. In the end, we agreed ten minutes before the curfew was about to start. This was how we managed to acquire valuable technology and know-how critical for building our own nuclear power plants later on.

Once we finished the negotiations, I hurriedly got in my car, and my driver tried to beat the curfew, which was just minutes away. Unfortunately, as we approached one of the bridges across the Han River, I noticed the local police and military guards already had their barricades set up. We were stopped at the checkpoint.

I got out of the car and walked over to a man who seemed to be in charge. "My name is Lee Myung-bak and I am president of Hyundai Construction." I continued, "I was in an important meeting with a foreigner since this morning, negotiating for our national interests. The negotiations just ended, and I would appreciate if you would let me go home so I can get some rest."

The man asked me, "How far away is your home? How long would it take you to get there?"

I replied, "I live in Apkujung so it'll take me about five minutes from here, maybe less."

The man said, "Then go. But if you get caught by anyone else, you mustn't tell them that I let you through."

I thanked him, and went home to sleep that night.

When it comes to building nuclear power plants, possessing the capability and actual experience is extremely important, for safety reasons. So as KEPCO began the bidding process to build nuclear reactors 3 and 4 at the Young-kwang plant, it was critical that a company that had experience be selected. It was obvious to everyone that Hyundai was the only capable candidate to take on the project. Thus, the ideal situation would be for the government to sign a private contract with Hyundai. However, a project of such magnitude involves an extraordinary amount of money, and in order to prevent any accusations of favoritism or fraud, the law prohibited the government from entering into a private contract with a company.

In addition, the government didn't want to give such a huge project to Hyundai. Chung and the government had had yet another falling out the previous month in which the two butted heads (again) over the management of the Far East Petroleum Corporation. The government decided to exercise its influence, which caused a rift, and another messy affair had erupted between the two. Then the accident at Three Mile Island took place. The news of the tragic accident triggered worldwide concern over the safety of nuclear power plants. Footage of the partial core meltdown caused widespread panic. Images of radioactive waste spewing out and contaminating the environment caused much fear among the people. Antinuclear activists began calling for the shutdown of all the nuclear reactors in the world. Questions were raised about the safety of these plants. Soon, companies that had no prior experience building nuclear reactors were being excluded—by law—from all future construction projects. Due to heightened safety standards, Brown & Root (B&R)—one of the world's leading construction companies—had to abandon a nuclear power plant project that it was carrying out in Texas. B&R failed to pass the new safety standard test conducted by the Nuclear Regulatory Commission and had to hand over the project to Bechtel, suffering nearly $1 billion in losses.

With mounting public concerns about the safety of nuclear power plants, the Korean government was in a bind. It knew that Hyundai was the only company capable of satisfying the new safety standards. However, it still didn't want to give the project to Hyundai. So KEPCO was ordered to conduct open bidding with new requirements attached. The bidding announcement was advertised in the newspapers. Applicants to the first round were screened, and Hyundai was the only company that passed. KEPCO announced a second round of bidding; the result was the same.

According to law, if the same company passed the second round of bidding, it was eligible to enter into an exclusive private contract. During those days, any company that won a government-ordered project would have to put up political funds; however, due to the nature of this particular project and the intense interest it generated at home and abroad, politics had no room to wiggle in. For those who were used to getting hefty payments whenever such a project was awarded, Hyundai winning the bid was a nightmare come true.

After making sure that our bid was secure, I boarded my flight to Singapore. The purpose of my trip was to check on our various projects in Southeast Asia. And while I was away, the unthinkable happened. The deputy prime minister and head of the Korean Central Intelligence Agency and other high-ranking officials got together and started to claim that Hyundai's bid was full of loopholes and irregularities. Afterward, the deputy prime minister went on national television to give a press conference announcing the annulment of the contract, saying that the government intended to re-open the bidding process.

After speaking with Chung in Singapore, I hung up the phone and stood for a while, thinking of my next move. I knew it would break protocol to cancel my visit to Thailand at the last minute, so I decided to go ahead with my original plans. I also knew that the government couldn't initiate the new bidding process in one or two days. The government would need much more time.

I arrived in Bangkok at 2 a.m., and after checking-in I went to sleep. At 6 a.m., I was woken up by Chung. "I still think you'd better come over right away."

Fully awake, I told him, "Boss, you and I should prepare for a long battle. My business here could be done in two days. After I wrap it up here, I'll fly right over. Don't worry."

Chung was agitated. "What do you mean, don't worry?"

I explained calmly, "Think about it. A project like this can't be decided by a handful of politicians. The government's making a big mistake. We have a good chance if we present them with an argument based on the validity of our contract. I'll take full responsibility."

Chung seemed slightly reassured, since I was so confident. "Fine. I don't know what you're thinking, but get back here as quickly as you can." And he hung up.

After finishing my business in Thailand in two days, I was back on the plane headed to Seoul. As soon as I landed, I went straight to work. My assistants had already set up a series of meetings I had requested. First I met with the deputy prime minister, Mr. Chung In-yong, and then the chairman of KEPCO, Mr. Park Chung-kee. Then I went to see the minister for energy, Mr. Choi Chang-rak. I told them how deeply embarrassing and outrageous it was for the government to annul a contract purely for political reasons. To each of them I emphasized that this project mustn't be interfered with by politics; it was far too important. None of them budged. They had already made the announcement, and none of them were willing to go and tell the president otherwise.

However, Park Chung-kee of KEPCO changed his mind. He understood that constructing a nuclear power plant was no ordinary project, and he knew very well that Hyundai was the only company capable of carrying it out. He decided to go against the government and honor the contract that Hyundai had won.

It was a courageous move, and he had to pay for it. The Chun administration succeeded in dismissing Park, who was the only man among the top government officials who had graduated from the same high school as President Chun (a connection considered extremely powerful in Korea) and who was also President Chun's junior class-mate at the military academy. The government seemed desperate, making such a drastic move.

Park's successor at KEPCO was a man named Han. When I met

him, I said, "Mr. Han, since you weren't here when all this mess started, I'm sure you can look at this objectively and hopefully do the right thing." He was initially skeptical that there was any way for him to reverse what had already been decided by the government. But he did agree to look into it. He soon realized that there was nothing wrong in Hyundai winning the contract.

As the new chairman's view became known, the government was forced into a corner. Finally, the minister for energy asked for a meeting. By now, Hyundai was preparing to file a suit against the chairman of KEPCO and the minister for energy. All legal preparations were finalized.

At the meeting, the minister simply said, "Mr. Lee, I hope you and Hyundai will acknowledge the authority of the state. Even if you think this is unfair, the state cannot rescind its decision. I wish for Hyundai to enter the new round of bidding together with Dong-a, which also has experience in building nuclear power plants."

The minister was again breaking the rules, but I decided to accept his proposal. What the minister said about respecting the authority of the state meant giving the government a chance to save face. I also took this chance to put in a request of our own. "We can't agree to have a total-amount bid. Instead, we want an itemized bid. As you know, building a nuclear power plant is extremely complex."

The reason I made this proposal was that an itemized bid requires an extensive review by a group of experts. Without experience, it was almost impossible for a company to calculate an accurate estimate of a project under the itemized bid procedure. If the government agreed to have an itemized bid, I was certain that we would win the contract.

I was correct; Hyundai won the bid to build units 3 and 4 of the Young-kwang Nuclear Power Plant. It was an odd victory—the same company winning the bid for the same project twice. It also marked the first time in Korea that a private company didn't have to put up political funds after winning a government-ordered infrastructure project.

During the Sixth Republic, when the opposition party won the majority in parliament, there were hearings into KEPCO, particularly regarding the bidding procedure for the Young-kwang Nuclear Power Plant Project. Former president of KEPCO Park Chung-kee and I were called as witnesses to testify at the hearings. The members of parliament (called the National Assembly in Korea) were suspicious of illicit activities during the bidding process. They were intent on proving that KEPCO, with the government's backing, had awarded the lucrative project to a private company of its choosing: Hyundai. The National Assembly was in the process of getting rid of any remnants of the Fifth Republic, and this became a symbolic case of rooting out the corruption that was so prevalent during the Fifth Republic.

Before taking the stand, I was required to give an oath. When this was done, I asked the members of the National Assembly if I could spend a few minutes explaining the details of the nuclear power plant industry and the related bidding process before taking any questions. They agreed. I proceeded to talk about the nuclear power industry. I first spent about ten minutes briefly outlining the history of Hyundai's experience in building nuclear reactors. I explained how we had first started out as a subcontractor of Westinghouse and how we later became the only company in Korea capable of building a nuclear reactor on its own. I then explained to them how other countries selected companies. "What happens in other countries is that when a nuclear power plant contract that is open to competitive bidding goes to the lowest bidder, its parliament conducts a thorough investigation and carries out an audit to see if there were any irregularities involved. Korea is the exact opposite.

This is because many of us lack understanding of how crucial safety is when talking about nuclear reactors. Some people even equate building nuclear reactors with building highways. But if cracks appear on highways, they can always be repaired. If a nuclear reactor breaks down—just once—the result is catastrophic. You can't just go in there and fix it. Therefore, emphasis must be placed on whether the candidates are capable of building safe and reliable nuclear reactors, not whether the bidding process is open or competitive." When I was done with my presentation, I invited questions. There were none.

My ordeals at Hyundai weren't limited to annulled contracts, interrogations by questionable agents in secret locations, and arguing about the future of the Korean economy with military officers. It was also about fighting this unseen monster called Bureaucracy. It often felt as if I was inside Kafka's "Castle," an endless abyss where everything vanished. Utter disregard for the rule of law, lack of common sense, feebleness, and cowardice—such were the traits of an authoritarian regime and the bureaucrats who pledged allegiance to it. It was sad and worrisome.

11 | LEARNING TO WORK, LEARNING TO LIVE

My success will be remembered by others; I don't have to constantly remind myself. However, I must always remember my failures, for if I forget, I'm bound to repeat them.

The government and the bureaucracy weren't the only places where reason, common sense, and logic went missing. Hyundai also had plenty of faults that needed fixing and traditions that were hard to get rid of. Once I became an executive, I set about changing them.

One was the practice of providing an executive with many perks, such as a chauffeur, a secretary, and sometimes even a cook. In the 1970s I met a foreign executive while I was working in Thailand. He told me he was astonished when he saw Korean executives enjoying such lavish perks. I was embarrassed. When I became an executive, I got rid of such unnecessary traditions. Executives were told to drive themselves to and from work and to use a chauffeur only on official business.

I also vastly streamlined the reporting process. Since Korea is a strictly hierarchical society, memos at Hyundai had to travel a long and winding road before they finally reached an executive or the chairman. The fallout was that this process provided little incentive to the original architect; the one who drafted the memo would be excluded as the memo was tampered with and altered by the people signing it. So I streamlined the process so that the one who came up with the idea could take part from start to finish and would take full responsibility as well as credit.

Another practice that I adopted as an executive was to answer all late-night calls myself, regardless of the time. Many executives would tell their staff to call them "anytime," but rarely would they answer the phone. Even if they did, they would sound tired or half-asleep, which would discourage anyone from calling them ever again at night. But I consider time to be of the essence, especially for an executive who is involved in international business. Critical decisions must be made regardless of time; sometimes a few minutes can mean the difference between closing the deal and losing out to your opponent. When someone called me at home in the middle of the night or early in the morning, I would make sure to answer the call with a clear voice, even if I had been asleep. I became an expert at this, and soon people wondered if I ever slept at all! After talking on the phone, I would hang up and immediately fall back to sleep. (Another habit was to always write down memos during those calls, lest I forget in my sleep.)

Ever since the days when Mother had woken us up at 5 a.m. every morning, I never slept past 5 a.m., whether I was in Korea or abroad. Time differences didn't matter, since I would never sleep during my flight; as soon as I arrived at my destination, I would go straight to the gym or squeeze in a game of tennis and then go about my business. After that, I would be dead-tired at night and would have no trouble falling asleep or getting up at five in the morning.

Many people ask me how I keep fit when I'm always so busy. I answer them—I can do all this and more *because* I'm so busy. If I had all the time in the world, I wouldn't have achieved as much. I saw many new employees at Hyundai who excelled at their work in the beginning, but once they reached a certain point, they would wither and fall. I wondered why this happened to some people and not to others. The reason was that those who continued to do well invested time and energy into learning the basics.

A good example is provided by the volleyball teams of Korea and Japan. Korean high school volleyball teams always beat their Japanese counterparts. This is because in Korea the coaches teach their student athletes the tricks of winning the game. In Japanese high schools, only the basic skills of volleyball are taught. When these two high school teams compete, it's natural that the Korean team would win. However, the situation is completely reversed once it reaches the professional level. Since Japanese players no longer need to learn the basics, they spend time learning new and difficult techniques that vastly improve their skills, while the Korean players are slow at learning new tricks, since they haven't mastered the basics.

Similarly, once a person has a firm foundation in the fundamentals, that person is able to add new techniques that allow him to become even better at what he does. He will also be good at managing his time, and ultimately he will dominate his work and not the other way around. Anyone can be a hard worker, but it's much more valuable to become a smart worker.

Because I learned this lesson early on, I was able to keep myself busy *and* do what was really important, such as taking care of my family, talking with my wife, and enjoying the many joys that life offered. I always had the time to play tennis twice a week; talk to my children, even if it was for brief moments on the phone when I was away; and listen to music or read a good book. I also learned from my failures and mistakes. I would always tell myself that it is best to forget the good stuff and instead remember the bad. This is because my successes will be remembered by others; I don't have to constantly remind myself of them. However, I must always remember my failures, for if I forget, I'm bound to repeat them.

On the other hand, those who were dominated by work were always busy, with no time for other important matters. And I noticed that such employees were the ones who constantly complained about their workloads and their bosses and everything else that was wrong with their lives. Rarely, if ever, did these people blame themselves. To such people, no job or boss is ever going to be satisfactory. Expecting to get a dream job with a great boss is foolish and naïve. To me, life has always been about doing my best and being content, whatever the circumstances. I never blamed my parents for being poor and never used poverty as an excuse. I never resented being born in a poor country. It was just another reason I worked hard at whatever I did; I considered it my duty to work hard.

In November 1977, I felt abnormally tired and was on the verge of collapse from fatigue. When I went to the hospital to see what was wrong, I was diagnosed with hepatitis B. Since my condition was considered severe, my doctor advised me to check into the hospital. I was surprised at the test results, so I agreed. But I soon regretted it. Hyundai was going through one of its toughest moments, and it was a critical period that could determine the fate of the company. I had to go back to work.

So, every morning I would wake up at 5 a.m. and go straight to work from the hospital. (Every morning we had our staff meeting at 7 a.m., so I needed to be in my office by 6 a.m. at the latest to check the cables and memos from our overseas offices that came in overnight.) My schedule remained the same—a series of meetings, giving out instructions, dinner with foreign partners, and more late-night meetings. I would return to the hospital around midnight. After about a week, my doctor decided it would be better to send me

home and to send over a nurse each night at midnight to check up
on me and to give me intravenous drips.

My family thought I was just tired from work; no one at the
office was aware of my condition, either. As my condition continued
to deteriorate, however, I finally decided to visit the leading special-
ist in liver disease. Dr. Kim Jung-ryong carried out a thorough test
and informed me that my numbers were dangerously high; I was
diagnosed with chronic hepatitis. He went on to insist that I stop
working immediately so I could recuperate. He warned me that will-
power alone would not cure this disease. I told him I was needed at
work. I also told him I would rather die while working than spend
the rest of my life confined to the hospital, trying to cure the disease.
Dr. Kim then told me he could not accept me as his patient. I told
him that was too bad and went back to work.

For the next two months, I was unable to visit the hospital
because I was too busy. I finally went to see Dr. Kim two months
later; he agreed to see me, and after examining me he told me that
my condition had not gotten any worse. He asked me if I took time
to rest. I told him no, but that I was taking his advice to heart and
doing my best to take good care of my body. Dr. Kim stressed that I
mustn't drink any alcohol. I told him I would do my best. So, whenever I was entertaining a guest or when people were out drinking, I
would pretend to take a sip of beer, and when no one was watching
I would drink some water to wash it away.

However, my condition was still serious. I had a hard time digest-
ing food. I took many pills after every meal (when people asked
about them, I said they were vitamins). I would have to go to the
bathroom very often. All the while, I prayed to God, telling Him that
I couldn't die, not yet. I knew I had a lot more to do with my life. It
wasn't about simply wanting to live longer; I had to live in order to
do what I was meant to do.

Luckily, my condition began to improve. Once in 1988 my condition deteriorated, but I soon recovered. Finally, in 1990, when I went for my regular checkup, my doctor looked at my results and was amazed. He told me that the hepatitis B virus was gone. Incredulous, he conducted another set of tests, but the results came back the same. My body had miraculously developed an antibody to the disease (my doctor emphasized that this was an exceptional case).

Some would say that I was reckless to risk my life for work, but I continued to work because I still had a lot to do in life. Besides, I took extra care so that the disease wouldn't spread. I had regular checkups, exercised more often, took full rests whenever I could, quit drinking alcohol altogether, and ate healthy foods and took vitamins. I never tempted fate. All I did was live my life as I always had—working smart, working hard, and always being grateful.

12 | INTO THE WORLD

"My people have been working day and night to try to get rid of poverty and to make our country prosperous. Yes, I am a businessman and I work for my company. But in a capitalist country, companies play a crucial role, and the success of a company is success for the country."

Entering Iraq

Hyundai was fast becoming a global corporation, and no market or country was off-limits. We were constantly seeking new markets, and one was Iraq, which was quickly emerging as a promising country in the region. However, we couldn't find a way to enter Iraq. When Saddam Hussein became president of Iraq in 1979, it became even more difficult, as the Iraqi government refused to issue visas to South Korean nationals. Saddam Hussein once said that he deeply admired the late Kim Il-sung[21], the "Great Leader" of North Korea and the father of Kim Jong-il, the current ruler of North Korea. Iraq has always had a close relationship with North Korea, and it was an open secret that thousands of North Koreans were in Iraq, disguised as military advisers, tae kwon do instructors, and businessmen. To North Korea, Iraq was an important ally, and North Korea had few allies. Thus, North Korea invested heavily in cultivating its ties with Iraq, and it made sure Iraq would not become too close to South Korea. As a result, animosity and distrust of South Koreans in Iraq were widespread.

Nevertheless, Iraq was an attractive market for Hyundai. As the Saudi market became saturated and problems began to surface doing business in Saudi Arabia[22], Hyundai started to look for other markets in the Middle East. And Iraq's new government was just beginning to implement ambitious plans to develop the country. It announced its intention to invest $45 billion between 1976 and 1980 and another $75 billion between 1980 and 1985. As a result, Iraq quickly emerged as the second-largest market in the Middle East, after Saudi Arabia. The problem was that, due to the visa restrictions, we couldn't go in.

Our first breakthrough came in 1978. My colleague Chun Kap-one, who was vice president for overseas operations, managed to win the sewage treatment plant construction project in Basra, Iraq's second-largest city. The only reason he was able to win the contract was because the bid price was the lowest. It was a desperate attempt, but this was the only way for Hyundai to make inroads to Iraq. We were determined to suffer financial losses to gain access to this vast, untapped market.

At that time, I was president of Hyundai Construction's overall domestic operations. However, Chung asked me to help out with the overseas operations whenever time permitted. So when Hyundai won the Iraq contract, I made sure that all the arrangements were in place for our engineers and technicians traveling into and out of Iraq, including measures to ensure their safety. Also, we needed to go about our project creatively. We needed to be prepared for unexpected difficulties doing business in a country with no diplomatic ties, and where people's sentiments were less than cordial.

To check all these matters myself, I traveled to Kuwait and entered Iraq by land. I was the president of a company that had just won a contract in a country I was not allowed to enter; I was given no visas. I felt like a secret agent in a spy thriller. It took me several days to reach my destination in Baghdad. After moving surreptitiously through the streets of Baghdad guided by a local staffer, I was finally able to meet the Iraqi official in charge of our project. The first words he said were, "How in the world did a *South* Korean company win the contract?" He couldn't believe it. He looked bewildered and a bit amused. We sat down, had tea, and talked for a while. I promised him that Hyundai would do its best and asked that he help us. He promised he would help, but he seemed only vaguely interested.

Our entourage stayed in Baghdad for many days, trying desperately to find some connection—any connection—with the new revolutionary leadership. We knew this was critical. One day, as we were sitting in a nightclub called Moulin Rouge in Baghdad contemplating our next move, an Asian lady came over and asked if she could join us. She introduced herself as a Japanese national.

When I got up to go to the washroom, she came after me without being conspicuous. She looked around to make sure no one was watching, and then she asked me in a whisper, "You came from South Korea, right?" She was actually Korean. I had thought that we were the first South Koreans to set foot on Iraqi soil after the revolution, but we had been beaten by this frail-looking woman. It turned out she had come to Iraq after hearing that she could make money here. She married a foreigner (a marriage of convenience) and came into Iraq; she told us that if the authorities found out she was a South Korean national, she would be deported instantly. She then asked me, "What brings you to Baghdad?"

I was struck by the woman's temerity and admired her guts. She was risking a lot by staying in a Muslim country that had just gone through a revolution. And here I was, head of Korea's largest construction company, being asked by a Korean woman in a nightclub in Baghdad what I was doing.

A few days later, our first break came. A local helper suggested we meet with the mayor of Baghdad, whose name was Wahab. It turned out that Mayor Wahab had very close connections with Saddam Hussein. When Saddam Hussein was planning his revolution, he and his comrades would meet up in Mayor Wahab's house. This was when Wahab was attending law school.

We found out about Wahab only after we were tipped off by our local helper. This was how ignorant we were about Iraq and its new leadership. We had no reliable intelligence. All the information we managed to gather came from the U.S. Embassy in Seoul, but it was information you could find in any ordinary travel brochure.

As we'd expected, it was almost impossible to set up an appointment with the mayor. We made repeated requests, but all of them were denied. I approached the interpreter who was working at city hall and pleaded with him. "Please convey to the mayor my sincere wish to see him just once. Please tell him not to consider me a businessman from South Korea but a man from the Far East who wishes to meet a young Iraqi revolutionary."

Iraq was unlike any other Middle Eastern country in that it didn't use intermediaries or agents when awarding contracts to companies. Therefore, Iraq was a relatively clean country where we didn't have to pay either official fees or unofficial bribes to anyone. So I figured the only way for me to meet with a high-level official was to appeal to his softer side. I knew that revolutionaries prided themselves on being honest, clean, and above corruption.

My guess was right. I was finally granted an audience with Mayor Wahab. But I was given only ten minutes.

I walked into his office. It was simple and modest. Although the mayor was a civilian, he was wearing what appeared to be a military uniform, and he also had a pistol strapped to his waist. I thanked him for giving me the time and said, "You seem to be fully committed to the revolution, a person who has dedicated his life to making life better for your people. I admire that. And I believe being able to do that for your country is a true blessing."

Wahab simply remarked, "Yes." He then went on, "I only sleep three to four hours a day. It's because we're all determined to make this country a better place. So, we all have no time to sleep. In fact, right now I'm splitting my busy schedule to meet with you."

I replied, "Thank you. I also sleep no more than four hours a day. I think we may have more similarities than you think."

Wahab looked at me and asked with a puzzled look, "You tell me you're a businessman. Why is it that you sleep only four hours a day?"

By now, my ten minutes was up. But I continued to keep him interested. "My country was extremely poor when I was born. Even today, there is poverty. My people have been working day and night to try to get rid of poverty and to make our country prosperous. Yes, I am a businessman and I work for my company. But in a capitalist country, companies play a crucial role, and the success of a company is success for the country."

I went on, "I was born into a very poor family. We had to work hard, and I have worked ever since I was a young boy. So for me, work was always a part of my life. This is why I'm here in Iraq. I know I can be useful to you and also be useful for my company and my country. We already won a contract, but because there are so many restrictions, we're having a hard time. And I wanted to tell you that we're different from others. We Koreans are known to be diligent and extremely hard-working. We're also very honest. We consider you our partner and friend. We are both trying to make our countries prosper." Wahab listened carefully. "And I've worked in many other countries in the Middle East, but I have never seen any country as free of corruption and as clean as yours. This is another reason I really want to work here."

When I was done, Mayor Wahab unfastened his pistol from his waist and eased into his chair. He later told me he was wary of South Koreans because he knew how close South Korea was to the United States, a country he considered imperialist. After listening to me, he slowly began to open up, and we started talking about different topics. He spoke of his desire to revolutionize his homeland; I talked about our own experience in economic development and the work I had done at home and abroad. He displayed keen interest when I talked about all the overseas projects I had worked on and what Hyundai planned to do in Iraq. We also spoke about the history of Iraq and Korea and how there were many similarities. Each of us spoke passionately about our homeland. We even talked about our families.

Soon, Mayor Wahab instructed his assistant to postpone all his meetings to make sure that we were not disturbed. More tea was brought in, and we continued our talk. After two hours, I finally got up to leave. But before leaving, I asked him if it would be OK to leave a small gift that I had brought for him. He asked me what it was, and when I told him I had left it with his assistant, he told his assistant to bring it in. It was a model of a "turtle ship" that was first built by Korea's most famous admiral, Yi Sun-shin, during the sixteenth century[23]. I told him the battleship symbolized the unbreakable spirit of the Korean people. "It would be an honor if you would display this in your office." Wahab said he would be glad to. He also told me to come see him the next time I visited Baghdad.

Although my meeting with Mayor Wahab turned out to be more fruitful than I had expected, problems persisted. I came back to Korea, and the first thing I did was take care of the entry visas of our engineers. My meeting with Wahab hadn't made all these problems disappear. Since Korea didn't have diplomatic relations with Iraq, our workers had to go through Kuwait. There, they waited weeks for their visas. Visas would be issued on an individual basis, so we had no way to plan their entry en masse. A Korean consulate-general in Iraq would have expedited the process a great deal, but when I contacted our foreign ministry, they replied that the relationship between Korea and Iraq wasn't nearly close enough to warrant the establishment of a consulate-general.

I returned to Baghdad and requested a meeting with Mayor Wahab. He told me to meet him at the Hunting Club at noon. The Hunting Club was an exclusive club patronized only by the top elites. Members were mostly cabinet-level officials with close ties to the leadership. Once we sat down, he asked me about the situation in Korea. After ordering lunch, he asked me a lot of questions about our economic development model. Then suddenly he said, "As you know, Iraq has close ties with North Korea. I suggest you be very careful when you do business here. I'm sure you're going to encounter a lot of difficulties."

This was what I was hoping for, a chance to gently raise the issue of visas. I said, "Yes, we are experiencing a lot of difficulties. But what's more disturbing is that your state project is falling behind schedule. This is what worries me more than the troubles we are going through. I'm the president of Hyundai, but it took me four days to get into Baghdad. Four days! Imagine how long it takes for my employees to get here. The engineers and technicians have to wait for weeks. We have hundreds of them just sitting around all day waiting to get in. So we're having a hard time finishing the project. Something needs to be done, Mr. Mayor."

"What do you suggest?" he asked.

"First of all, it would be great if Iraq could issue us a block visa. That's normally how other countries do it, too."

Wahab immediately replied, "Done! Just give me the papers for this block visa." When we finished lunch and as we were about to say good-bye, Wahab gave me a bear hug. "Lee, I'm so happy that we have become good friends! We are like brothers, my friend. No, we *are* brothers!"

Wahab was knowledgeable about literature and he was greatly interested in the arts. He would often quote from ancient scripts and impress me with his extensive knowledge about philosophies of the east and the west. He was of course a man deeply involved in politics, but I noticed a softer side. This was the side of him that made him a key player in the revolution, a revolution in which he earnestly believed and worked hard for.

Wahab also kept his word. The next day he called to tell me happily that the Iraqi Foreign Ministry would be issuing a block visa to our workers as a special favor. It was a gesture of goodwill and a reflection of his stature within the revolutionary government. I was grateful and also quite impressed.

A month later I went to Iraq for my third visit. This time I invited Wahab to lunch. I told him I must repay him since he had treated me to a sumptuous meal and solved a vexing problem of mine. I made sure to reserve seats at one of the best restaurants in Baghdad. He said he would be bringing along two of his close friends. One of them was the minister for housing and construction and the other was minister for industry, both powerful men. Both were also Wahab's revolutionary comrades. In particular, the minister for industry was widely believed to be one of the most influential men in government.

Wahab introduced me to them, and we all sat down and ordered our meal. Wahab said, "These men are like my brothers, Lee. If you want to continue doing business in Iraq, you will need their help, believe me." The minister for housing was the man in charge of overseeing our project. I knew it would have been extremely difficult, if not impossible, for me to arrange a meeting with him without Wahab's help.

I was relieved when both men seemed to get comfortable after a while. The minister for industry was very interested when I told him about Hyundai's experience building power plants. Pretty soon, we all became good friends. It was surprising how quickly we became so close. Iraqis are known to be a fiercely proud people. Historically, Iraq has always been a major force in the region, and they were intensely proud of that fact. But they also had a side that respected diversity and had a fondness for the arts and culture. They valued friendship and honor above all else. This made it easy for anyone to become close friends and remain friends for a long time.

When lunch was over, the two ministers bade us farewell. We promised to meet again in the near future. Wahab and I stayed behind to talk some more. When we were alone, I briefly mentioned the idea of opening a consulate-general in Baghdad; however, I noticed Wahab become nervous, and I quickly changed the subject.

A month later when I visited Baghdad for the fourth time, I was contacted by my Iraqi friends as soon as I checked into my hotel. They already knew of my visit from their sources in Baghdad. The minister for industry called and asked me to join him for dinner. I gratefully accepted his offer. As I was getting ready, I received a call from the minister for housing, who also invited me for dinner; when I told him I already had an appointment, he was disappointed.

The minister for industry invited me to a restaurant situated along the Tigris River. The building was built more than four hundred years ago. It offered magnificent views of the majestic river beneath. When we arrived, I was greeted by Mayor Wahab, the minister for housing and another "friend" I didn't know. They explained that they had all decided to come out that night to welcome me. I thanked them for their kind gesture. Their friend turned out to be the minister for heavy industry and mineral resources.

The minister for industry explained how he had been impressed when I told him about Hyundai's work in building power plants. He thought then that I should get to know the minister for heavy industry and mineral resources, since power plants fell under his portfolio. I was grateful.

We all enjoyed the night. Our drink that night was very similar to Korea's *soju*, and the name even sounded similar. Quite a lot of it was brought over. We were also surprised to learn that many of our words sounded similar. For instance, the Korean words for "father" (*ae-bi*) and "mother" (*ae-mi*) are pronounced almost the same in Arabic. This was not altogether that surprising, considering that historical records since the fifth century BC, when Korea was ruled by the ancient Shilla dynasty, show seafaring traders from Arabia coming to Korea. Arab merchants brought with them Middle Eastern culture. Korea and Iraq were at opposite ends of the Silk Road.

Throughout the night, all of us talked about how close our two countries were in many aspects. One of them also spoke passionately about the new Iraq's desire to engage with Korea on a deeper level. He pointed out how Iraq always worked with countries like Japan, Germany, France, and the UK, but how they felt none of them treated Iraq as an equal partner. He went on to say how he hoped our two countries could work more closely together.

The revolutionary leaders of Iraq were deeply committed in the beginning; they were intent on transforming their country, and they were looking for new partners they could trust. I happened to be at the right place at the right time, creating a golden opportunity for Hyundai.

Soon, Hyundai was winning contracts in Iraq. Hyundai was able to beat rival Japan to win the $720 million Al-Mussaib thermal power plant project on a turnkey basis. Later, Hyundai also won the $820 million housing project to be completed in Fallujah. As for the thermal power plant project, the Iraqis knew that our firm was technically incapable of delivering the plant on a turnkey basis. Nonetheless, the Iraqis awarded us the project and even advised us to use Japanese technologies and import materials from Japan, if needed. The reason for this was twofold: they wanted to be able to say to the advanced countries that they were no longer the "old" Iraq, and they wanted to protect their national interest.

Our foray into Iraq began to quicken. My friendships with Mayor Wahab and the others continued. Thanks to Wahab, I was able to meet with the man in charge of Iraq's economic policies. He was reputed to be the one who was running day-to-day business. Iraq had its own cabinet, but apart from this the Revolutionary Council dictated and made most of the major decisions. Saddam Hussein was the chairman of the council, but this man was actually running it.

Wahab took me to the palace where the man was waiting for me. Television crews were also present, and the image of the two of us shaking hands was broadcast on the evening news in Baghdad. After exchanging greetings, we sat down, and tea was served.

As I was coming over, I asked Wahab what I should say to the man. Wahab was considerate; he suggested I raise the issue of establishing diplomatic relations.

The man told me that this was the first time he had met with a foreigner in charge of construction. He said that he had heard a lot about me from his colleagues. He thanked me and wished me good luck. I nodded and told him I would do my best. I then gently told him there was one thing I was hoping for. He asked me, "What is that?" I proceeded to explain the difficulty of continuing and finishing the construction project due to the many restrictions. As soon as

I uttered those words, the man understood where I was headed, and I saw his face turn grim.

A while before, during the ceremony to celebrate Iraq's revolution, a large delegation from North Korea headed by vice premier Park Sung-chul came to Iraq. It is said that the North Koreans vehemently protested the Iraqis allowing a South Korean company into Iraq; the Iraqis assuaged the North Koreans by telling them that Iraq's relationship with Hyundai was strictly business and that Hyundai was doing what North Korea was not capable of. The Iraqis told the North Koreans, "You are always welcome to do whatever it is Hyundai is doing. That is, if you can. We're just working with the South Koreans. Our relationship with you is still the same, so don't worry." The North Koreans weren't pleased, but they had nothing to say, I was told. Still, the Iraqis were caught in a dilemma.

I told the man that I wasn't asking for immediate action but requested that he at least look into the matter. He replied, "I'll consider it carefully." It was neither negative nor positive, so I saw hope. In business and diplomacy, it's important to nudge your way in when you see even the tiniest opening.

Later, when I was alone with Wahab, he asked me what Hyundai would offer in return. He needed something to take back to his people. I offered him Hyundai cars. I thought it would be good publicity and a show of our new friendship if Hyundai cars roamed the streets of Baghdad. However, Wahab said, "We already have enough cars. How about pick-up trucks?"

I said, "Of course!" (Even though, at the time, Hyundai didn't make pick-up trucks.)

Wahab said, "Excellent! Then send us your pick-up trucks and I'll see what I can do about setting up a consulate-general."

I told him, "Thank you, my brother. I assure you we will do our best to help you rebuild Iraq. Trust me."

I returned and reported my meetings to the president's office back in Seoul. I was worried that our own government would be overly cautious in establishing diplomatic relations with Iraq, due to our relationship with the United States. So I emphasized that the Iraqis had given me positive signals about establishing full diplomatic relations to make the deal more attractive. I then waited a week before the president's office gave me the go-ahead to donate our pick-up trucks.

As soon as the request was granted, we set up a separate manufacturing assembly line at our Pony plant and built customized pick-up trucks. The factory turned out pick-ups by working overtime. We loaded the trucks onto a special freight to Kuwait. The ceremony in Iraq to commemorate the donation of the pick-up trucks was so elaborate that we all thought we already had diplomatic relations.

When I returned after attending the ceremony, I was visited by a high-ranking agent of the KCIA. He explained that his agency had been working behind the scenes to establish ties with Iraq through our embassy in Kuwait. He boasted that his agency had made much progress and warned me that this was a matter that must be dealt with between governments. He advised me not to disrupt the negotiations. In short, he wanted me to butt out.

During the 1980s, it was considered a tremendous accomplishment when new diplomatic ties were opened. Beginning with the Park Chung-hee administration, there was competition between the two Koreas regarding the number of embassies that each had abroad. It was a race among various agencies within Korea to gain as many friends as possible. It often turned comical, as in this case, where each agency tried desperately to claim victory.

I understood the nature of the bureaucracy and let them take the spotlight. After all, they needed to look good to their superiors; to me, it didn't matter who got the credit as long as Hyundai was able to do more business in Iraq with fewer restrictions. I told the agent from the KCIA that I had no intention whatsoever to claim credit or even share any of it. A few days later, I was contacted by a high-level official from the Foreign Ministry, who basically said the same thing. I smiled bitterly to see these people all of a sudden so interested in Iraq. As far as I recall, I was never once contacted or helped by any of them when I went into Iraq. And even afterward, they had no interest in my activities until the issue of diplomatic relations came up.

In the end, Korea was finally allowed to open a consulate-general in Iraq. I invited Wahab and the minister for industry to Korea. I was pleased to have the chance to pay them back for their friendship and hospitality. They visited many sites in Korea, and I made sure to show them how much Korea had been able to achieve. They were profoundly impressed by our progress and fell in love with our culture and, most of all, with Korean cuisine. I made sure they were fed well at every meal.

After the opening of the consulate-general, many Korean firms were able to go into Iraq, and the construction industry entered its second Middle East boom. Unfortunately, in 1979, just a year after setting up our consulate-general, the Iranian Revolution took place. The Iranian monarchy was ousted, and a new Islamic Republic under Ayatollah Khomeini was born. Iran had a new government, and the following year the Iraq-Iran war started. We had no choice but to leave Iraq as the war intensified. Our Korean companies were once again forced to look for new markets.

Baghdad Exodus

The Iraq-Iran War brought about unexpected changes to Hyundai's presence in Iraq and also to my personal fate. There's a saying—

"You win the battle but lose the war." I was triumphant in my quest to break open the Iraq market, but I lost the "war" afterward as a result of a real war.

Hyundai was hard hit by its loss in Iraq; our sudden pull-out was a tremendous strain on our finances. Rumors started to circulate that because of Iraq, my relationship with Chung and my status within Hyundai was shaky. Some were speculating that I would soon move to another company or that Chung was going to fire me. Some predicted that I would choose to walk away with dignity, quit business, and become a politician; others were saying that I had been offered a cabinet post and that I would accept at any time.

Regardless of such talk, I was still confident that Hyundai's entry into Iraq was the right thing to do at the time. I was also sure that once Iraq regained stability, Hyundai would be given another chance. In the meantime, since we were unable to receive our payments because of the war, we agreed to be paid in oil.

Perhaps Chung blamed me for all the trouble Hyundai had to go through. I was the one who had spearheaded our drive into Iraq. But Chung never voiced his inner thoughts to me. Nor did we ever engage in discussions regarding the Iraq debacle. There was, however, an awkward silence between us after Iraq during which we talked less. This in itself was quite unusual, considering the kind of relationship that we had. It was certainly no small matter, and it was quite painful for me.

While we were giving each other the silent treatment, we attended a dinner hosted by a government official with whom I was close. I had arranged this dinner because the official had asked me to introduce him to Chung. During dinner, this official looked at Chung and said, "Chairman Chung, Mr. Lee is a person I greatly respect and admire. I hope you will continue to take care of him." I never asked the official to say anything on my behalf; I still don't know if he was even aware of the awkwardness between me and Chung. It is my guess that he was just trying to repay my favor in introducing him to Chung and that, out of courtesy, he was putting in a good word to Chung. Chung looked at me and said, "Well, this man here is someone who will never surrender, even if he's on the ground and someone's stepping on his throat. He doesn't really need anyone to take care of him. He's one tough son of a bitch."

I managed to smile, and we moved on to different subjects. But what Chung said that night stayed with me for a long time. Did he mean that I *was* on the ground and that I was not giving up, even though someone was stepping on my throat? Or did he mean that I was someone who always manages to get up, with or without anyone's help? I don't know. One thing I did realize that night was that Chung Ju-yung could very well be the person to step on my throat one day.

Interestingly, my uneasy relationship with Chung was eventually brought back to normal in the same place where the trouble began. In December 1982, shortly before we pulled out of Iraq, we boarded a plane from Kuwait headed for Baghdad. We were taken to the tarmac and checked and frisked; we were then told to load our own baggage into the cargo space of the plane. This was to prevent bombs from being placed on board. If a bag was left unattended, that meant the bag had no owner and probably contained explosives. Only when all the bags were accounted for and loaded were we told to board the plane. The plane was outdated and absolutely dilapidated; I think Chung Ju-yung and I are probably the only business executives in the world who were reckless enough to ride such a plane.

Once we arrived in Baghdad, we met up with our old friends. Our "brothers" in Iraq promised that they would look after Hyundai and make sure that we would not suffer unduly.

Then Chung and I took time to visit our construction sites. A war was going on, and mortars and rockets were always flying overhead, but Chung was unperturbed. He was back to being the field general, a role he had relished years ago. He seemed to be enjoying the rush and the commotion and all the grit. When Chung noticed something he didn't like, he would invariably ask who was in charge and yell, "You! I want your resignation letter. Now!" and then move on. Most people knew that he said that a lot and rarely meant it. Those who weren't familiar with his outbursts turned pale.

The night before we were to depart, Chung hosted a farewell dinner for all the site managers from around Iraq. Liquor was hard to find in Iraq at that time, but our resourceful managers enlisted the help of our local staffers and managed to rake together a substantial amount. With that, forty-plus men sat around drinking. It was a rowdy affair. We slaughtered many lambs and brought over a famous Iraqi dish called *maskouf*—a large fish that was caught in the Tigris River—from a nearby restaurant. People relaxed and forgot about what was going on, at least for a few hours. They drank late into the night, dancing and singing.

As the partying got more intense, I told Chung, "Mr. Chairman, why don't we return all the letters of resignation before we go?"

He replied happily, "Oh, that's right! OK, no one's fired!" and continued to drink.

Chung was having a great time. Years later, he would reminisce about that party in Iraq as one of his best memories. He would say that he felt true camaraderie there, drinking with men who were risking it all and fearful of nothing. He told me that those were real men, real warriors. He was proud to be their boss.

At 4 a.m., we packed up our things after the all-night party and headed toward Kuwait by car. I couldn't help but grimace for a moment, thinking about the long ride ahead. We had to travel fourteen hours and pass Basra, where intense fighting was taking place. But none of this seemed to matter. We were both reminded of the beginning, when all of this started. Chung and I were back to normal. And our work continued.

Malaysia, Mahathir, and the Penang Bridge

One leader I admire and call my friend is former Prime Minister Mahathir[24] of Malaysia. Mahathir is a modest man who dislikes pomposity and formalities; he is action-oriented and has dedicated his life to improving the lives of ordinary Malaysians.

The first time I met him was during the late 1970s, when Hyundai was building the Kenyir Dam in Malaysia. One of my jobs when traveling overseas was to meet with the various leaders of the countries, and Mahathir was one of those I met. However, although Mahathir was deputy prime minister at the time, he had no real power. This was because he was reinstated by Prime Minister Hussein Onn only when the public demanded that he be brought back after being ousted from the ruling party for defying the party line. Mahathir was brought back from exile and appointed as deputy prime minister, but he was given no responsibilities. Mahathir would spend his days alone in his office.

Whenever I was in Malaysia, I would drop by his office. This was 1981, when we were competing against France and Japan to win the contract for the Penang Bridge, which would be the longest bridge in Malaysia and the fourth-longest bridge in Southeast Asia. Japan's Marubeni had already won over many members of the Hussein government with bribes and gifts. Naturally, I was completely shut out and prevented from meeting any of the important decision-makers. So instead, I went and talked with Mahathir. Whenever I called on Mahathir, he would look at me and ask in his gentle, quiet voice, "Mr. Lee. I have no power to help you. Yet you still come see me. Why is that?"

I would say half-jokingly, "Well, Mr. Deputy Prime Minister, after every overseas business trip, I'm required to report who I met and what we talked about. But my Japanese competitors have effectively prevented me from meeting any of your colleagues, so I tell my boss that I met with the deputy prime minister so he thinks I'm doing my job. This will make him feel as though I'm meeting with someone very important."

Mahathir smiled back and said, "If that's the case, then you're welcome anytime, Mr. Lee. But on one condition: I hope you'll tell me about what's going on in your country."

From then on, we met more frequently. Mahathir was interested in our experience in ending poverty. He was a learned man and knew about our history of being colonized by Japan and how painful this was. He knew about our history of war and division, our military dictatorships and years of oppression, our strategic decision to invest in industrialization and develop our heavy industries, and much more.

He was particularly interested in our *Sae-ma-eul* (or "New Village") Movement, which played a pivotal role in eradicating poverty in our countryside. He understood that the most important factor enabling any country to escape poverty was reforming the minds of its people. If the people were willing, then anything was possible. Mahathir wanted to wean the Malaysian people from the complacency they had come to accept following decades of British colonial rule. He wanted the Malaysian people to embrace their destiny, to instill within them a sense of purpose and mission. This was one reason he was fascinated with Korea's experience, one that was in many ways quite similar to Malaysia's.

We became engrossed in our intellectual exchanges, and I often found myself proffering advice. Some of this advice was brutally honest, but Mahathir always listened carefully and with respect.

We would often go out for lunch together. No one recognized him when we walked into a restaurant. I'm sure Mahathir felt the indifference, and I'm sure he was biding his time, all the while conceiving and fine-tuning his vision for Malaysia. However, he was unaware of what was about to come. And I certainly had no idea that a big surprise was awaiting me. Mahathir would later play a decisive role in helping Hyundai win the Penang Bridge contract. Contrary to what he had said to me when we first met, he did have the power to help me.

I first heard about Malaysia's plan to build the Penang Bridge when I was working in Thailand during the late 1960s. The Penang Bridge, once completed, would span 14.5 kilometers, linking the island of Penang to mainland Malaysia. The total cost of the project was estimated at $300 million, and it quickly became Malaysia's most important national priority.

There were several reasons the Malaysian government considered this project so significant. One was the need to rein in the wealthy island of Penang and integrate it into the mainland economy. Penang is widely known for its scenic beauty and its potential as a major international tourist destination. It also had considerable value as an industrial base. Its value was so great that when Singapore gained independence, the Chinese residents initially asked to be given Penang instead of what is now Singapore. Another reason was political. Penang was effectively controlled by Chinese Malays, making it the hub for trade and industry. Penang was a provincial state, but its economic influence rivaled that of Singapore. By linking Penang with the mainland, Malaysia would not only benefit economically, it could also influence the powerful Chinese Malay community.

The bidding for the Penang Bridge began in early 1981. Hyundai devoted tremendous time and energy to the bid. Forty-one companies from seventeen countries took part in the bidding. Almost all the major construction companies in the world were eager. I was placed in charge of the process for Hyundai, and following our costly withdrawal from Iraq, I was determined to succeed.

Our plan was to first of all disregard the Europeans, who were less competitive in terms of overall cost; our focus was solely on our Japanese competitor, Marubeni. But the first-round results were a surprise. The French company Campenon Bernard came in first, with Hyundai a close second, followed by the Marubeni Corporation of Japan and a West German firm in fourth. These four companies then proceeded to the second round. The West German firm withdrew, so it was a contest between Hyundai, Campenon Bernard, and Marubeni.

Marubeni was a tough competitor. It had an inexhaustible supply of funds and an unbeatable network within Malaysia. So we decided to eliminate our other opponent and then focus all our efforts on beating Marubeni. It was a long shot, but it was worth trying. We convinced the Malaysians that we could finish the job much earlier than the French. Although the French bidding price was lower than ours, we explained that Malaysia could recoup that difference by collecting tolls much earlier than expected.

So the real problem was Japan. The Japanese were intent on overturning the disappointing results of the first-round vote, and they used everything they had. The Japanese embassy and government were fully involved. Japan offered enticing incentives, such as long-term loans at almost no interest. They also engaged in a negative ad campaign accusing Hyundai of negligence and poor technical skills. The main source materials for their campaign were the articles *Joong-ang Ilbo* had published unfairly attacking and defaming

Hyundai. And Japan made sure that I would not get anywhere near
the prime minister's office, let alone have an audience with the
prime minister.

The only person in Malaysia to whom I could turn was Mahathir.
Mahathir was sorry that he couldn't be of any help. I was touched
by his concern, but he was right. There was nothing we could do to
turn the tide, and the outcome seemed all but sealed. I came back to
Seoul having done my best.

After six months, I headed to Malaysia again. I didn't have any
hopes and I knew our chances were slim. I was aware of the
domestic turmoil and political upheaval that was going on in
Malaysia. In the spring of 1981, Malaysia saw a public uprising
calling for the ousting of the government, and there were talks about
the Hussein government collapsing. But I didn't realize how serious
the situation was.

When I arrived at the airport in Kuala Lumpur, however, I could
feel that the mood was very serious. Then I saw a newspaper headline in English that read: "Prime Minister Hussein Onn Dead." I
immediately dialed Mahathir's number. The phone was answered by
his secretary, and I promptly asked if I could see the deputy prime
minister. Considering the state of emergency, I fully expected my
request to be denied. Surprisingly, Mahathir came on the phone and
readily agreed to see me. However, he told me he had to fly out to
Singapore urgently, so he had no time to see me in his office. He
told me to go to his residence, since he was on his way home to
pack his bags and change clothes. I thanked him and headed
straight to his residence.

While I was chatting with his wife over tea, Mahathir arrived,
and we greeted each other warmly. I asked him, "Is it true? Are you
going to be prime minister?" Mahathir answered, "Let's wait and see.
Everything will be decided after I return from Singapore." I could

see that he was being cautious, but I also detected confidence in his eyes. I was also dying to ask him about the Penang Bridge bid. Prime Minister Hussein had not made any final decisions about the project before he died, so the Penang Bridge bid would now be decided by Mahathir! But I couldn't bring myself to ask him about the bid right then.

That afternoon, Mahathir was designated as the party chairman and simultaneously became the new prime minister. As soon as he became prime minister, Mahathir was able to carry forth the vision that he had honed during his time in the political wilderness, and he called for reform. His "Look East Policy" and "Clean Government" were the two main pillars of his new administration.

The "East" clearly indicated Korea. Mahathir was now putting into practice what he had formulated in his head. He was confident that he could learn from Korea and even overtake its progress. As a Korean businessman, I was proud. At the same time, I felt a sense of urgency, because I knew a man like Mahathir could very well deliver on that promise.

As for the bidding for the Penang Bridge, everything went back to square one. To a reform-minded new prime minister calling for clean government, accepting political funds in exchange for awarding a major state infrastructure project was totally out of the question. It was Mahathir's firm intention to root out the corruption that was prevalent under the previous administration; that was the essence of his Clean Government message.

Now my job was to convince Mahathir's new cabinet. We compared ourselves to the French and the Japanese and explained that we were better in terms of lowering costs and delivering reliable quality. We emphasized our commitment to becoming a trustworthy partner of Malaysia. The most appealing card of the Japanese—the loan at no interest—was thrown out as a result of Mahathir's call for reform. This was because scores of previous cabinet members who had served under Hussein were convicted of receiving bribes. This led to Marubeni losing all credibility.

In the end, Hyundai was awarded the Penang Bridge project. To this day, I consider the Penang Bridge one of my proudest accomplishments as a businessman. I felt fortunate that I was able to develop a lasting friendship with Mahathir. I was also pleased that the Penang Bridge had become a landmark and a source of pride for the Malay people. Even today, many Malaysians remember Hyundai, and many of them think of me as the architect, which is a great honor.

For the opening of Penang Bridge, after its completion in 1982, Hyundai prepared an elaborate ceremony that would showcase the grandeur we had managed to erect. Looking back, to be honest, the ceremony was born out of my own hubris. But I was sincerely grateful to Mahathir and the Malaysian people for believing in us, and I wanted to pay that back. We had experts flown into Malaysia; we erected a high podium for dignitaries and various VIPs. We made a large tent over the VIP section to block the sun and installed a specially designed console with buttons that would ignite massive fireworks. We placed two large chairs for Mahathir and the first lady that were distinguishable from the rest. In short, we replicated what our own government did in similar events back home.

A day before the ceremony, the chief of staff and an agent in charge of the prime minister's security visited the site to check whether all had been done according to protocol. They were shocked. The chief of staff looked around and asked me, "Why is there a tent over the VIP section? If you're going to have a tent over the VIPs, then what about the five thousand guests who'll be attending? Are you planning on setting up a tent for them, too?" I was dumbstruck. I had never thought of that. My only concern was with the VIP section.

The chief of staff then asked me, pointing at the chairs reserved for the prime minister and the first lady, "Why are those two chairs larger than the others? As far as I know, my prime minister's, um, behind isn't any bigger than the others."

That night, after replacing the chairs so that they were identical to the rest, we succeeded in setting up a tent to cover all 70,000 square feet where the ordinary guests were to be seated. One company couldn't erect the entire 70,000 square feet in time, so a total of twelve companies were selected, and each went about setting up approximately 6,000 square feet of tent. The chief of staff was right; Mahathir certainly didn't have a big behind, and he most definitely didn't have a big head, either.

Marcos and Imelda

After our victory in Malaysia, our next stop was the Philippines, where we were knocked out by our rival, Marubeni of Japan. And our loss was due to the peculiar and very personal nature of Philippine politics at the time.

The international bidding for a $150 million power line project took place just a year before President Ferdinand Marcos and his famous first lady, Imelda, fled the country. As in most developing countries with leaders who have been in office for far too long, all decisions made in the Philippines were made by those with power. And there were two figures in the Philippines who had equal amounts of power and who were above everyone else—President Marcos and his wife, First Lady Imelda.

Marcos and Imelda were an odd couple. Since it is known that they were quite a happy couple, a power struggle between the two seems unthinkable. Nonetheless, politics in the Philippines revolved around these two eccentric characters. They each had their own backers, who operated separately and often against each other. For foreign companies trying to win government contracts, it was crucial to decide where to place your bet. During most of the Marcos era, the Philippine construction market was dominated by the Japanese, especially the Marubeni Corporation. Marubeni was infamous for being the company that bankrolled the Marcos regime, and in return received almost all of the government contracts. But we were determined to win this project.

When the first-round results came in for the power line project, Hyundai came in first, while Marubeni came in second. Hyundai was working with a figure who had direct access to President Marcos, whereas Marubeni was working with someone belonging to the Imelda faction. And both sides knew what the other was up to at all times. Back then, anyone could "buy" government documents for a small fee.

Soon, our contest turned public and ugly. Agents representing each side started to attack the other. This public spat soon ripped the Philippine government into two camps—Marcos versus Imelda. It was a stark and disturbing lesson in state governance. It was disheartening and even painful to witness such a lovely country with vast potential spiral out of control, manipulated by corrupt officials looking to cash in. Of course, Hyundai had no choice but to go along with the infighting to win the bid—business was business. But it pained me nonetheless.

In the end, the project was awarded to Marubeni. When I asked our agent, who was a confidant of President Marcos, why Hyundai had lost, he simply answered, "Marcos lost to Imelda. It's as simple as that."

Following the assassination of Benigno Aquino Jr., the dramatic fall of Marcos, and subsequent revelations about their corruption (and the international headline-grabbing discovery of more than 2,500 pairs of shoes in Imelda's closet), Ms. Corazon Aquino, the widow of slain Benigno Aquino, was elected president. President Aquino was a world apart from the former president.

I had a chance to meet her when we were hosting a reception to commemorate the opening of the headquarters of the Asian Development Bank in Manila, which we built. General Fidel Ramos, who was serving as President Aquino's chief of staff of the armed forces (and later as minister of defense), was also present. As with Mahathir of Malaysia, both of them were different from the usual politicians.

When President Aquino gave a brief congratulatory remark, I noticed General Ramos sitting quietly in the back. He was then widely believed to be the new president's closest confidant, yet he exuded humility and shunned attention. President Aquino was also extraordinarily impressive with her mild manners, but her steely resolve was evident. She was accompanied by just two bodyguards.

During cocktails, President Aquino kindly approached me, and we exchanged greetings. Then I asked her, "Madam President, is it OK for you to travel with just two bodyguards? Shouldn't you have more security?" The horrible footage of Senator Benigno Aquino lying on the tarmac was still vivid in my mind; it was only natural for anyone to be concerned about her safety.

President Aquino smiled at me warmly and said, "President Lee, I was elected by the people because they yearn for freedom and democracy. That's why I ran for president in the first place. Democracy is my people's wish. With or without Aquino, democracy will continue in the Philippines. Regardless of who becomes president from now on, democracy will prevail. It is fate. So why should we spend all that money on protecting the president when the people are having such a hard time? I'll be fine."

Those words deeply impressed me. Later I was able to meet with General Ramos as well. General Ramos looked at me and said, "Do you remember the Philippines helping you during the Korean War? Back then Korea's per capita income was just $60, while the Philippines' per capita was $700. But now, we are seeking your help. Do you know why? There's only one reason—bad leadership. But fortunately, our leadership has been restored, and our politics are back to normal. Hopefully, we'll be able to catch up."

That was my hope as well. General Ramos was instantly likeable, and I knew he would continue to play an important role for his country. And he did, by becoming president following President Aquino. As I had expected, he became an extremely good president, widely admired and beloved by his people for revitalizing the economy and returning political stability to the Philippines.

13 | UNFORGETTABLE

When Korea was still a poor country, many of us considered our jobs solemn duties...It wasn't simply about making money, although for many that was what had brought them there. It was much more than that. The country needed them, and they answered its call.

Building bridges that connect land and people, power plants that brighten lives and sustain industries, and highways that enable growth and prosperity to spread is a thrilling experience. You can see and touch what you built, and what you built lasts a lifetime. It is one of the most rewarding jobs any person can ask for. But it is also extremely hard and very often dangerous. So it can also be heartbreaking.

When Korea was still a poor country, many of us considered our jobs solemn duties. Many men and women decided to sacrifice their lives so that their families and others could have better lives. And all of them had the firm conviction that they were serving a higher cause; that is why they bore the hardships, knowing that their work would allow others to enjoy what they themselves were never able to. It wasn't simply about making money, although for many that was what brought them there. It was much more than that. The country needed them, and they answered its call.

Hundreds of thousands went out to the deserts and the jungles overseas; women went abroad as nurses, and men went deep inside the coal mines of Germany, working eighteen hours a day. While building our first expressway in Korea, seventy-seven workers were killed on the job. During the 1980s, thirty to forty workers died every year on construction sites. This was partly because of a lack of awareness about safety regulations and poor protective equipment, but it was mostly because the work itself was fraught with danger and risk. Often, we were doing things for the very first time, not knowing the dangers involved. Today, we know through experience what to avoid and strictly abide by high safety standards. We are also able to utilize advanced technologies. But back then, it was all about doing work with your bare hands. That is why the stories behind so many of these men and women are so poignant and sad. To me, they are unforgettable.

One story I vividly remember was about a man named Choi. I first met Choi, a hard-working and quiet man, more than thirty years ago, when I was a new recruit working at the Thailand office as an accountant. Choi was in charge of the local workers. Choi had received very little education, and he came to Thailand so that his son wouldn't have to suffer like he had.

One day, the local Thai workers shot Choi over a minor dispute. Choi was shot seven times in the chest, but he miraculously survived. I would go visit him at the hospital after finishing work. Many others took turns taking care of him.

One day at the hospital, Choi asked me for a favor. He told me he was certain that I would one day rise to become an important person in the company. He then asked me not to ignore his family if they came to see me asking for help. I told him I wasn't sure about becoming someone important, but I promised him nonetheless that I would help his family as best I could. Soon afterward, Choi died in Thailand with no one from his family by his side.

Twenty years later, I became president of Hyundai Construction, but I had forgotten what he said to me years earlier. Then one day I received a message from a lady who said she was the widow of Choi, who used to work with me in Thailand. She said, "If you remember him, then I wish to see you. If you don't remember him, then I won't bother you." Suddenly, memories came flooding back. I told my secretary to call the lady back and tell her to come see me.

The lady came to my office the next day. She pulled out a yellow, tattered letter. It was the letter Choi had sent her while he was in the hospital. The letter said, "Dear wife, I'm not sure if I will be able to go back to Korea alive. I just wanted to tell you about a man I came to know and respect. His name is Lee Myung-bak, and he is a young accountant. He is a diligent man, and he is also a good man. If I die and you encounter any difficulties while taking care of our son, go see Lee just once. He promised me that he will help our family in any way he can. I know he will become someone important one day and that he will keep his promise. Life's not going to be easy for you raising our son alone, but after he graduates from high school, if you need help, please go see Lee. I'm sorry to leave you. Good-bye."

Tears welled up. I saw Choi in his hospital bed, gaunt and nearing death. And I remembered my promise.

I found out that his wife had raised their son alone and managed to get him through vocational high school. But his son couldn't get a job. It was then that she was reminded of the letter her late husband had sent years before. I asked her how I could help; she told me that she would like to see her son get a job and be allowed to go overseas. I told her, "Don't worry. I'll take care of it."

She was obviously not well off, but poverty didn't strip away her dignity. She reminded me of my mother. I then asked her if there was anything else she would like me to do. She told me, "No, President Lee. My husband made it very clear to ask you for only one favor. Even if there was anything else, I wouldn't bother you. Thank you so much." Her son was hired by my company, and he was soon sent overseas. She never asked me for anything else.

Another heart-wrenching story was when sixty workers died when Korean Air Flight 858 was blown up over Myanmar[25]. All 115 passengers on board, including sixty Hyundai workers and eleven crew members, were killed. No bodies were recovered. Those sixty workers had been working in Iraq, and many of them were coming home for the first time in years. Of those who died in the bombing, one was my close friend and associate, Mr. Kim Deok-bong, who was then our executive director for overseas power plant facilities. Kim and I were the same age, and we had traveled together on many overseas trips. He was known as one of the preeminent experts in building power plants, and we went to Iraq on numerous occasions when Hyundai was building the Al-Mussaib thermal power plant.

Kim was in love with his work, so he had no time to date. I was the one who implored him to get married, and fortunately he later married. When others his age were sending their kids off to college, he had a son who was just entering kindergarten.

In late 1987, Kim and I were involved in finalizing the Al-Mussaib plant deal while trying to win another deal in Iraq. Our negotiations with the Iraqi government were almost over, but we needed to resolve a financing issue.

One day Kim came to me and said he wanted to go to Iraq to close the deal. I told him he should postpone his trip since it was the holiday season, but he kept insisting. Normally people tend to avoid traveling during the year-end holiday season. I appreciated his willingness but suggested that he go to Iraq a week later, since there were pressing concerns in Korea, too. But Kim kept insisting, "I can't lose this opportunity. Timing is important. I think I can get this deal done if I go now." Kim left the next day.

A few days later, I received a telex saying that Kim would be returning. I telexed him back, instructing him that before he returned to Korea, he should stop over in London to take care of business concerning the purchase of equipment. He replied by telex that he would "return to Korea and visit London next time." After dispatching what would be his last telex, he immediately boarded that fateful plane.

When I heard the news of the incident and confirmed that Kim had been aboard, I visited his widow. She was devastated. She refused to attend the joint funeral for the deceased Hyundai employees, believing that her husband was still alive. When she was told that Kim was the highest-ranking employee among those who were killed, she changed her mind and attended. She knew that if she didn't attend, she would be dishonoring the other families.

I was asked to deliver the eulogy. I announced the company's decision to promote Kim from executive director to vice president. As I read his eulogy, I cried.

Another unforgettable memory was of a man named Hwang. When I was at one of our regional offices a long time ago, Hwang was a heavy machinery operator. He was a Hyundai veteran, having worked at Hyundai much longer than I had. Hwang sent me a letter while he was working in Iraq: "Mr. President, I have been working at Hyundai for over thirty years," the letter read. "Although I've been working for such a long time, I know I will remain just a laborer and will not be able to become a full-time employee of Hyundai. My only wish is that my son will become what I was never able to, a full-time employee at Hyundai Construction. My son will be graduating from college this year, but my wife tells me that his grades aren't good enough. I feel responsible for this because I was never there for him when he was growing up." The letter ended by asking me to favorably consider his son's application as a favor to an old and loyal "Hyundai-man."

I was touched because I knew what Hwang had gone through. I knew that spending your entire life as a laborer was in itself something to be applauded and respected. I knew that Hwang was one of those who sacrificed his own life for his family. He volunteered to go overseas whenever he could so he could send back more money. And as a father, he couldn't be there to see his children grow up.

When I checked his son's grades, it was as Hwang had told me— they weren't good enough. However, I discovered that his son was gifted in other areas, so I decided to hire him. Sometime later, I received another letter from Hwang. It read, "Mr. President, thank you so much for your kind consideration. I am deeply grateful. You have granted this old man his last and greatest wish! My son also met a fine woman after getting a job, and now he's going to get married. I plan on going back to attend his wedding. When I'm in Seoul, I hope I can go and visit you." Sadly, Hwang was also on Flight 858.

Being the president of a company is a privilege with many entitlements, but whenever such tragedies occur, I'm also reminded of the awesome responsibilities that I must fulfill. I'm allowed to do what I do because of people like Kim Deok-bong, Choi, Hwang, and many others. Without their selfless dedication and sacrifice, I wouldn't be where I am today. It has been an honor working with them; my duty will be to always remember, to never forget.

14 | SOMETHING NO ONE'S EVER DONE BEFORE

I knew that my ascension this time was different; I knew that my days at Hyundai were numbered and that it was now time for me to do my last bid for the company I had helped create...I needed to steer Hyundai in a new direction.

Entering a New World

In March of 1988, the year South Korea hosted its first summer Olympics, I was promoted to chairman and CEO of Hyundai Construction. I became the leader of one of Korea's largest and most profitable companies twenty-three years after entering it. I was forty-six years old. As usual, the press went berserk. I was immediately dubbed the "Idol of the Salarymen." It was flattering, but as always, I was slightly spooked by all the attention and ignored the hype. Also, I knew that my ascension this time was different; I knew that my days at Hyundai were numbered and that it was now time for me to do my last bid for the company I had helped create.

The year before, a major shift had begun taking place within Hyundai. Chung Ju-yung decided to hire professionals to take charge of his many subsidiaries, while he placed his brothers and second-generation Chungs in various positions with the group. Chung Sae-young was promoted to chairman of Hyundai Group, and Chung Ju-yung became the honorary chairman (in reality, Chung Ju-yung was still the undisputed leader).

With one pillar being held up by professional managers and the other by the up-and-coming second generation of Hyundai heirs, I was left to ponder my own position within the group. I had always considered myself as belonging to the first generation, together with Chung Ju-yung. If Chung was taking a step away from everyday operations, then I would follow. The professional managers were to prepare the way for the eventual rise of the younger Chungs as they took over the group.

I knew I would be forced to make a decision soon. I didn't intend to retire and spend the rest of my life moping around or waiting for some plum retirement package. Instead, I started thinking about my post-Hyundai career. But before that, I needed to steer Hyundai in a new direction. Hyundai desperately needed to change course to adapt to its new surroundings.

Hyundai had always managed to transform itself in ten-year cycles. During the 1960s Hyundai became the first company in Korea to venture overseas; the '70s were spent exploring new markets, such as the Middle East, and becoming a global company. It was crucial for any private company to read the trends and to adapt and transform itself. When companies become complacent and too comfortable with the status quo, they start to fall behind. Innovation, reform, and pioneering new frontiers were the only ways forward. This was what Hyundai needed, and it was itching for a new sense of purpose, a new mission to fulfill.

As for Chung Ju-yung, he was becoming increasingly disillusioned and disgusted by politicians. Beginning with the hearings during the start of the Fifth Republic, he and his beloved company had been constantly under attack. During the Sixth Republic, the situation didn't get any better, and he had to battle negative perceptions by the public as well. His sufferings caused morale to plummet within the Hyundai Group, and we needed to turn the tide.

During this period, I spent considerable time in front of a world map. I was looking at the possibilities and figuring out where Hyundai needed to go. I was asking myself, where is the New World for Hyundai? This is when my mind turned toward the "Northern Territories" or "Northern Countries."

Geographically, the Northern Territories included the northern area adjacent to the Korean Peninsula, such as the former Soviet Union, China all the way to Eastern Europe, and of course North Korea. It was a vast region inhabited by millions of people. For us, it was virgin territory, a land where we had no diplomatic relations and where no South Korean company had ever set foot.

To South Koreans who still remembered the Korean War, the Northern Territories were a feared place, a land that once invaded our country. It was the untouchable land, a place we knew nothing about. From a political standpoint, "Northern Diplomacy" was ultimately aimed at Pyongyang (the capital of North Korea); Moscow and Beijing were stopovers to reaching Pyongyang. However, from a business perspective, this was far too short-sighted and narrow in scope. The former Soviet Union and China were immensely important to Korea—politically, economically, culturally—and they have influenced both Koreas for centuries. And I was certain that they would become even more important to the Korean Peninsula in the coming years.

Even as I was traveling the world doing business, I was always frustrated that we were in fact doing business with just half the world. Korea was an ally of and close friend to the United States, but it considered its immediate neighbors enemies. The communist world was always out of reach. The proximity of China and the maritime province of the former Soviet Union (the southeastern province of Russia) made me wonder how we could remain enemies, especially on the cusp of the twenty-first century. Thus, my next project began to take shape. Entering the communist world was going to be my last project as a businessman, and my last tribute to Hyundai.

Entering the Soviet Union

There was no way for me to pry open the door to the vast Siberian tundra. I knew where I wanted to go, but I had no idea how to get there. Korea didn't have any diplomatic contact with the Soviets, let alone a consulate-general or even a liaison office. A private company getting its foot in the door was unthinkable. But I was determined. And knowing how hard it would be, I became more enamored by the idea.

Soon my breakthrough came. A Japanese colleague with whom I'd worked on many projects in the Middle East came to see me one day. He was a manager for the Nissho Iwai Corporation of Japan, and we had worked together as partners to build the Al-Mussaib power plant in Iraq. During our meeting I complained, "We need to find new markets now that the Middle East is no longer a viable option. We're looking for bigger, more attractive markets, like the Soviet Union. My hope is to build something big over there, something no one's ever done before." I searched for any reaction. It came. The manager perked up and said, "Mr. Lee, are you interested in the Soviet market?"

I was thrilled that my bait had worked. "Well, it's nothing specific right now. As you know, we know how to work in deserts that are above forty degrees Celsius, but we've never worked before in places that are forty degrees *below*."

The manager quickly suggested, "Chairman Lee, we have a branch office in Moscow. Out of all the Japanese companies that have been doing business in the Soviet Union, my company is by far the most engaged."

I told him, "That's interesting. I wish I could go visit Moscow someday. Do you think I could visit?"

The manager said that it wasn't going to be easy, but it would be possible if I were to receive an official invitation from the Communist Party. He promised me that he would speak with his colleagues and get back to me. The reason he was so eager was not because we knew each other, but because he knew that it would be beneficial for Nissho Iwai to form a partnership with Hyundai when working in the Soviet Union. He was aware of Hyundai's strengths. And he considered us a valuable asset, especially when working in harsh conditions such as the Soviet Union.

However, even with Nissho Iwai working as an intermediary, the path to the Soviet Union was arduous. Lack of diplomatic relations prevented the Soviets from issuing me an invitation.

Then one day in the fall of 1988, I was told by Nissho Iwai that my chance had come. A member of the Soviet Chamber of Commerce had told the Japanese that he was willing to stop by in Korea on his way to Japan. This man told them that after meeting me in person he would make the final decision whether to invite me to the Soviet Union. I was ecstatic and set about preparing for his visit.

When I met the man, I was reassured of our prospects. He seemed very interested in working with Korea; he was also quite familiar with Hyundai and our achievements. Once he got back to Moscow, he briefed the reporters by telling them that his visit to

South Korea had been "a success." He then proceeded to inform me that the possibility of me visiting Moscow was "open," and he asked for a list of people who would be accompanying me.

Chung Ju-yung hadn't been informed of my secret project. After securing word from the Soviets that my visit would be realized, I went into Chung's office and said to him, "Mr. Chairman, let's go to the Soviet Union."

Chung's first reaction was lukewarm. "The Soviet Union? What's there to do in that cold place?" Chung wasn't all that interested in the Soviet Union, but I figured it would be more symbolic and effective for the head of the Federation of Korean Industries to be the first businessman to enter the Soviet Union, rather than me being the first to go.

Despite Chung's bland first response, I didn't give up, and I tried to convince him of the great potential and the limitless business opportunities the Soviet Union offered. Chung was always interested in new business opportunities, and the best way to convince him was to appeal to this side of him. During a business trip to New York, I sat next to him and explained the thinking behind my Soviet interest throughout the entire flight. The Soviet Union has the world's largest reserves of natural resources; Korea has none. This was one reason we needed to venture into the Soviet market. Once we succeeded, we would have a stable, safe, and cost-effective supply of natural resources. Yes, North Korea, which lies between us and the Soviets, could easily prohibit the transit of goods. However, I argued, this shouldn't discourage us. Since North Korea was also in desperate need of energy, it could easily be made into a partner. As our industries grew, our need for energy would only become greater. If we could supply our energy needs by land through a pipeline and not import by sea, it would be as if we were using our own resources and not those of others.

Chung slowly began to show interest. On our way back from New York, I continued to explain to him the attractiveness of the proposal. Apart from the economic benefits, I highlighted the symbolic meaning and the historical significance of being the first to open the Soviet market. As a final push, I told Chung, "Mr. Chairman, you have to start thinking about what kind of legacy you wish to leave behind. If you are able to open up the Soviet market and be the first person to do so, you will be leaving behind a great legacy for yourself and doing a great service for your country. That would be a fitting finale to your career."

Chung was finally convinced. "You're right. Let's do it. Besides, I like snow."

As soon as I got back to Seoul, I began negotiations regarding our visit. When I informed our own government, its reaction was one of mild indifference. This was because no one had any hopes of us achieving tangible progress. One agency did react sensitively, however, and that was the KCIA, the intelligence agency. They made us promise that we would not go beyond talking about business and business-related activities. Only after we signed a pledge to that effect did they grant us permission to go.

With the necessary papers and all the arrangements in place, we set about packing our luggage. But since no one had ever visited the Soviet Union before, we didn't exactly know what to bring along. It was January, so we guessed it was probably freezing cold; we told our staff to buy the warmest parkas, boots, and matching hats.

Our delegation consisted of five people, including Chung Ju-yung and me. Of the five, two went in first, on January 5, 1989, as part of an advance team; the remaining three—Chung, myself, and one other colleague—went in two days later via Tokyo. As we boarded the Aeroflot flight, we were excited. We exchanged jokes to get rid of our uneasiness. As the plane reached its altitude, a vast expanse of land with no end in sight came into view. It was the Russian tundra. As I sat in my seat looking down through the window, I knew this was where the future of Hyundai, and that of my country, lay.

Vodka

Our first meeting with the Soviet Chamber of Commerce took place on January 10, 1989, a Monday, at 8 a.m. We went straight to business. First, we explained that we needed to have a system in place if we were to initiate and promote economic cooperation between our two countries. This would expedite Korean companies' entry into the Soviet market. The Soviets asked us which area we were most interested in; as the first joint project, we suggested Hyundai be allowed to take part in developing the Siberian region. Then, we made another bold proposal: to set up a Korea-Soviet joint economic cooperation council.

We realized we were pushing the Soviets on our very first talks. Back in Korea, the press was attaching significance to the visit itself, emphasizing that it was the first visit of its kind to the Soviet Union by a Korean company. The Soviets were ready to explore the possibility of quietly working with South Korean companies, but they were certainly not prepared to make it official by setting up a joint council. Still, we had more ambitious plans.

The Soviets became uneasy when they heard our proposal. Their first reaction was one of caution. They made it clear that they did not wish to make it public that they were working with South Korean companies. It was obvious that they also had to keep in mind the North Koreans. However, we were looking beyond all that. Our ultimate objective wasn't simply to win more business for

Hyundai or promote economic cooperation between Korea and the Soviet Union. I always thought that our advancement into the Soviet Union would be the start of eventual diplomatic relations. We would be making the Soviet Union our friend and not the "feared enemy." This was what we wanted, more than just winning the rights to develop Siberia or build power plants. However, the Soviets were firm, and our talks weren't able to move forward.

I was the chief negotiator for our side, and I was updating Chung on the progress. When I told him about the Soviet reaction, Chung was disheartened. We had just started, and already we were at an impasse. "Maybe it's better we go back now. If they continue to be like that, tell them we're going back. Or, you can assume full responsibility and try to convince them." He was aware that a lot of Korean companies back home were eagerly waiting for good news.

I went back and told my Soviet counterpart that we were prepared to leave if the Soviets were unwilling to talk about our proposal. They told us, "Do as you wish," and said no more. If we were to end our talks like this, our plan to enter the Soviet market had surely failed, not to mention our dream of setting up diplomatic relations.

Chung was hoping to keep the talks alive. I kept reminding myself that I was dealing not with ordinary businessmen but with *communist* businessmen, who had to answer to their superiors, including the much-feared KGB. When dealing with Western businessmen, all I had to do was convince them and try to reach a deal. Here, I wasn't just dealing with those sitting across from me at the table. There were others looming behind them, those with the power to make (and break) deals. Thus, we began to wonder if we needed to talk to the man himself, Mikhail Gorbachev.

The negotiations were temporarily put on hold. I then invited the deputy chairman of the Soviet Chamber of Commerce, a man named Vladimir Golanov, for a private dinner. We ordered a bottle of vodka along with our food. They say if one wants to do business with the Soviets, one must be able to drink vodka, and a lot of it. I found this to be quite true. Usually, Soviets liked anyone who could drink vodka; they would treat you as an old friend. It was similar to Koreans liking any foreigner who could drink *soju* or any of the local brews.

That night Golanov and I ended up drinking a lot of vodka. As usual, I managed to stay sober despite the near-fatal dosage. Near the end of dinner, I mentioned to Golanov our proposal once again. "If you're not in a position to make the decision, why don't you let my boss meet with your boss? You tell me your boss isn't in Moscow at the moment, but I think he is."

I knew why they were reluctant to have the chairman of the Chamber of Commerce get involved in our negotiations. First, they didn't want to give the impression that they were too eager. Second, they didn't want to have the chairman bear the burden in case the negotiations fell through. It wouldn't look good.

Still, I shared my honest opinions with Golanov and explained to him why it was important for this negotiation to yield results. I told him how Chung, as head of the largest private organization representing the interests of all the major Korean corporations for the last ten years, was in a position to exercise a lot of influence back in Korea. I also told him that I had been the deputy chairman of the Korean Chamber of Commerce for the last thirteen years. I emphasized to Golanov that we were the two individuals he should be able to trust and rely on if the Soviets were serious about working with the Koreans. I also told him how even without establishing diplomatic relations, Korea and the Soviet Union could cooperate economically by having a joint business council or having the chambers of commerce work together. I closed by assuring him that the North Koreans would not be provoked (of course, I had no way of knowing this). I asked him to relay this message to his superiors. Golanov responded by saying, "OK. Let's talk about this more tomorrow." I sensed the vodka had worked its magic.

No one was going to blame us or criticize us for coming back empty-handed on our first visit; we could easily say that ideological differences or lack of investment potential prevented us from making any progress. But I didn't want to lose the opportunity.

The negotiations resumed the next day. By the afternoon, we got word from the Soviet Chamber of Commerce that they were willing to sign an agreement. They proposed we proceed with a signing ceremony. It was the breakthrough I was hoping for.

On January 11, 1989, the Republic of Korea and the Soviet Union signed what would be their very first official document. It was a historic moment. For a businessman, there is nothing more exhilarating than the moment you sign an agreement. The scratching of the fountain pen, closing the cap, then handing over the document and finally shaking hands—this was what business was all about. Although we didn't yet have any specific agreements, the fact that the Soviets came back to the table and signed an official document was momentous. Both Chung and I were ecstatic that we had managed to open an official channel with the Soviet Union, our foe for the previous fifty-plus years. That night we hosted a celebratory dinner for our Soviet friends (again, vodka flowed).

After a successful first trip, we traveled to the Soviet Union numerous times until 1991. Hyundai's chief executives alone made seven trips to the Soviet Union during this time. We visited Moscow, Leningrad, Nakhodka, and the Yakutia Republic[26]; we traversed the massive region from west to east, north to south. If there was an opportunity, we went.

Every morning, we would wake at dawn and set off to visit new places. We met with provincial governors, federal government offi-cials, and leaders of the various republics to discuss business. We would work until midnight, after which time we would either attend or host social functions (yes, more vodka). We would travel more than ten hours by helicopter, the rides so rough that even local offi-cials accompanying us would get sick and vomit along the way. But Chung and I were fired up. We felt we were back to the old days of running around day and night looking to finish a job and find more things to do. We were excited to be out in the field. We charted our course, took notes, and asked questions. We believed we were usher-ing in a new era and we were determined to bring about real change. We were on a mission.

The Soviet officials were amazed at this Korean pair who were so focused and energetic. They were startled and admitted they had never seen anyone so passionate. Our efforts did pay off—Hyundai won numerous contracts, including an aluminum refinery in Leningrad, a joint forestry venture in the Maritime Provinces, a joint petrochemical venture, construction of a pulp factory in Olga Harbor, coal exploration and building of a railway in the Neryungri mine area, and gas exploration in Yakutia.

Almost the entire investment and business portfolio of Hyundai in the Soviet Union was mapped out during the short period between 1989 and 1991, when those of us at Hyundai—including Chung and myself—combed the entire region personally. Many of these projects began shortly after being agreed to; many more began soon after. But of these many ventures, the one project I was personally most fond of was the gas exploration project in Yakutia Republic.

In 1989, before my first visit to the Soviet Union, a reporter asked me what I intended to accomplish there. I told him it was my first trip; I didn't know what to expect, so I had no concrete plans. He persisted and asked me why I was going to the Soviet Union. On the condition that our conversation was off the record, I proceeded to explain to him my dream.

I told the reporter that the twenty-first century was going to be dominated by energy. To be more precise, it was going to be about how to develop and use clean energy. Of all the fossil fuels that were in use, only natural gas was considered clean. Therefore, demand for natural gas was bound to explode as countries began to develop at a rapid pace. Natural gas can be found in many countries in the West, but our problem was that we needed to transport it via sea. We also needed to liquefy the gas to transport it by sea, and we needed a separate plant for this process alone. This meant added cost. Also, we needed to build specially designed ships to transport these lique- fied natural gases, separate storage facilities, and a separate facility to restore the liquefied gas to its original state. As such, the entire process was costly, it required extra facilities, and it was extremely complex. Moreover, natural gas from reliable sources in many of the western countries was already dominated by Japan. The only source that had yet to be tapped by Japan was the Soviet Union. When we looked at the natural gas reserves known to be in the Soviet region, we could see that a lot of it was near the Korean Peninsula. I told the reporter that my dream was to develop and bring this natural gas into Korea by land.

Unfortunately, the reporter broke his promise and ran a story with the headline, "Siberian Natural Gas to Be Brought into Korea via North Korea." I was tricked by the reporter (he secretly recorded our conversation and aired it during the evening news). But I was increasingly hopeful of realizing my dream when I vis- ited the Soviet Union.

In early 1990, when I was in Moscow, the Central Committee of the Soviet Communist Party invited us for the first time to discuss the state of bilateral relations and the future prospects of economic cooperation. During this meeting, the head of the committee's international division told us that the Soviet Union had considered Korea an attractive business partner for some time, way before Gorbachev, *perestroika*, and *glasnost*. The official told us that many in his department were wary of attending the 1988 Seoul Olympics[27] because they knew that Korea was a close ally of the United States and believed that many Koreans had prejudicial ideas about the Soviet Union. That was one reason the Soviets decided to take a large contingent of world-class artists and performers: to relieve some of the tension between Korea and the Soviet Union. However, the official told us he was surprised to note that the level of hostility among ordinary Koreans toward the Soviet Union was much lower than expected, and as time went by they even found Koreans to be welcoming. In the end, the Soviets were pleased with the results of the 1988 Seoul Summer Olympics and went home encouraged.

They also became quite interested in working with Korean companies, such as Hyundai, Samsung, and Daewoo. The Soviets had analyzed in great detail the strengths of each company and were already thinking about which areas would best suit each. With regards to Hyundai, the official knew that we were the most suitable partner in the areas of construction and heavy industries, and considered us ideal for developing the Siberian region and other infrastructure projects.

During this meeting, the deputy prime minister for the Yakutia Republic was present. The official said that the deputy prime minister flew seven hours to Moscow in order to meet with the Hyundai delegation. As soon as the briefing by the Central Committee was over, the deputy prime minister pulled out a map of his country and began to explain in earnest. We were stunned. We knew the Yakutia Republic was one of the world's richest areas in terms of natural resources, but we were completely blown away at its extent and diversity. It is said that when God was creating the world, He went around sprinkling natural resources throughout the lands and the seas; however, when God came upon the skies over Yakutia, it was so cold that He accidentally dropped all that He held in His hands. After hearing the briefing, it wasn't hard to believe the story.

Upon finishing his presentation, the deputy prime minister said that he hoped Hyundai would visit the Yakutia Republic. We promised that we would. Six months later, we were there.

Yakutia Republic is situated just north of China. If we took a plane from Seoul and flew straight north, we would arrive there in just three hours. The country lies in the same longitude as Korea, making it an ideal place to do business, since there is no time difference.

When we arrived at its capital, Yakutsk, the government officials took us to the state guesthouse. The air smelled of fresh paint and the walls looked brand-new. We checked in, washed up, and met with the prime minister as well as the deputy prime minister. Afterward, we headed straight to the fields.

The first site we surveyed was the Kisir-Sir gas field, located on the outskirts of the town of Vilyuysk. It was two hours by plane from the capital. The gas field was still undeveloped, but in terms of reserves, it was the second-largest in the Soviet Union. One could see the bluish-gray flame coming out of the gas field illuminating the night sky; it was eerily beautiful.

Then we boarded a helicopter and visited a diamond mine near a place called Mirny. This particular diamond mine had the world's second-highest production rate, second only to South Africa. A diamond-processing plant was situated nearby. The next morning we got up early and went to a town called Aldan. This time we visited a gold mine.

Then we visited a coal mine in Neryungri. The coal mine was the largest open-pit coal mine in the world. The sheer size of it took our breath away. There were literally mountains of coal, and all you had to do was shovel it. I thought of the miners back in Korea who had to dig hundreds of feet below the earth to extract coal. I thought to myself, God didn't just drop whatever He had in His hands over Yakutia; He blessed the entire land with the most precious gifts imaginable to man.

Befitting the scale of the mine, the transport equipment there was equally impressive. The enormous transport machines weighed 80 to 120 tons apiece. Millions of tons of coal from this mine were being imported by Japan every year.

Then the Yakutia officials took us to an undeveloped but extremely promising coal mine nearby. This was the mine they hoped we would develop for them. Their ambitious plan called for us to develop this mine and to export the coal to South Korea.

For this plan to materialize, several things needed to be done. First, the mine had to be connected to the Trans-Siberian Railway so the coal could be transported to Vladivostok; then, from Vladivostok, the coal would be transported to the port of Posyet, which was north of the Tumen River (a 521-kilometer river serving as a boundary between China, Russia, and North Korea on the northernmost tip of the Korean Peninsula). From there, the coal would be brought to South Korea either by ship or over land. The project had two main pillars: one was developing the mine, and the other was laying the railway infrastructure that would connect it to the Trans-Siberian Railway.

The Yakutia government and Hyundai began to examine these projects. We were particularly interested in the possibility of utilizing the land route over North Korea. If possible, we would be able to transport the coal from Vladivostok over the Tumen River through North Korea and finally to South Korea, all by land. For days, high-level officials from the Yakutia government joined us in mapping and carefully surveying the land. We traveled by helicopter for hours on end.

As specific talks regarding the development of Yakutia's vast coal reserves moved ahead, the dream of tapping into the enormous gas reserves of Yakutia was still burning in my mind. It was estimated that Yakutia's gas reserves were approximately six billion tons. This was an amount that would satisfy our energy needs for the next fifty years, even after factoring in the rapid rise in consumption.

Since Yakutia's population was a little less than one million, the domestic market was not big enough; they had to export the excess. The issue was where to export it. Europe was geographically too far away and thus not an economically viable option. That left the Far East. We needed only to transport the gas 3,800 kilometers to reach Korea. This gas was destined for Korea, a land with practically no natural resources to call its own. I felt as if God had blessed Yakutia for our sake.

Of course, there were many obstacles to be scaled before I could realize this dream. First of all, even if we reached an agreement with the Yakutia government to develop its gas reserves, we needed to obtain permission from the federal government. And even if we managed to address all the procedural and legal requirements, we had to face one of the harshest working environments on earth. During winter, the temperature in Yakutia drops to negative 40 degrees Celsius, and the night seems to go on forever. During summer, the temperature rises to more than 40 degrees Celsius, and the sun is up for close to nineteen hours a day. Basic infrastructure such as roads and housing were absent.

Due to such extreme conditions, many countries and private investors had come, marveled at the potential, and turned back, shaking their heads. However, this was precisely why Yakutia was so full of promise for Korea. To others, it was enticing but unreachable; to us, it was feasible. Hyundai was used to extreme conditions.

For any country, bringing in resources over land is fundamentally better than bringing them over the sea. The Europeans had laid a 6,500-kilometer pipeline to get access to natural gas east of the Ural Mountains. We needed a pipeline only 3,800 kilometers long. I was also thinking ahead to transporting the gas from Yakutia through North Korea and on to Japan by building an underwater tunnel linking Korea and Japan. The underwater tunnel between Korea and Japan would need to be only 200 kilometers.

Such a project would not only deliver in natural gas, it would create a Northeast Asian economic zone. A pipeline running through this vast region would be a string binding together these different zones. When the Maritime Province, Jilin and Heilongjiang provinces in northeastern China, and North Korea began development, which was only a matter of time, these regions' thirst for energy would become insatiable. And for these regions, having a secure source of energy would become vital. With a pipeline in place, this region had the potential to become a robust hub of economic activity. Trade and other activities, as well as massive infrastructure projects, would naturally follow. This was my grand design, my ultimate dream.

After finishing our exploration of this treasured land, we drafted an agreement with the Soviets aboard a yacht on the Lena River. More than 4,000 kilometers long, the Lena is a majestic river flowing across the plains of Yakutia. It was one of the three longest rivers in the Soviet Union. The river travels across the tundra of Siberia before flowing into the Laptev Sea. At one point, the river is twelve kilometers wide, making it impossible to see the shore with the naked eye if one is floating in the middle of the river. The people of Yakutia were stylish and had class. The luxurious yacht on which we traveled was imported from the Netherlands and was packed with the latest gadgets. Plenty of food and fine wine had been pre-pared. But despite the delicious food and beautiful scenery, busi-ness was business.

We engaged in fierce negotiations. At one point, the deal was on the brink of collapse. Each side would huddle at opposite ends of the yacht and discuss strategy. For two hours, we would stare at each other without saying a word, hoping the other would give in. Fortunately, the deal was sealed at the last minute. And as always, reaching a deal after going through so much effort is rewarding. We came to respect each other, which is an integral part of any business partnership.

We reached a final deal and laid out the terms of agreement regarding Hyundai's participation in developing Yakutia's natural gas and coal mines, as well as laying the railway network. We flew to Moscow to seek permission from the federal government, which was granted almost immediately. We then proceeded to sign our agreement aboard a yacht on the Moskva River (the Soviets seemed fond of signing such agreements aboard yachts). The deputy prime minister of Yakutia, Chung Ju-yung, and I were the signatories.

Regrettably, the projects were put on hold as Hyundai became involved in domestic politics. (Chung Ju-yung became involved in politics, to be precise.) Also, the political situation within the Soviet Union became more volatile, and inter-Korean relations deteriorated, causing further delays to our projects. As such, doing business in the former Soviet Union was not easy. But all of it was worthwhile. We were also lucky on many occasions, such as when we were given a chance to meet one of the most impor-tant political figures of the twentieth century. I believe the proj-ects will resume one day, hopefully soon. Until then, my dream will continue.

Meeting Gorbachev

During my seventh visit to Moscow, in November 1991, I was urgently summoned by Nikolai Petrakov, who was then the special adviser for economic affairs to President Mikhail Gorbachev. Petrakov asked that I come see him alone. I sensed he wanted to discuss something important. As soon as I walked into Petrakov's office, which was located just opposite the Kremlin, he asked me, "Are you interested in meeting President Gorbachev?"

I was surprised but calmly replied, "Of course, Nikolai. We would be honored to meet with His Excellency! It's always been our greatest hope. We would be delighted to explain to His Excellency what our plans are for the Soviet Union and to find out what His Excellency thinks."

Since Petrakov was sounding me out, I guessed he had already broached this subject with the Kremlin in some way. In any case, it was quite an unprecedented gesture from the Soviets. Petrakov told me to provide him with a list of people who wished to attend the meeting. He also made me promise that I wouldn't tell anyone about it.

When I got back and reported my meeting to Chung, he excitedly said, "Lee, prepare what we're going to say to President Gorbachev. And you know, the KBS [Korea Broadcasting Service] news team's in town. Negotiate with the Kremlin so that those guys can go in and film our meeting."

The next morning, I was summoned by Petrakov. He again wanted me to come alone. Petrakov said, "Your meeting with President Gorbachev has been set for tomorrow at 5 p.m., inside the Kremlin. Only Chairman Chung Ju-yung and you, plus one interpreter, will be allowed in. Please let me know who you'll be bringing as your interpreter."

That was when things started to go wrong. We had no official schedule before our five o'clock meeting the next day. As it happened, our Moscow bureau chief informed Chung that he had set up a meeting with the president of the Russian Soviet Federated Socialist Republic, since Hyundai was doing a lot of business with Russia. The meeting was set for 2 p.m. the day before our scheduled meeting with Gorbachev. The bureau chief assured us that meeting the head of the Russian Republic would help business greatly. So Chung and I, along with our Moscow bureau chief, went to visit the head of the Russian Republic. We had a productive meeting, signing an agreement stating that Hyundai Corporation would supply the goods needed by the republic and that we would receive payment in the form of raw materials. Television crews from Korea and Russia filmed and aired the signing ceremony. Our signing ceremony was broadcasted on state television, and newspapers ran the story as well. One of the items in the list of raw materials to be provided by Russia was petroleum. Trade in certain resources, such as petroleum, natural gas, and gold, needed approval from the federal government, but we were not aware of this provision at the time.

Afterward, Petrakov called and said he wanted to see me immediately. I ran over to his office, sensing something was wrong. When I walked into his office, he was visibly upset. "You guys made a huge mistake," he fumed. "You've violated one of the most important policies of the federal government. Your meeting with the president has been cancelled, and you can expect no help from us in the future."

I was shocked. "What do you mean? We weren't even aware of such a policy! If you want to blame anyone, you should blame the Russian Republic for signing that agreement, knowing that such a provision existed. Fine, it's too bad our meeting with the president has been cancelled. But I cannot accept what you said about not cooperating with us." Petrakov was unmoved; he told me the meeting was over.

When I told Chung what had happened, he was extremely disappointed. He went into his hotel room and didn't come out. It seemed our entry into the Soviet Union was now over. We later found out that the shaky relationship between Gorbachev and Boris Yeltsin, the president of the Russian Republic, was already falling apart by then. Being unaware of this development, we couldn't respond accordingly. We had inadvertently stepped into a battle that was raging between these two giants.

I first calmed myself. I tried to think of a way to resolve this issue. I realized I needed to speak to Petrakov and mollify him. Then I decided that I needed to communicate with him in Russian. Speaking English with him wasn't sufficient to convey my true feelings. I needed a Russian interpreter.

I asked for Mr. Yoo Hak-gu. Mr. Yoo had been born in South Korea, but when the Korean War broke out he had fled to North Korea and finally settled in the Soviet Union. He was a historian by trade and the director for East Asian affairs at the Moscow State Institute of International Relations. Mr. Yoo was scheduled to be our interpreter during our meeting with President Gorbachev, so his name had already been submitted to the Kremlin. (Later, Mr. Yoo served as President Roh Tae-woo's Russian interpreter during President Roh's summit meeting with President Gorbachev.)

I took Mr. Yoo along to meet with Petrakov. Petrakov coldly rebuffed my meeting request several times. When I informed his office that I wanted to say something to him before going back to Korea, he finally agreed to see me. It was 5 p.m. I pleaded with Petrakov, "Look, Nikolai, I'm sorry if we offended you, but I assure you we didn't mean it. I know you are the architect of President Gorbachev's *perestroika,* and we are grateful to you for showing us the way. We've always been eager and dedicated to paving the way toward a relationship that was mutually beneficial. But if all our effort goes down the drain just because we made one mistake, then I'm afraid this will be terrible for all of us."

He looked the other way when I was speaking in Korean, but he began to listen when Mr. Yoo repeated what I said in Russian. I went on. "Nikolai, I'm asking you as your friend. We will regret not meeting with President Gorbachev. But it won't just be Hyundai that will regret it. It is also a big loss for your country. Please don't do anything that you know you will regret later." When Mr. Yoo was done interpreting, Petrakov told us to wait while he stepped outside.

I was nervous. I didn't know whether he was giving us another chance. While I was waiting patiently, Chung called me; he was also anxiously waiting for news.

After a long time, Petrakov came back. He said, "I understand what you're saying. Let me make a proposal to you, then. I want you to give a press conference with Tass News Agency and to read this statement." He handed me a piece of paper. It said basically that Hyundai was nullifying the agreement with the Russian Republic because Hyundai signed the agreement without being aware of the trade provision. Petrakov told me he would reconsider once a story along this line was printed in the newspapers.

Unwittingly, we found ourselves caught in a fight between the federal government and the Russian Republic. We had to be cautious; no one knew for sure how the political drama would unfold in the Soviet Union. We couldn't risk alienating one over the other. We didn't have the liberty of picking sides.

After much thought, I decided to go ahead with the press conference. Petrakov agreed to send a designated reporter. For our meeting with President Gorbachev to go ahead as planned, we needed this article to appear in the papers by 5 p.m. the next day. We didn't have much time.

The next day, a reporter from Tass came to us early in the morning. He was fully informed of the situation. I made small changes to the statement Petrakov had given me; I felt I needed to hedge my position. I wasn't about to take sides, especially when the situation was so precarious and unpredictable. I inserted statements such as, "We are not 'nullifying' this agreement" and "We are simply pointing out the fact that it is impossible for us to faithfully implement an agreement that has been signed by parties who mistakenly overlooked certain policies." I was playing with words.

The story of my press conference appeared in the press before noon. I then received a phone call from Petrakov asking me to come see him. I was obliged to explain the differences in the statement. "You told me yesterday to annul the agreement, but if you think about it, an annulment applies to lawfully signed documents. Our agreement with the Russian Republic violated existing policies, so technically it's an invalid agreement that cannot be annulled. Therefore, saying that it cannot take effect until it is revised is a much stronger phrase than simply using the word 'annulment.'"

Petrakov nodded and went into the other room. When he came back he was in good spirits. "Good! You've been allowed to meet with the president at 5 p.m. today, as scheduled."

I excused myself and informed Chung. While I was in good standing, I asked Petrakov for one more favor. I asked him to allow the KBS news team to film our meeting. At first Petrakov cited security concerns, but soon relented.

We arrived at the Kremlin on time and were shown to the waiting room. At exactly 5 p.m. a secretary came to inform us that the president was running a little late. She asked us to wait ten more minutes. Fifteen minutes later, the secretary appeared again and cordially asked us to wait fifteen more minutes. I was impressed by President Gorbachev's thoughtfulness. It was normal for businessmen to be kept waiting thirty minutes or even up to an hour without any explanation when they had a meeting with a head of state. There wasn't much we could do. We were certainly not going to complain.

Finally, President Gorbachev arrived. After a photo op, we sat down, and he began by apologizing. He said, "I'm very sorry to be late. I had to receive credentials from ambassadors from five different countries. It's not often that I get to meet with ambassadors, so I decided to have tea with them. But, as you know, ambassadors are talkers. They have a lot to say. Again, I'm sorry for the delay."

Gorbachev was extremely knowledgeable when it came to the histories of Korea and the Soviet Union. He was also very frank. He shared his concern about the future of the Soviet economy and said that his country needed help from Korean businessmen. "Two hundred years ago a famous scholar who founded what is now the Soviet Academy said that the development of the Soviet Union will come from the east. If we wish to develop our far-eastern region, then we must cooperate with our friends in the Far East. This is why I'm hoping that Korea will play an important part."

Then he said something that struck us as very unusual, especially coming from the leader of the communist world: "When the Korean Peninsula was divided into North and South Korea, North Korea was far more advanced, with the latest industrial complexes, and its per capita income was greater than that of South Korea. Back then, your country subsisted on agriculture and a few primary industries. But today, North Korea is much poorer than you. Do you know why?"

We couldn't fathom what he was getting at. Then Gorbachev said, "It's because North Korea chose communism, while you chose capitalism."

It was revealing to listen to the president of the Soviet Union admit that communism had failed. We were just two businessmen from a country that didn't even have diplomatic relations with the Soviet Union yet. But Gorbachev saw the arc of history, and I think he knew where the world was headed. At least he seemed to know where his country was headed. And I think it was because of his ability to see the world as it was and to honestly admit past mistakes that he was able to steer his country toward stability despite the tumultuous upheavals and ideological battles that would soon engulf it.

Gorbachev continued. "It was the Soviets who urged the North Koreans to adopt communism. Therefore, the Soviet Union is responsible for many of the problems that North Korea is facing today. Before the peninsula was divided, I know that the two Koreas shared the same language and the same culture. You were one people. I don't know when the time will come, but when South Korea and the Soviet Union establish diplomatic relations and begin to expand our economic cooperation, let's share the fruits with the North Koreans. The Soviet Union has a moral responsibility to do so."

I was impressed by his foresight and his vision. Gorbachev encapsulated the significance of economic cooperation between South Korea and the Soviet Union. He was honest in sharing with us his vision for the future of our two countries and emphatic when it came to strengthening our bilateral relationship. He also did not forget to promise us that he would do all he could to promote and support Korean business within the Soviet Union.

Our meeting with Gorbachev was a success. Chung was buoyed by the meeting and seemed revitalized. Chung told me, "Now that we've met Gorbachev, let's go and meet Bush!" We did end up visiting the United States, as well as China, and finally Pyongyang, the capital of North Korea. I think Chung began to think that he had an important political role to play. In fact, he was the first person from

South Korea to make such historic headway. In that regard, he was a pioneer. And he would always be proud of this.

As for me, I was glad to have conveyed what I considered my final tribute to Hyundai.

15 | LEAVING HYUNDAI

I looked back at my life. I had no regrets. And I saw that it was now time for me to embark on a new path.

On December 31, 1991, I took my family to the island of Jeju, which is a famous vacation and honeymoon destination for many Koreans. It was our first family vacation. My wife and four children were excited to be going on a family trip, but I was preoccupied. One more day, and it would be a new year, and I had to make the decision.

Should I leave Hyundai?

I was at a crossroads. I would soon turn fifty, and I had to make a decision. In Korea, when a person turns fifty years old, we say that the person is mature enough to discern the will of heaven. And the first thing one must do to know the will of heaven is to look into the past. Without coming to terms with the past, one cannot go forward or discern the will of God.

So, I looked back at my fifty years. My life had never been easy. Nothing was given to me on a platter, so I worked hard. Many people say that my twenty-seven years at Hyundai was an easy ride; some call me a legend. But to me, nothing was easy.

I went for a walk along the beach. I stood and looked at the horizon. I felt an odd connection with the sea. This was the sea where our family was shipwrecked as we were coming home from Japan forty-five years earlier; it was this sea that took away what little we had and left us penniless. In a way, I was back to my origins. I looked back at my life. I had no regrets. And I saw that it was now time for me to embark on a new path.

I told my wife that I'd decided to leave Hyundai. As always, Yoon-ok was supportive. She told me, "Do as you wish, dear. I'll be here as always to support whatever you do. We trust you. I trust you." I thanked her. And I knew that Hyundai would continue moving forward without me.

I came back from our family trip and went to work on January 3. Every year on the first day of work, all the employees attend a sort of opening ceremony to mark the beginning of a new year. It was a time to wish each other good health and success in the coming year. Chairman Chung Sae-young sat at the head of the large oval table. I sat to his left with Lee Hyun-tae; to my right were Lee Choon-lim and Chung Mong-koo, the son of Chung Ju-yung and nephew of the chairman. We all exchanged greetings, and the mood was relaxed. Suddenly, Chung Ju-yung, who was by then the honorary chairman, walked in. Chung usually woke up early and walked to his office wearing sneakers; after he arrived at his office, he would change into a suit and begin work. However, that day he walked into the first meeting of the year wearing sneakers and a track suit. It was highly unusual of him to deviate from his normal pattern.

Chung Sae-young hurriedly got up from his seat to make room. Chung Ju-yung sat down with a hard look on his face. Without any pleasantries, he said gruffly, "As of today, Lee Myung-bak, Lee

Nae-hun, and I have decided to enter politics. We are hereby resigning from Hyundai, effective immediately." With those words, he got up and left the room.

No one said a word. Chung Sae-young broke the silence by giving his prepared remarks and brought the ceremony to an end. After the ceremony, all the executives shuffled out to board a bus to one of Hyundai's training centers on the outskirts of Seoul. It was an annual tradition for the executives to spend a day there to discuss company business. I didn't join them.

I went to Chung Ju-yung's office and knocked on his door. Chung was alone in his office; I stood in front of him and said, "I'm sorry, Mr. Chairman. I can't help you. I'll go now." Just as his announcement had been brief, mine was brief as well. It was sufficient. I thereby gave Chung my answer to his final ultimatum, which he had presented to me the year before.

At the end of the previous year, Chung had set forth a hasty schedule—he was going to found a new political party at the beginning of the new year. I was given until the end of the year to make up my mind whether to join him in his new endeavor. I resented his unilateral announcement. I considered his decision an abuse of his privilege as the owner of the company. I was being coerced; I never gave in to coercion, and I didn't intend to start now.

So when I announced to Chung in his office that day my intention to leave Hyundai, he got up from his chair and said, "Let's meet in a few days."

I told him, "I'll think about it."

My response was a clear refusal; I never gave such ambiguous answers whenever I discussed matters related to business, and Chung knew that I meant what I said.

I left his office and closed the door behind me. I went back to my office. I felt no regret, and I was prepared to leave. Reporters came in to ask me questions. Many of them thought I would follow Chung into politics. I told them I intended to think about it; I wasn't about to enter politics simply out of personal loyalty. If I did something, I needed to know that I was doing the right thing.

Chung proceeded to found his own political party. I tried to dissuade him, to no avail. I tried three times, each time giving him a different reason why he shouldn't.

One was to discourage him from entering politics out of spite. It was known that Chung was on bad terms with President Roh Tae-woo's chief economic adviser. Around that time, the National Tax Service slapped Hyundai with a fine of approximately $200 million. It was uncalled for, and Chung believed he was being singled out and persecuted.

On my second attempt, I tried to persuade him to support as many independent candidates as possible and to help them get elected. Once the election was over, I told him, he could bring together those he had helped elect and found a political party (my guess was that he wouldn't have a sufficient number at the start to form a negotiating bloc within the National Assembly). This didn't work, either.

My third and last attempt was to appeal to his pioneering side by encouraging him to find and develop new blood. I told him I would be willing to support him in such an effort, since he would be sending a strong message to young voters that he was committed to genuine change. I figured that was worth a try, since Korean politics was considered tainted and ineffective. I saw the value in such a pursuit. I also told him that it would earn him much respect from the public. Unfortunately, this bid failed as well. Despite my pleas, he wanted to do it himself.

Chung became irritated that I was being difficult. But to me, it was more complex. It was about business ethics and responsibility to society at large. Chung was undeniably one of the greatest and most influential business leaders of Korea. He was also the owner of one of the wealthiest companies in the country. I expected him to exercise restraint and responsibility befitting his stature. When I told him how hard it was going to be for Hyundai to pick up the pieces if he failed in his political efforts, he said, "Even if I fail, *I'm* the one failing and not the company."

I was dismayed. All my years, I had worked as if I were the owner of Hyundai, always considering first how my actions would affect the company. That was always more important to me than my personal wishes.

In January 1992 I stood in front of five hundred Hyundai Construction employees to deliver what would be my farewell remarks. "Beloved colleagues, I am about to leave Hyundai, which has been my home for the last twenty-seven years. There are many reasons I'm leaving Hyundai, but now is not the time to dwell on that. I leave knowing that Hyundai will live on because it is blessed with so many talented and dedicated individuals. We are all owners of this company as long as we work here. All of us here devoted our lives to building this company and making it prosper. Those who join us later will continue to carry on this legacy. Whether we are owners by right or owners in spirit, we are and will remain part of this legacy. That is why whoever we are and wherever we may be, we mustn't do anything that will harm our home. I, of course, will abide by this rule."

It was the last message I wanted to share with my colleagues; it was also a message going out to the owners, reminding them that the company was not theirs to use for personal gains, of whatever sort.

This was my last duty to Hyundai. I was not a "blue blood" and did not belong to the Chung family. Nor was I in any position to claim a piece of Hyundai. I was simply a hired salaryman who had risen to become a professional CEO. Deep down inside, I was just another worker, no different from the welder, the mechanic, and the machine operator. But I was immensely proud of what I had done, and I considered Hyundai my own.

With that, I said good-bye to Hyundai.

16 | POLITICS

I wanted to apply to the world of politics what I had learned in business. I believed my years in the field would be beneficial to the country.

In March 1992 I became a member of the National Assembly and began my new life as a politician. For the previous twenty-seven years I had been a businessman, immensely proud of being in the center of my country's remarkable economic progress. Now, I was beginning a new life—a second life, so to speak—as a politician. I decided to enter politics because I wanted to apply to the world of politics what I had learned in business. I believed my years in the field would be beneficial to the country.

I had always felt privileged to be a part of my country's phenomenal economic growth. Now, as a newly minted politician, I felt if I did my best to bring my convictions and principles to my new profession, I could achieve results similar to those I had achieved in the business world. Yet I was prepared for what lay ahead. I knew enough about politics and had dealt with a sufficient number of politicians to know that it wasn't going to be easy. Many people said that my time at Hyundai was the stuff of legend. Although I was flattered by such a label, I also knew that most people saw only what I had achieved; they weren't aware of the immense personal sacrifice that I had to endure along the way.

Much as I thought I was prepared, the world of politics surprised me nonetheless. The inefficiency and sheer waste was much worse than I expected. Politicians were defined by which group or faction they belonged to; loyalty to the party was of paramount importance. Many politicians made decisions only to further their personal agendas. Convictions and principles mattered little, if at all. Politicians would argue, often vehemently and sometimes with physical force, yet once the discussions had ended and the cameras stopped rolling, they would slap each other on the back. To a man who spent more than two decades in the world of business, a world where even the smallest decisions had enormous consequences, such behavior was simply incomprehensible.

Ironically, though, I was thrilled. I hoped, indeed was determined, to bring real change to a world filled with debilitating inefficiency and dreadful waste. I have always believed that corporate management and state governance were fundamentally the same. Corporate management entails looking far ahead and making decisions accordingly. It seeks to maximize gains and minimize waste. I was sure that if I could manage to incorporate such practices into politics, then I could create yet another legend.

I intended to stay above political tricks and manipulations. I wasn't about to get mired in old-school practices, which would inevitably lead me to lose sight of why I entered politics in the first place. I knew that such convictions would soon cause friction within the establishment. I knew that I was looked upon as a maverick and an outsider, yet I didn't entirely mind. I chose to remain focused on the job that lay ahead.

Lessons from the World of Politics

The presidential election was set to take place on December 18, 1992, and all eyes were on Mr. Chung Ju-yung, the charismatic chairman and founder of the Hyundai Group. Mr. Chung had founded his own political party—the United People's Party—and was creating a massive political storm and generating much publicity. Politicians were becoming increasingly uneasy with his growing popularity with the public.

By this time, I was already seated in the National Assembly as a member of the ruling Democratic Liberal Party, having been elected by way of the proportional representation system. As I described previously, I was one of those who had emphatically tried to persuade Mr. Chung not to run for the presidency. Having worked with him for close to thirty years, I deeply cared for him and did not wish to see his achievements tarnished by political ambition. I knew his chances of becoming president were practically nonexistent, despite the great enthusiasm his candidacy was generating at the time.

As a member of the Democratic Liberal Party, I was instructed by the party to give a televised endorsement speech for our candidate, Kim Young-sam. In fact, the speech they planned was less about endorsing Kim Young-sam than slandering Chung Ju-yung and was a desperate attempt by Kim's public relations team to clinch the election. The party wanted me to use this opportunity to demystify Mr. Chung in public, to talk about his shortcomings, and to criticize his personal life on national television. The party was calculating that if Lee Myung-bak was heard saying something negative about Chung Ju-yung, the public would accord it extra credibility.

I told the election committee that this was not acceptable to me, saying that I believed slandering a presidential candidate in such a way would drag Korean politics further into the dirt. But on a deeper level, I felt such actions went to fundamental issues of loyalty and character. Although Chung and I were now on different sides politically, I wasn't about to attack a man with whom I had worked for so long, merely for political gain. I told the election committee that if I were to give the speech, I would use the opportunity to highlight the strengths of Kim Young-sam, certainly, but not to attack Chung.

I set about drafting a 20-minute speech. In it, I tried to be candid and convincing. I explained why I believed Chung should withdraw from politics. I also debunked point-by-point one of Chung's most controversial campaign promises: to provide apartments to the public at half price. All of this was based on my personal experience and expertise learned as a result of running Hyundai Construction. In my conclusion I set forth what I believed were essential qualities for the next president—honesty and integrity— and pointed out that Chung had once told me, "Kim Young-sam is an honest man."

After finishing my draft, I gave it to people in various fields and sought their advice. Professors, journalists, and party members all provided me with useful comments. However, when the election committee read it, all hell broke loose. They fumed, saying that my draft was tantamount to an endorsement of Chung.

The election committee insisted I read the speech drafted by them, word for word. I again refused, saying that not only would it make me look foolish and morally incompetent, it would also cost Kim a lot of votes. In the end, the election committee abandoned their attempts to convince me to read their draft and reported to Kim that I had refused to give the speech because of my loyalty to Chung. My television appearance never happened.

Dream

As I recounted earlier, after graduating from high school in my hometown of Pohang, I came to Seoul, where I lived hand-to-mouth in run-down neighborhoods. It was then that I became painfully aware of how important it is for a person to have a job, both for economic reasons and for reasons of personal dignity. It was during these hard times that I came to believe that one of the government's primary goals must be to ensure jobs for its people.

Once in Seoul, I decided to enroll in college. I knew even then that in order to escape poverty, I needed an education. However, money was again a problem. If I wanted to pass the extremely competitive college entrance exam, I needed to devote myself full time to studying. In order to study, however, I needed books. If I wanted to buy books, I needed to work. This is what is meant by the term "yoke of poverty."

Luckily, people stepped up and helped me out. I was able to acquire textbooks from one of the many second-hand book stores that used to line the Cheonggyecheon area in central Seoul. Once in college, I worked as a janitor to pay for my tuition. When I worked in the marketplace, the shopkeepers gave me extra work so I could earn a bit more. I was grateful, because while these people were only slightly better off than me, all of them had what we Koreans call *jeong* (roughly translated, it means compassion, empathy, or emotional bond). As I went to college, matured, and grew up, the people of Seoul were always there to help me. They weren't from privileged families with time and money to spare; they were ordinary folks who led tough lives. I had always dreamed of repaying this kindness, and I did not abandon this dream when I entered politics. Later, when I ran for mayor of Seoul, I thought hard about these people and of all the things I could do to improve their lives. And so it was that my next goal in life started to take shape.

Standing Up to the President

In June 1995 I registered as a candidate in the party's primary for mayor of Seoul. I already had a clear goal as to what I intended to do if elected; my plans were in place, waiting to be implemented. It turned out that I was the only one who registered for the primary. Initially the staff at the president's office responded positively, saying that I had a very good chance of getting elected. Then one day, President Kim Young-sam invited members of the ruling party to the Blue House for an unofficial dinner and announced that he did not wish there to be a primary election of the mayoral candidate. Instead, President Kim stated, he wished to nominate Chung Won-shik (no relation to Chung Ju-yung) as the party's candidate. President Kim went on to say that since I was still relatively young, I should head the election campaign committee.

The secretary general of the party summoned me and informed me of the president's decision and asked me to withdraw my name from the primary race. I could see that this was shaping up to become another trial in my short life as a politician.

After thinking about the proposal, I decided to refuse. This was not a question of my political ambitions; it was a test of whether or not I was willing to stand up for what I believed in. Journalists were intrigued, since they had rarely witnessed anything like this—a first-time lawmaker standing up to the president. In a society that values hierarchy and seniority, a political world that is heavily governed by factions, and a system whereby the president has almost unlimited power as both head of state and head of his party, this was unheard of. In the Korea of the 1990s, if the president wished for something, it usually happened.

With both sides adamantly refusing to budge, an impasse was inevitable. Finally I suggested to the party leadership that they should convene an executive meeting and announce that they were canceling the primary. The party leaders, however, insisted that I agree to remove myself from the race. That way, they said, the matter would solve itself.

Finally I received a call from the president's senior secretary for political affairs. Perhaps the president felt he needed to talk to me directly in order to resolve the issue. The senior secretary and I met at a downtown restaurant for lunch. As soon as we sat down, the secretary told me the president wanted to meet with me. I cordially but firmly refused.

The senior secretary was nonplussed. His face betrayed his thoughts: how could a first-term lawmaker refuse to meet with the president when the president himself had requested it? I told him I had no desire to meet with the president if he was simply going to order me to withdraw. The senior secretary became visibly upset. He said this was unacceptable and that there was no way he could go back to the president and report that I refused the invitation for a meeting. He went so far as to say that this was unprecedented in modern Korean history.

"Mr. Lee, perhaps you don't quite understand. Maybe it's because you haven't been around long enough. But let me tell you one thing: a lawmaker never refuses a one-on-one meeting with the president, especially when the president is the one who is calling the meeting. I will not go back and tell the president what you just told me."

Our lunch soon ended, but before parting I made it clear to the secretary that my only wish was for the president to allow for the primary to go ahead, as originally planned.

A few days later the senior secretary called again, and we agreed to meet a second time. At this second meeting he reiterated his demand that I meet with the president. Our talk went on for almost three hours. Then, in the middle of the conversation, the secretary got a call. After stepping outside to take the call, he returned to tell me that the president was willing to hear what I had to say. So I agreed to the meeting. The secretary emphasized that I was to keep my meeting with the president strictly confidential.

On May 2 I arrived fifteen minutes early to my 7:00 a.m. breakfast meeting with the president. Back when I was in the business sector, I would visit the Blue House with pride, thinking that I was there as part of the dauntless business warrior class. Today, however, I had mixed feelings and was in fact quite uncomfortable.

When I arrived at the main entrance to the president's office building, I noticed the chief of staff was waiting outside. Under Blue House protocol, the chief of staff normally greets guests deemed especially important, such as party chairmen or the like. I wondered who else was coming to our meeting. Sensing my bewilderment, the chief of staff remarked with a solemn face, "I'm here because this is an important meeting."

The president arrived five minutes early and greeted me warmly. I bowed slightly, shook hands, and sat down. Breakfast was simple, and both of us finished in fifteen minutes. The table was cleared, and tea was served. Then the president started talking about his recent overseas trip to attend the Asia-Pacific Economic Cooperation (APEC) summit. As his monologue continued I grew impatient, knowing that Blue House breakfast meetings usually lasted thirty minutes, forty at most. If the president took up all the time talking about his diplomatic trip, then I would be left with no time to state my case. So, despite the discourtesy, I interrupted him.

I said, "Mr. President, I came here today to listen to what you have to say, but I am here also to offer you my own candid opinion." As soon as I said this, the mood turned palpably cold.

President Kim's voice rose slightly, and he simply said, "Go on."

I continued, "Mr. President, let me first of all reiterate how deeply

I admire what you did to bring democracy to this country. I know what you had to endure and what you did to defend democracy."

With the utmost courtesy and sincerity, I went on, "When you were fighting for democracy, I myself was involved in student activities in pursuit of these same goals. When my friends who took part in these movements decided to pursue politics, I decided to devote my life to bringing economic prosperity to our country. And I am quite proud of the job that I did. Through meetings with many heads of state and government officials I have learned how the global economy works. And when I decided to enter politics, I was confident that my background would serve me and my country well. I hope, Mr. President, that you recognize and respect my experience and will keep it in mind as you listen to what I have to say."

I continued calmly, "Mr. President, if I become the mayor of Seoul, I can fully utilize what I learned over the years as a businessman. Do you remember what I told you when I first became a member of the National Assembly? It is because of what you did to establish democracy in our country that our party today is conducting primaries. In accordance with these same democratic principles, our party's constitution clearly stipulates that we hold primaries to select candidates to run for office. All I'm doing is abiding by those rules. If you were to cancel the primary and designate Mr. Chung as our party's candidate, this would be tantamount to reversing not only the party constitution but what you stand for. I urge you, Mr. President, to reconsider for the sake of advancing democracy."

President Kim listened intently. After a while he said, "As you know, Mr. Chung helped me by serving as the chairman of my election committee back in 1992. I owe him. Mr. Lee, you are still young, you have much promise, and you can achieve a lot. I hope you will consider helping Mr. Chung."

I knew then that this issue wasn't about me. I could sense that the president had no ill feelings toward me; rather, he was intent on rewarding a dear colleague who had helped him become president. The president then reiterated his wish not to hold a primary. He went on to explain the consequences of holding primaries by discussing what happened during the 1992 presidential primaries[28].

After listening to him, I said, "Mr. President, the effects of the 1992 primary were not because of some flaw in the scheme but because the participants didn't abide by the rules. You yourself have always advocated holding primaries. Also, in my opinion, designating Mr. Chung as the candidate just to send him off to an election that will be determined by the voters doesn't seem like a respectful way to treat him, either. I think you should appoint him to an important post instead."

President Kim replied with determination in his voice: "Believe me, Mr. Chung *will* get elected."

I said, "Mr. President, you're probably right. However, you know that anything can happen in an election. Nothing is certain, and I believe you should prepare for all contingencies."

"Mr. Lee, let me tell you something," the president went on. "Mr. Chung is a great speaker. Whenever he gives an endorsement speech to a crowd, he's absolutely terrific. During television debates, he's also a formidable opponent. I know a thing or two about elections."

I proceeded to explain to the president what would happen in the event that Chung lost the election.

"Mr. President, let us assume that the man you designate loses the election. The blame will be on you. On the other hand, if you allow the primary to go ahead, then all the responsibility lies with the party, since it was the party who elected the candidate. The fact is that a candidate who wins a primary emerges with powerful momentum going into the general election. You said you're worried about the side effects of holding a primary, but I assure you that I will fully respect the results, as long as it is held."

I took pains to assure him that I would not be a sore loser or do anything to undermine the president or the party. I could see that he was now clearly exasperated; it was his desire to end this discussion on his terms, but I was not accommodating his wish. He tried hard to convince me. We were both adamant.

"Mr. Lee, you will have lots of opportunities in the future."

President Kim seemed to want to offer me something in return for my withdrawal, and so I quickly cut him off.

"Mr. President, I agreed to meet with you because I want to be the party's candidate for mayor. If you were to offer me something else, and I accepted, what would that make me? I have always stood by my principles. I'm afraid I will not be able to do anything while you are president."

For more than two hours we sat there arguing. We each emptied five or six cups of tea. Finally I decided that I was placing an enormous burden on the president and prepared to leave.

"Mr. President, thank you for this opportunity, and thank you for sharing your thoughts with me candidly. I will go back now and pray over this matter. I hope that you will also think about what I said today."

President Kim seemed fully aware that I was unwilling to budge, and he sensed that there was no easy answer to this problem. The president got up and walked me to the door of the small, private dining room. We shook hands. Clearly, he was not pleased.

I was unwilling to abandon my principles in this matter, but equally important, I believed that holding the primary was good for the party as well. By demonstrating to the people that the party was committed to democratic ideals and procedures, the party would gain more support from the people. A primary would also make the party itself much more democratic, both in terms of procedure and political ideology. However, I was also reminded of the sad truth that very often in politics, changing the system isn't enough.

My meeting with the president was leaked, and the media ran the story the next day. Journalists called me nonstop. They were following the story closely to see how my foray into politics would unfold. They were also musing about what would happen to me as a result of my refusal to acquiesce to the demand of the president.

Initially, I denied ever meeting with the president. Then a reporter for *Yonhap News* told me that the senior secretary for political affairs had already confirmed the meeting. I called the senior secretary and told him, "Mr. Secretary, if I had accepted the president's proposal after meeting with him, then it would have been appropriate to announce the fact of our meeting to the press. But don't you think it places the president in a bad light if you tell the press of our meeting knowing that I still haven't accepted the president's offer?"

The senior secretary seemed finally to grasp that he had made a mistake, and he also understood that I was not going to change my mind. He promptly thanked me, and we hung up. Later I was told that he praised me as a rarity in politics: a courageous politician who stuck to his principles. Although I considered what I had done as something quite ordinary, his was a compliment I would nonetheless cherish.

Soon after the news of my meeting with the president was released, ominous headlines started to appear: "Lee Myung-bak's private life and wealth to be scrutinized," they announced, and rumors about an investigation began circulating. Close acquaintances and friends wondered whether I would be able to weather the storm. I assured them that an investigation into my private life would be a blessing in disguise. I was confident that I would come out stronger.

As the story began to unfold, there were slight, yet unmistakable,

shifts in the media. Initially, many reporters assumed that my registration for the mayoral candidacy was largely symbolic, a move to
gain publicity. Now, however, they were beginning to understand
that I was serious about my bid. Changes among the younger reporters, in particular, were palpable. They were clearly excited to see
someone stand up to the president. I could see that they were rooting for the underdog; they admired someone who was willing to
instigate change and infuse new life into what many considered to
be a stale, corrupt, and inefficient political establishment. Some of
them visited me in my office just to offer encouragement. Many
wrote articles depicting my resolve, taking pains to portray me in a
positive light. These same reporters were also often indispensible
sources of valuable information regarding my pending investigation.

While all this was happening, the Democratic Liberal Party began
preparing to endorse Chung, and for that purpose they convened a
meeting of district chairpersons amid rumors of my impending
defection from the party. This time, the senior secretary for civil
affairs called me and invited me over for lunch.

After exchanging greetings, I went straight to the point. "Mr.
Secretary, did you find any irregularities in my private life? Any
wrongdoing? Because if so, then I suggest you tell me right now. I
have nothing to hide. If I had problems with my personal life, do
you think I could be elected to lead close to fifty thousand public
employees belonging to the Seoul Metropolitan Government? "

He answered that the investigation had found nothing improper.

"Good," I said, "So let's forget about all this and enjoy our meal."

I always considered the senior secretary a man of integrity, and I
respected him. It was this respect that allowed me to be frank. After
my lunch with him, the meeting of district chairpersons was postponed, and soon afterward, I received a call from the secretary-
general of the party.

He said, "Mr. Lee, I'm calling to ask you not to leave the party for at least another day or two." I said, "Who said I'm leaving the party? Mr. Secretary General, I expect the primary to be held. At least, that's what I hope for."

Once again a meeting with the district chairperson was scheduled. The night before the meeting I arranged to have a chat with some of my close friends in the media. Many of them were younger reporters who supported my bid, and several of those I met with that night were thinking that I had had a good run and that tomorrow it would all be over. They had concluded that the next day, when the party announced its decision not to hold the primary, the only remaining question for me would be whether to accept the decision and withdraw from the primary or quit the party.

One of them asked me, "Can I just write that you're going to leave the party?" Another said what many had wondered all along: "Why are you trying to do what's impossible?"

I told them, "Listen guys, we still have about twelve hours left until the party announces its decision. That's plenty of time, and anything can happen. In business, it may take months to prepare and implement something, but it may take less than ten minutes to make a decision. So, there's plenty of time. Let's just wait and see."

I was still hopeful.

The next day, the district chairperson's meeting was cancelled, and immediately after that I got a call from the party. The president had decided to hold the primary.

Later, after the primary had been held, pundits who knew Korea's political history and the president himself commented that this event was epochal. Nonetheless, many started to worry about me and my future.

The reaction from the public was completely different. The general consensus was that the decision to hold the primary was a momentous political victory and, more importantly, a giant step forward for democracy in Korea.

Had any irregularities in my financial life been found as a result of the investigation, I'm sure I would have been forced out of the primary, and most likely my political life would have ended prematurely. But the investigation into my personal life and fortune proved to be my blessing; I was given a "clean bill." Then, when I continued to insist on holding the primary, many party leaders complained that such a thing was unprecedented.

Well then, it was time to start setting precedents.

Running for Mayor

The primary race for mayor of Seoul was now on. I was excited but also worried. The fact that the primary was being held at all was significant in modern Korean political history, making my participation far more than a personal victory. However, leaving aside the historical significance of the event, the outcome of the race was almost a foregone conclusion. This was because a primary race was voted on by delegates appointed by the party, not the voters at large. As a candidate who'd fought against the party leadership, my chances were slim, to say the least.

On May 12, 1995, more than 7,700 delegates gathered in the Olympic Gymnastics Stadium in southern Seoul. The stadium was packed, the largest gathering for such a political event in recent memory. A party convention to choose a candidate should be an occasion to celebrate democratic ideals at work. It should be an opportunity for like-minded people to voice their collective opinion by choosing the candidate who will best help them realize their aspirations. Instead, this particular convention was fraught with mishaps and blatant, dishonest mismanagement from the very start. One such mishap was a curious technical problem with the microphone system, whereby the volume would diminish to an almost inaudible level whenever I spoke. If I would raise my voice to be heard, then the mysterious microphone would miraculously correct itself.

During the actual balloting, districts voted according to instructions given by the district chair. Since many delegates traveled together and moved as a group, the district chairs had ample time to thoroughly educate their delegates so as to ensure that they would vote correctly.

Many of my supporters were aware of such practices. It was a sad reminder that politics in Korea was rough and often brutal. Some of my supporters suggested that I boycott the procedure, but I insisted that I must remain until the end. And I did. I believed that staying in the race was important, even though the procedures were flawed.

The results were as expected. I lost. There was nothing more I could do. I was consoled by the fact that the primary took place at all.

I received a total of 2,884 votes, or 37.4 percent, of the votes cast. My opponent received 4,701 votes, or 61% percent. Given the systematic efforts by my opponents to undermine my bid, we considered the fact that I was able to gather 37.4 percent of the votes to be quite impressive under the circumstances.

During my concession speech, I thanked President Kim for deciding to hold the primary race, and I went on to congratulate my opponent.

When everyone had left the stadium, I stayed behind, contemplating the significance of the event, the agonizing moments when I had to make difficult decisions, and the excitement of realizing that I had helped bring about a real and significant step forward for democracy in Korea. My supporters, who remained behind with me, hoisted me on their shoulders and began to chant, "Lee Myung-bak! Lee Myung-bak!" I noticed some of them were crying. I was grateful to all of them.

The next day I received many phone calls congratulating me for what I was able to achieve and consoling me for my loss. One of them was from President Kim Young-sam himself.

"Mr. Lee, I was deeply impressed by the dignified way you handled yourself. I think what you did was admirable, holding the hand of Mr. Chung and pledging your support. It reminded me of a similar event in my own political career. In 1972, Kim Dae-jung, Lee Chul-seung, and myself were locked in a fierce primary battle to win the party's nomination for president. I had an agreement with Mr. Lee that if the primary voting went into the second round, he would throw his support to me. However, Mr. Lee broke our promise and sided with Kim Dae-jung, and I ended up losing the primary. Although I lost, I kept my part of the bargain and traveled around the country campaigning for Kim Dae-jung, as I had promised. And look at me today. I've become the president."

I was thankful that President Kim called but, to be honest, I wasn't very comforted by what he said.

The 1995 primary for the mayor of Seoul was a seminal event in Korean politics. For the first time, a truly free primary race was held to determine the party's candidate. Afterward, all the political parties would consider it natural to hold primaries when selecting their party's candidate for mayor of Seoul.

Residents of Gung-an Village

I've met many individuals over the years, but there is one entire village that I remember fondly. It was called Gung-an, and I first met the residents of this distinctive district when I was running for the parliamentary seat of Jongno, the prestigious district representing central Seoul.

As the race heated up, I decided to campaign in the area near Gung-an village. As soon as I aired my wish, my campaign staff voiced strong disapproval. They reminded me that that part of town never voted for the ruling party and that it was useless to even try to garner their votes. They said I should instead devote my time to consolidating my support in other districts. The majority of the residents of the village were from a province traditionally at odds with the ruling party. It was an old wound, one that had been plaguing Korea for centuries, and it was still very much alive in the middle of Seoul.

However, I didn't share in those prejudices, and I wasn't about to engage in regionalism. If I was to become a national assemblyman representing the Jongno district, then I intended to represent the residents of Gung-an as well, regardless of where they were from or whether they voted for me.

In fact, the more my staff attempted to dissuade me, the more intrigued I became and the stronger grew my resolve to campaign there. Realizing this, my staff eventually stopped pointing out the futility of my visit and started making efforts to prepare for it. But it wasn't easy. Overall, the village was hostile to outsiders, especially politicians from the ruling party, and rumor had it that there was no way to guarantee my security. Later on we found out that even the police were reluctant to go into the area, so security was practically nonexistent, making my visit quite dangerous.

As it turned out, mine was the first such visit by a member of the ruling party in more than forty years. I arrived at around ten in the evening. Many of the residents were day laborers and lived hand-to-mouth. After working fifteen or sixteen hours a day, they would stop by at a makeshift tent that served as a local tavern and down a few glasses of *soju*. As I have described earlier, I myself used to live in just such a shanty town, although this place was in fact far worse. The entrance into the village was barely wide enough to allow one adult to pass through. The village itself was dilapidated, and some shanties were on the verge of collapse. The residents looked on with open hostility; many of them had been living illegally on other people's property for more than forty years, and the threat of forced eviction was always real. As we waded into their territory, the animosity and suspicion toward us was unmistakable.

Inside, the village was like a maze. Paths were built haphazardly, and it was easy to get lost. After some time we arrived at a tiny open space that functioned as the village square or plaza. It had the village's only working well. The well was where the people would draw drinking water, wash their clothes, and take a few moments to rest from their back-breaking labors.

I asked one of my aides to hand me the bullhorn, and right away I started to let the residents know I was there. People started to shout obscenities and told me to shut up. I've heard some vulgar remarks in my time, but what I heard that day surpassed them all. They were indeed a lively, colorful bunch. But I was determined. I wasn't about to back down.

I knew all along that it was useless to talk policy with these people. This wasn't because they were incapable of comprehending, but because they were indifferent to politics altogether. These people believed that what went on outside their village, the actions of politicians and the government, wasn't in the least for their benefit. They considered themselves complete outsiders. They were hardened. I knew where this feeling came from because I know what debilitating poverty means and what it can do to a person's self-esteem and outlook on life.

I looked at the handful of people standing in front of me and said, "Listen, folks, I'm not here today to ask for your votes or anything like that. I know I'm not going to get any votes here. I'm not so sure any of you will vote at all. Anyway, I came here today to share with you a little secret. I'm here to tell you the secret of making money."

I was getting worked up. I knew what these people were thinking and what they had to endure. I began to realize how exciting it would be if I could help them escape from poverty. This was real policy. This was what politics was about!

"I used to live in moon towns[29] like this myself when I was growing up," I continued. "I used to collect garbage and did all sorts of odd jobs. I know hard work. I also know what it's like to wait in line every morning just to use the toilet. But I worked hard. I worked really hard. And I became the head of Korea's largest conglomerate. I made a lot of money, too. Today, I'm willing to share with you the secret of my success and also the secret to making money."

People started to gather around me. Those who had told me to shut up quietly came and sat down. I put down my bullhorn. I laid down some newspapers, sat down with them on the ground, and started to talk.

"When I was growing up, and when I was poor, I didn't give a rat's ass who was running for office. I didn't know who represented me, and I wasn't interested. But one thing I *was* interested in was how I could escape from this wrenching poverty. How in the world can I make money? Others around us in similar predicaments were complaining all the time; they were blaming others, or they simply gave up hope. My family was different. I was different. When there was a local election and we had a day off, I never drank like the others or chose not go to work. I found work to do even on my days off, and I worked like mad. Being poor makes life inconvenient, but it isn't something to be ashamed of. And if you want to escape poverty, then you must really work hard. No one else can do it for you. Let me ask you, has any other elected official from your district ever come over to do something for you? I assure you I won't be any different. You know why? It's because there's nothing I or anyone else can do for you! Do you want your kids to inherit this poverty too? I know what goes through your mind when you worry about marrying off your son or daughter."

By then it was getting late, but none of them seemed to want to go. One of them stood up and asked me if I would come again. He thought that others should listen to what I had to say.

A few days later I visited them once again. Unlike my first visit, this time many people were already gathered in the square before I arrived. Like last time, I laid out a few pieces of newspaper and sat down on the ground. As soon as I got comfortable, I noticed more people starting to gather around. I could sense that the residents were much more accommodating, even welcoming.

"I know many of you will not vote for me. I understand. If I am elected, I'm quite certain there isn't much I can do for you. All I can say is that I will try to be helpful as much as I can, whenever I can."

One issue that I could help with was the forty-year-old dispute between the residents and the owners of the land.

"I know about your long dispute with the landowners. When I was in business, I resolved countless incidents involving landowners, reparations, and the like. I'll try my best once I'm in office to bring an amicable settlement to the issue. I know my predecessors probably promised a lot, but rarely, if ever, did any of them follow through."

I knew my remarks went straight to the point. That night the residents and I talked about a whole host of issues. To them, I wasn't the former CEO of Hyundai Group or a political candidate, I was just Mr. Lee Myung-bak, dispensing advice, listening to their concerns, and sharing with them my personal thoughts. Later, prior the election, when the landowners and the residents got into a disagreement, one of the residents came to me asking for help. I kindly sent him away. I was careful not to promise anything when I hadn't even been elected.

"Please come back when the election's over," I said, "and I promise you that I will try to help regardless of whether I win or lose."

Election day brought a powerful upset. Contrary to expectations, I beat my opponent handily, garnering 40.5 percent of the votes, much more than expected. The runner-up, Mr. Lee Jong-chan, received 33 percent, while Mr. Roh Moo-hyun[30] received 17 percent. More than anything, I was pleased when I learned that I had won in Gung-an village. The reason for my victory was that ordinary voters chose me. This, above all else, made me proud of my victory.

After my upset, those who had predicted I would lose—badly— avoided me. Understandably, they were embarrassed. One day, one of them came to see me and apologized. I told him an apology was unnecessary. I said, "Your predictions were right, based on the facts as you knew them. However, the times have changed. People have changed. You just made the mistake of ignoring this change."

What I was saying was that the old politics no longer worked. Regionalism and stereotypes no longer worked among voters who were becoming much more sophisticated and less prone to such manipulations. My victory in Jongno was stunning for many reasons, but most of all, it gave me renewed hope that we can overcome such prejudices. After all, Jongno was the embodiment of the establishment and the privileged; yet as home to residents like the ones in Gung-an as well as Seoul's rich and famous, it was also the place where divisions and animosities were prevalent.

New politics meant that I now had to try my best to help everyone, not simply my supporters. Like a company, I needed to cater to the needs and wishes of my "customers." New politics would be about doing our best to listen to the concerns of all the constituents. If we marketed our "products" as best we could, then I was certain we could overcome even the regionalism that was a source of so much division and dissention.

After winning the election I went to Gung-an village again. I had not promised them anything, so technically I had no obligations. Regardless, the residents greeted me with open arms and shook my hand, congratulating me. The sense of mutual trust and affection was gratifying. I vowed to remember that these people were the reason I had decided to become a politician.

17 | A NEW BEGINNING

I believed in the 1 percent possibility, the idea that if there is even a 1 percent possibility of success, a project can be realized by the addition of hard work.

November 15, 1998. I was on my way to Gimpo International Airport. I was thinking about my past life and the things that I had done, thinking of the nearly thirty years I spent as a businessman, traveling all across the world, entering politics and fostering my newfound passion: helping people. I had been honored to win the coveted seat representing the Jongno district and deeply pained when, having been charged with exceeding the legal spending cap during the 1996 election, I decided to resign. However familiar I was with trials and hardships, this one was particularly wrenching. Nonetheless, I considered this situation to be of my making. I didn't intend to blame anyone. I have always believed that whether in business or in politics, one has to exercise responsibility.

Giving up my seat—and being unemployed—gave me time to reflect. It was also the first time in my life that I had a lot of time on my hands. Eventually I decided that this was the perfect opportunity for me to study. I recalled the case of my good friend, former Prime Minister Mahathir of Malaysia. There was a period in this exceptional man's life when he was forced to the sidelines after having served his country admirably for many years. During his time in the political wilderness, Mr. Mahathir didn't idle away the hours or become remorseful; he turned it into an opportunity by traveling around the world, studying what others were doing. On his travels he would carry with him a small video camera. Visiting major factories, he recorded the steps they were taking to improve quality and global competitiveness. Once back in politics, Mr. Mahathir didn't waste a single day—he immediately implemented what he had learned abroad. I knew I wasn't going to waste my time either. I decided I would pursue my other passions.

Nineteen ninety-eight was a time of great expectations and much uncertainty as people anticipated the coming new century. I wondered how the Americans were preparing for the future. Fortunately, I was offered a position as a visiting fellow at George Washington University, in Washington, D.C., where I planned to spend a year studying business management and state administration and governance.

About that time, Korea's leading daily newspaper published the findings of an opinion poll. *Chosun Ilbo* was celebrating the fiftieth anniversary of the founding of the nation and had asked respondents who they thought were the most influential individuals of the past fifty years. I was chosen as one of the ten leading figures in the field of business. My autobiography, which had been published in 1995, was selected as one of fifty important publications of the year. Both were gratifying consolations to me as I prepared for a new beginning.

Before I left for the U.S., a group of close business associates and family friends hosted a small dinner reception for me and my wife. I told them that I intended to step aside from politics and business for a while to study what others were doing to prepare for the new century. I also told them I considered it a great blessing to be able to look back on what I had accomplished and to prepare for the future. I knew I had shortcomings, and to have the time to study and improve myself was truly a blessing.

On the cusp of a new millennium, I wanted to develop a new and different vision for my country, to set myself apart from the usual politics. Although I had been unable to breach the high walls and rules set by the establishment, I was as determined as ever to change things. In order to do so, I knew I had to arm myself with new ideas and new visions. I still harbored a desire to apply what I had learned in the private sector to the public sector, and I instinctively knew that that was what Korea would need to prosper in the coming century.

When my wife and I arrived in Gimpo International Airport, a throng of well-wishers was there to bid us farewell. We hadn't told anyone our exact departure date or time, so it was surprising—and deeply touching—that so many of them showed up to say good-bye. I shook hands with each of them and thanked them. Some had become teary-eyed, and I too was overcome with emotion. I thanked them once again and assured them that I would come back a better man, a better leader. I didn't have to say anything more. I knew that I would demonstrate my resolve through my actions.

A Second Honeymoon

I had spent countless hours on airplanes during my days as a business executive, but this day was different. Whenever I had traveled as a business executive, I flew first class. Now, for the first time, I was seated in economy class on the midnight flight, the cheapest available.

I felt sorry for my wife. What was even more depressing was the fact that I was stuck next to an enormous man who took up a lot of space. I became annoyed, but there was nothing I could do. Before leaving for the States, I had promised myself that we would live frugally. I made this promise to my wife, and she readily agreed. So complaining about a lousy seat was out of the question.

Our red-eye flight landed at 6:00 a.m., Washington time. After a long and tiring (and very cramped) flight, all I wanted to do was rest. Life was hectic back in Korea, and the emotional toll of the past few months had sapped me of my energy. I was longing for a hot shower and a nice long nap. When we arrived at the hotel, however, we learned that our room would not be available for another few hours. Unless we paid for an extra day, we would have to wait until the afternoon check-in time. In the past, I would have simply paid for another day, but under these new circumstances, I decided to wait in the hotel lounge.

My wife and I found a sofa in the hotel lobby and settled down as comfortably as we could. Then I looked over at my wife. Suddenly I realized that I hadn't looked closely at her face in a long time. I was surprised to notice that her once beautiful face was now show-ing unmistakable signs of age.

My wife and I had not had time for a proper honeymoon, because as soon as we had been married I went back to work, trav-eling to faraway places. During these years I would often be gone for weeks and months at a time, and even missed the births of our four children. In my absence, my wife had to take care of the kids all on her own. Whenever something happened in the family, she would have to make all the decisions and take care of it herself. She was a strong woman, a terrific mother, and a caring, loving wife who had endured a lot over the years, and I was reminded of how lucky I was to have her as my companion.

Fortunately, our stay in the hotel didn't last too long. We were able to find our own place through the help of an old friend, Professor Park Yoon-shik, who was teaching at George Washington University. During our first week in Washington, Professor Park's wife showed us around town so we could choose a house. The first house she showed us was a handsome two-story home with a large front lawn. My wife was immediately smitten with the house. She found the lawn especially enchanting. However, I told Mrs. Park that we wanted to see a smaller, more modest place. I didn't even set foot inside the house. I told her that we would prefer a small apartment near the university.

Mrs. Park protested that the house wasn't big at all by Washington standards. She insisted that it was no larger than a house in which an average Korean news correspondent stationed in the area would live. She went on to say that since I would be entertaining many guests, especially reporters from Korea, I should at least live in a house similar to theirs. I told her that I had no intention of entertaining any guests during my stay and insisted she help us find a smaller place.

Mrs. Park finally relented. She led us to a neighborhood near the university and showed us a quiet little apartment. I decided that this was the perfect place for us to settle down. We signed the rental agreement and moved in immediately.

My wife and I had decided that we wouldn't buy new furniture, but living with a minimal amount of furniture turned out to be harder than expected. Our table was an upturned box, which also served as our telephone and fax console. My desk, as well as the blankets that we used, were given to us as gifts by our friends.

Such frugality and modesty wasn't an attempt to prove anything to others. It stemmed from my personal conviction that whatever the circumstances, one must try to learn from them. I am inherently an optimistic person and have an optimistic outlook on life. Now I was in self-imposed exile, so it was only natural for me to remain frugal. I told myself that the purpose of my stay in D.C. was to learn something new; there was no need to live lavishly. My mother was the one who instilled in me such an attitude. I never once saw my mother complain. Instead, she always gave thanks for whatever she had and tried to make the best of it. I intended to do the same.

At first it felt rather odd for me to spend an entire day with my wife. I had trouble figuring out what to say! For her part, my wife found it awkward that I was always home. She wasn't used to having me around during the day and was concerned that we would find living in a small apartment too cramped. Yet by our third month together, ensconced in our new life, we both became comfortable with our daily routines and didn't feel awkward being together all the time. We were, in fact, enjoying the most relaxing time in our lives. On Sundays we would go to church together and worship; afterward, we would take a short drive and continue talking. During the week, we would go out together to socialize and meet with friends. We spent a lot of time together and felt as if we were enjoying a real honeymoon for the first time.

Whenever I attended seminars, my wife would join me. If we had to drive for hours, we would take turns. Going to places we'd never been before was no problem at all. All we had to do was download a map and follow the directions. Since in the States all the streets had names, this was very easy, whereas in Seoul, finding a place even if you had the address was often a great challenge. For example, our house in Seoul was located on a street called Star Village Road. I was wondering how I could explain to my American friends where my house was located, given the irregular naming and numbering conventions of Korean addresses. I realized it was all but impossible. Suddenly I had an idea about how to regularize Korean addresses. This and many other ideas would begin to take shape as my time in D.C. progressed, perhaps none more ambitious than my plan for Seoul's version of Boston's Big Dig project.

The Big Dig Project

During my time as a visiting fellow at George Washington University, I studied business management and state governance. My prime interest was in learning how the United States was preparing for the new century. At a seminar one day, I realized that the environment was becoming a major area of study and a source of grave concern. Many academics and policy experts in the States were predicting that protecting the environment and ensuring sustainable growth were going to be among the most important concerns of the twenty-first century.

Boxes of books from online bookstores began to accumulate in the spare room of my apartment. Then one day, as I was looking at the boxes, a thought occurred to me: "A box is a box. But a box doesn't always have to be just a box." This thought came to me as I was thinking about how to protect the environment while at the same time ensuring continued growth of the economy. Sometimes a radical new approach is needed to solve problems. Why should a box be just a box? With some creativity, a box can be something else. Similarly, if we are trying to solve environmental problems in a time of limited resources, then we mustn't simply create new things to satisfy all of our needs; rather, we must limit our needs and transform the way our existing resources are being used.

As my interest in this topic continued to deepen, a friend of mine told me about the Big Dig project in downtown Boston. He suggested that I take time to visit the site myself. He said it was quite a sight, and that it was what preparing for the twenty-first century was all about.

Sometime later, I made the trip up to Boston and headed for the old elevated highway (Interstate 93) that runs from Charlestown through the North End and on through downtown. The highway, although still serviceable, was being demolished in favor of a massive tunnel that would both relieve traffic congestion and improve air quality throughout the city. The project was known as the Big Dig.

No one knew how long the project would take to finish. Some said ten years, others said twenty. Once the project was finished, however, traffic would run underground, and parts of the surface would be converted into a park, lush with trees and playgrounds. It was, in short, a fantastically romantic idea conceived by visionaries.

I found out that at first there had been serious disagreement surrounding the viability of the plan and whether to undertake such a massive public works project. In the end, however, Bostonians chose to become romantics and decided to support the project. For a man who was used to looking at charts and balance sheets, carefully weighing the pros and cons of any decision, I immediately realized that the benefits of this project were incredible. Once finished, the tunnel would not only make Boston a green city, it would transform the way the people lived and enjoyed life. At first glance, the project might have seemed unrealistic, even impossible, but upon closer examination, I understood that it had the potential to change the future of the city forever. In short, it was an outstanding investment.

I pictured how Boston would look in the future. The thought occurred to me that while with this project Boston was taking just a single step forward, down the road no other city would be able to match the breadth of this project's vision. Accurately reading the current trends, predicting where the future lies, and then taking the necessary steps now—this is what determines our fate.

While looking at the Big Dig and imagining the future of Boston, the image of downtown Seoul came to mind. Through the heart of Seoul a stream called Cheonggyecheon (the term means "clean stream") used to run. Unfortunately, as the city began to grow and the surrounding area became overcrowded, the stream became more and more polluted with garbage and sewage from the shanties that dotted the riverbank. This became a particular problem beginning during the mid-1950s, following the end of the Korean War. Everything was dilapidated, and the economy was shattered. As conditions along the stream worsened, city officials decided that the most viable option was to cover it over. Soon, roads and expressways were being built over the stream. Between 1955 and 1970, numerous construction projects were undertaken, and by the end of 1970, almost the entire stream (approximately 5 miles long) was completely covered.

For more than forty years, Cheonggyecheon had been one of the most chaotic and congested areas within Seoul. Underneath the expressway were strewn thousands of small stores, street vendors, and stalls. Development was out of the question; crime was rampant. Almost 170,000 cars traveled along the Cheonggye Expressway daily, and there was always the danger of collapse. Repair work necessary to prevent this potential disaster was carried out almost nonstop, leading to still more congestion. But these repair jobs were only temporary measures. A fundamental solution had to be implemented.

A further problem lent special urgency to finding a solution: the space between the original stream and the roads above was filled with toxic exhaust fumes. With no adequate ventilation system in place, the gases had been festering for forty years and seeping out into the surrounding atmosphere. In short, the heart of the city was in utter decay. Because the natural flow of the stream had been blocked, heat was also trapped. During summer, when the heat and humidity became overbearing, the average temperature around the stream was 2 to 3 degrees higher than in the surrounding areas. A heat island had formed right in the center of Seoul.

There was only one solution: restore the stream.

Seeking the 1 Percent Possibility

I began calculating the possibility of restoring Cheonggyecheon. Was it really feasible? Almost everyone agreed that the area had to change, but the big question was, who was going to undertake such a massive public works project? When, and how?

As soon as I returned to Korea, I sought the opinion of transportation specialists and urban planners. They were all in agreement about one thing: getting rid of an expressway that carried nearly 170,000 cars a day would precipitate a transportation crisis. That, I told one of the experts, was exactly what I had in mind.

After a moment, the expert understood and agreed. "It's about time we adopted policies to curb demand. We can no longer accommodate this volume of traffic and still expect to live in comfort. However, you're likely to face an enormous amount of resistance. The people are not ready, and they are not willing to put up with the inconveniences."

"Without radical change," I continued, "transportation paralysis will bring the city to its knees. Yet people will only realize the need for change when they see the paralysis with their own eyes. When it comes to transportation policy, the government has to be a step ahead of public perception, but in fact we've always been a step behind."

The more I discussed this issue with people, the more I became convinced that it was doable. I believed in the 1 percent possibility, the idea that if there is even a 1 percent possibility of success, a project can be realized by the addition of hard work.

Engineers agreed that technically it was quite simple to dismantle the expressway and restore the stream. In other words, the engineering challenge was the easy part; the hard part would be to convince people to endure the inconveniences.

The so-called policy experts were the most difficult to convince. They favored a simple approach and were adamantly opposed to any project requiring extensive preparatory work. A project of this scale, they argued, would invariably involve much negotiating, and the negotiations would eventually scuttle the project. They insisted that the project had the potential to become a political disaster.

I was crestfallen. Although everyone was aware of the pitfalls of having an ugly expressway in the middle of the city, threatening not only the safety of the motorists but also the health of those below, the consensus was that it was premature to undertake such a project. The experts swept away my concerns and plans as nothing more than wishful thinking and told me flatly that it was impossible. Many of them were also worried about the political fallout and did not wish to take actions that might threaten their careers.

Frustrated by the experts, I sought the advice of ordinary people. I asked my friends what they thought of my idea. None of them was an engineer or an expert in urban planning. The answers that I got surprised me. They all said, "If that's the case, I suppose it must be done!" They encouraged me to believe that I was on the right track after all.

These ordinary folks understood the stakes and recognized the need readily enough. They told me that the plan wasn't premature but rather almost too late. I became convinced that if we let this problem continue growing, the issue would become so complex that a solution would become forever out of reach.

However, I was just one individual. Restoring the stream wasn't a project that could be carried out by a private company. It needed to be carried out by a public agency. It wasn't just about dismantling an expressway; it was about ushering in a new era of better living. And it involved negotiating with countless actors. It was also about transforming the way we viewed urban life. In short, it was about planning for the future. By dismantling the expressway, I planned to get rid of a structure that symbolized the past, when indiscriminate development at all costs was the accepted norm. By clearing the city of this remnant, I believed we could convince people that life doesn't have to be entirely about development. Life can and must be about shared prosperity and opportunities; it must be about enjoying clean air and having the chance to take a stroll with your family.

This was when an idea that had been brewing in the back of my mind finally took concrete shape. I had found my next goal. I decided to become mayor of Seoul so that I might have the opportunity to provide those things for my family and following generations.

18 | BECOMING MAYOR OF SEOUL

I learned that most of the time, if we were pursuing the right policies, then dedication, clear strategies, and an abundance of patience could take us a long way.

After returning from the United States, I decided to enter the Grand National Party's primary race to nominate its candidate for mayor of Seoul. To my luck, my opponent withdrew his candidacy, and the party announced me as their candidate for mayor.

All previous Seoul mayors had come from the Democratic Party. Being the Democratic Party candidate meant that a win was almost a given. As such, the Democratic Party was confident that it would win the Seoul mayoral race yet again. This time their nominee was Mr. Kim Min-seok, a charismatic thirty-eight-year-old politician. Kim had once been a student activist who was known nationwide and had great appeal among young voters. As president of the student council of Seoul National University (one of Korea's most elite universities), he led the student movement for democracy and was jailed for his activities. Young voters in their 20s and 30s were saying that they would take part in the election so they could vote for him. He was hailed as the new face of Korean politics. Opinion polls showed that I was constantly behind by 1 to 3 percent.

Naturally, my supporters were bracing for a hard battle. They tried to comfort me by saying that the young voters would come around as the initial excitement subsided. Nonetheless, Kim was a formidable opponent. However, I remained confident. I realized I was trailing him in part on account of the age factor, but I also knew that I was armed with what really mattered: good policy ideas and a workable plan.

My predictions proved correct. As time passed, voters began to realize that this election was more about policy than about popularity. As I patiently and consistently explained what I intended to do if elected mayor, they started listening. I methodically outlined my plans for the restoration of Cheonggyecheon, and soon this issue became the central focus of the election. I was able to present a detailed plan and answer questions ranging from the cost to when it would be completed. I explained how living standards would improve and how the surrounding areas would be renovated. I assured the voters that a revamped public transportation grid would minimize traffic congestion during the restoration project. In short, I was dictating the narrative of the election and winning over voters.

During our television debates, Kim said he opposed the project, and I was forced to defend my position. Being the opposition candidate meant that it was difficult to attain even the simplest government statistics to back my claims; however, I was undaunted and persistent.

In the end, I was elected mayor of Seoul. I won by garnering 52.3 percent of the vote, and my margin of victory was a respectable 9.3 percent. On June 13, 2002, I was given the keys to the mayor's office and put in charge of the ten million citizens of Seoul as well as the 46,000-member Seoul Metropolitan Government. Considering that pundits and election experts, as well as politicians, had predicted the race would be "too close to call," my win was definitely an upset. And sweet.

Politicians and experts didn't realize it at that time, but ordinary voters, and especially the citizens of Seoul, were yearning for change. They understood what I was trying to do and gave me their support. The people on the streets wanted real change, and I was ready to deliver it.

Restoring Cheonggyecheon

During the mayoral campaign, and then after assuming office, I tirelessly explained the details of the project. When I said that the project would be complete in two years, people were skeptical. (Some quipped that my old nickname, Bulldozer, was especially apt now.) Yet it wasn't an unrealistic goal: with the preparatory work already underway, the actual demolition and restoration would take place over a period of two years. Before the summer monsoon season, we would run a preliminary test of how the stream would hold up, make corrections, and finalize the project. My intention was to minimize the inconvenience to the residents of Seoul and to all others whose livelihoods would be affected by the project.

The construction itself was fairly straightforward. We had to demolish the expressways, bury the water pipes and sewage lines below, and rearrange the streambed while landscaping the surrounding areas. If the stream had not been in the middle of a city of ten million people, the entire project could be finished in less than six months.

As it was, however, the project was akin to closing down entire traffic lanes and relocating thousands of shops on New York's Madison Avenue for two years (although the shops on Cheonggyecheon were definitely more modest than the ones on Madison Avenue). The immediate vicinity had more than ten thousand shops, represented by close to a thousand unions and owners' organizations. On top of this, there were hundreds of competing interests at work; shop owners and those who rented the space had differing, often conflicting, desires. For instance, those selling fashion apparel and the like welcomed the change; the ones selling hardware and household appliances opposed it.

We set out to convince them all. To do this, I set up a special division within the Seoul Metropolitan Government (SMG). Its task was to listen to the concerns of the shop owners, explain the need for restoring the stream, and describe how we intended to go about it. If the vendors and shop owners had concerns, then the team would deal with them. Every morning at 8:30 our team members would set out to visit the shops and vendors. Each evening, the team would come back to the office, write up reports, and handle the many requests made by the shopkeepers. This was our way of earning trust. After a while, the shopkeepers would call our staff whenever they had a complaint or needed something done. The staff did their best to help them in whatever way they could.

From July 2002 until June 2003 our team met with the shopkeepers a total of 4,200 times. We resolved close to 1,000 requests. As a result of such strenuous effort on our part, the shopkeepers and various organizations finally agreed to our plan just fifteen days before the scheduled start of the project.

Now, with the necessary administrative measures in place, we were set to begin our version of the Big Dig. Adjacent roads were expanded to allow for more traffic, but we also took measures to curb drive-alone cars by urging drivers to take public transportation.

Seoul's public transportation system was undergoing its own transformation, aided by the adoption of the latest technologies, so that traffic in the downtown area would not become overly congested. One-way streets were designated, and a central control center was created to monitor and adjust traffic patterns, depending on the flow at any given moment.

Korea's state-of-the-art information technology helped us immensely. Team members worked around the clock and ran countless simulations using the latest computer technology to prepare for all contingencies. The simulations warned us to expect some initial confusion and congestion, but they also predicted that the situation would resolve itself within two weeks.

Seoul's extensive subway system was helpful, too. We allotted extra cars during peak hours to encourage greater usage of the subway during the morning and evening rushes.

In the end we were fortunate, for the residents of Seoul adapted quickly to the new environment. Credit must be given to them for their patience and understanding. Koreans are infamous for being short-tempered and always rushing from one place to another. However, Koreans are also good at recognizing when an inconvenience is worth their trouble. Once they understand the value of something, they gladly bear any inconvenience to achieve the goal. The people of Seoul were now fully convinced that what we were trying to do was well worth the trouble.

Nine days after the starting date, once we saw that all was going well with the new traffic patterns, I ordered the commencement of the demolition of the expressway.

As promised, the Cheonggyecheon stream was restored in two years. For the first time in decades, people were able to enjoy fresh air and clean water in the heart of Seoul. Even migratory birds came back, and the residents found a place to stroll and relax. Office workers began to commute on foot. During weekends, people came out with their families and friends.

Cheonggyecheon quickly became a favorite tourist destination and a landmark of Seoul. World-renowned artists came to our city to perform, world-class art exhibits soon opened all across Seoul's many museums, and people started to appreciate the beauty that Seoul had to offer.

Because of Cheonggyecheon, surrounding neighborhoods also began to come to life. Traditionally, the downtown area was known as the old part of town. Rarely, if ever, would young people explore its rich history and quaint charm. Now the various streets in downtown Seoul were swamped by young couples out on dates and by teens armed with digital cameras. If the area south of the Han River, with its chic architecture and exclusive boutiques, was considered the hip part of town, then downtown Seoul became known for its historical beauty, fusion of old and new, and classy sophistication. The project quickly redefined central Seoul as a hip part of town all its own.

The project also gained international acclaim. At the 2003 Venice Biennale it won the Best Public Administration award for urban construction and was given extensive coverage by *Time* magazine (May 15, 2006). A documentary about the project was filmed by the Discovery Channel and was aired globally. Several European broadcasters took an inside look at the implications of the project and dubbed it a success, describing it as a feat that "killed two birds with one stone," both restoring the environment and fostering sustainable development. With global interest in sustainable growth catching fire, the Cheonggyecheon project served as a model for the future and an example of what urban planning should look like. We were able to show the world that protecting the environment and promoting clean development can go hand in hand.

Green Seoul

With more than ten million residents, Seoul is one of the world's most populated metropolises. If one includes the Greater Seoul area, the combined population exceeds twelve million. In Seoul alone there are roughly two million registered vehicles, and more than 2.8 million vehicles roam the streets every day. The foundation of the public transportation system is an extensive underground subway that crisscrosses the entire city and its neighboring areas. Buses are also widely accessible. Nonetheless, during my tenure as mayor, private bus companies were continually vying for the most lucrative lines with the greatest number of passengers. The result was a morass of redundant routes served by multiple companies in some areas and a scarcity of public transportation along other, less lucrative routes. The entire public transportation grid was in need of reorganization to improve efficiency.

Tackling this issue was, in some ways, even more frustrating than the restoration project at Cheonggyecheon. It meant having to deal with hundreds of private bus companies, and this at times led to nothing short of shouting matches and acrimonious finger-pointing.

These were just a few of the issues that I tackled while serving as mayor. It required a tremendous amount of skill for me to settle disputes and bring about amicable solutions. Sometimes it required arm-twisting. But I learned that most of the time, if we were pursuing the right policies, then dedication, clear strategies, and an abundance of patience could take us a long way.

With the completion of Cheonggyecheon and the transformation of our bus system, Seoul was fast becoming a model for other cities, particularly in terms of sustainable development. For example, government officials from Vietnam and China visited us to learn about our reforms of the bus transportation grid. This gave us an opportunity to share not only what we had learned but some of the mistakes that we made, too. Chinese and British officials came to study our transportation overhaul as they prepared for the 2008 Beijing Olympics and the 2012 London Olympics, respectively. The mayor of Istanbul was one of many foreign dignitaries who personally came to Seoul to learn about our experience.

As our success story became widely known, the press as well as government officials from countries such as Japan, the Philippines, Germany, Taiwan, and Indonesia asked for information. Our project was recognized with numerous awards: the Seoul Metropolitan Government was the sole recipient of the 2005 Sustainable Transportation Award, given by the U.S. Transportation Research Board during its 85th annual meeting. A special seminar on Seoul was hosted by the International Association of Public Transportation in 2004. In 2007, *Time* magazine selected me as one of their Heroes of the Environment. The *International Herald Tribune* ran a front-page article on the restoration project; the *Chicago Tribune*, *Financial Times*, *Frankfurter Allgemeine Zeitung*, and other leading international papers also wrote major pieces.

These were all flattering, of course, and I was deeply gratified by the many acclamations and awards. But more than anything, I was proud of what we had achieved for the people of Seoul and pleased that we presented them with an alternative vision of urban living. The staff and everyone at the SMG who worked so hard were also a source of great pride, and credit must be given to them as well.

On May 1, 2004, we opened the Seoul Plaza in front of City Hall. Previously the area had been an intersection so twisted and tangled in knots that tourists riding in buses thought they were being driven in circles; now that area has been transformed into a wide, open plaza laid with carpets of grass. Many people said they felt relaxed just looking at the plaza, while others told me that they took their shoes and socks off so they could feel the grass between their toes. Mothers with their babies in strollers, office workers having coffee, couples on dates, and parents with their children all flocked to the plaza. Throughout the spring and especially during the hot summer nights the plaza became a favorite destination.

From the mayor's office I could see the entire plaza and I was pleased to see so many people enjoying themselves. However, I knew that the people would no longer be able to enjoy the open space as temperatures dropped. Seoul winters are known to be harsh, but I wanted the people to enjoy the plaza despite the cold weather. It was then that I was suddenly struck by an idea—the Rockefeller Center ice rink in New York City. I immediately summoned my staff and explained to them my plan of setting up an ice rink on the plaza.

At first many of them were skeptical and some were outright against the idea. One reason was the fear that such a structure would cause irreparable damage to the grass and the supporting foundation. Others pointed out the difficulty of obtaining the necessary funding, while another said that by the time the ice rink was finished, it would be spring.

These objections were all legitimate, but I wanted to pursue the idea. I enlisted the opinion of an outsider who was an expert in staging and producing large-scale musicals. He responded that it was doable; if we were worried about damage to the grass, then the ice rink could be set up on one side of the plaza where there wasn't any grass. If size was a problem then we could fix that by allowing only figure skating, which required less space.

I stressed to my staff the cultural value of setting up an ice rink in the heart of the city, and the symbolism of the city government breaking the mold. Most of all, I wanted to offer the people the pleasure of enjoying the plaza even during winter. Soon, a plan was born. As for funding the project, I instructed the staff to pitch the idea to private companies for a sponsorship. Later, when the ice rink became a huge hit, the financial company that became our sponsor said that it was one of their most successful advertisements ever.

The ice rink was finished and opened to the public before Christmas. The rink ended up being much larger than the one at Rockefeller Center. It became an instant sensation. Soon, similar ventures sprang up all across Seoul and spread to different cities. We initially planned to close the rink in early February, but we extended the season seventeen days.

Another project that we completed was the making of the Seoul Forest. This was a project in line with my philosophy of achieving harmony between development and environmental protection. It was also another cultural symbol and the completion of my vision to establish a green network in which culture and environment complemented each other.

I envisioned an eco-friendly park in the eastern part of Seoul, much like Central Park in New York, where people could enjoy nature. It wasn't about building another amusement park where people lined up to ride roller coasters or crowds rushed about. Instead, it was a place of quiet contemplation and leisurely walks. I wanted a place where people could rest.

One problem, however, was that the area was set aside for a massive development project worth approximately five billion U.S. dollars. It was a substantial amount that was difficult to ignore. Nonetheless, I finally decided that having a nature park was worth much more in the long run. In particular, I was concerned about the lack of green space that was available to people living in Seoul.

Although there were obstacles, such as convincing landowners (who were expecting a lucrative buyout) and nearby residents (who were hoping to see an increase in their property values as the area developed into a major commercial district), and zoning issues, we managed to complete the project in a relatively short period of time. With the completion of this project my vision for a green network was finally materializing. Beginning in the heart of Seoul with newly formed pedestrian walkways and the restoration of Cheonggyecheon stream, and now the Seoul Forest, Seoul was no longer gray. A greenbelt was in place.

Along with establishing a green metropolis, an important goal of mine was to make culture an important pillar of Seoul. I was aware that the word "culture" had broad applications, but to me the essence of culture was about creating a fulfilling life. The ice rink, the Seoul Forest, and the Cheonggyecheon restoration were all about fulfilling life and upgrading the quality of life for everyone, not just a select few. My decision to upgrade the Seoul Philharmonic Orchestra was another project that would complete the picture.

Many world-class philharmonic orchestras are based in and supported by major cities such as New York, Vienna, and Berlin. They play an important part in not only advancing art to the masses, but reflecting the high quality and standards of their cities. Unfortunately, the Seoul Philharmonic Orchestra was far below standard. Despite Korea having an abundance of musical prodigies, the Seoul Philharmonic was always short of talent.

This all changed when I met Chung Myung-whun[31]. I remembered Chung once saying that his life-long dream was to help a Korean orchestra become first-class. I met with Chung and we shared our thoughts. Chung and I agreed that the first thing we needed to do was grant independence to the orchestra by making it into a foundation (previously it was under the auspices of the Seoul Metropolitan Government). Then we recruited a professional executive to manage the orchestra. With these structural changes in place, we proceeded to recruit the best talents. Chung agreed to become the art director and principal conductor of the Seoul Philharmonic

Orchestra. I promised him that the city would continue to provide the support that he needed.

In order to make a world-class orchestra, we would need to satisfy three criteria: we would need a world-class conductor, skilled members, and continuous support. With Chung on board we satisfied the first. The second would be easily satisfied, since I was confident that many of Korea's talented musicians would be interested in joining simply because of Chung's presence. As for the third, I reassured Chung that I would make sure that the city's support for the orchestra would continue even after I finished my term.

Another dream of mine was that the orchestra would reach out to people who would normally not be able to enjoy classical music. Chung also shared my dream. Soon, the Seoul Philharmonic Orchestra came up with a unique idea: "visiting concerts," whereby the orchestra would visit towns and villages and give free concerts in school auditoriums, outdoor plazas, churches, and gymnasiums. Some people were concerned that such an idea would be an insult to classical music; some were worried that the acoustics would be awful. However, I wanted to let everyone witness the rebirth of the orchestra, and I also wanted as many people as possible to enjoy classical music. The orchestra traveled all across Korea holding these concerts. I was happy when I heard that many elders in remote villages heard Beethoven and Mozart for the first time in their lives thanks to the Seoul Philharmonic Orchestra.

On August 15, 2005, as the country celebrated its 60th anniversary of independence, the Seoul Philharmonic Orchestra performed in front of City Hall. For the special event, I had City Hall completely covered with 3,600 Korean flags. In front of this building, the Seoul Philharmonic Orchestra gave an outstanding performance. When Chung finished with the last piece, which was aptly titled "Korean Fantasy," we were all deeply moved.

June 30, 2006, was my last day as mayor. Traditionally, the farewell ceremony for the outgoing mayor is held at 10 a.m. inside Sejong Cultural Center, which is Seoul's largest concert hall. When I was told that my ceremony would follow this tradition, I became curious and asked the section chief in charge, "What do you guys do after my ceremony ends until the new mayor is sworn in?" The chief replied, "We just do our routine work, sir." Technically, my term was terminated at midnight on June 30 and my successor's term would begin immediately. I knew that these ceremonies were all formalities and traditions and I saw no reason to cut short my last day. So, I decided that I would end my last day as mayor at 6 p.m., which is when the workday was supposed to end. I also told my staff that there was no need to prepare an elaborate farewell ceremony at Sejong Center; I told them to instead bring a microphone and a small speaker and to place them in front of City Hall. I wanted to say a few words to the officials who worked so hard throughout my term; I wanted to thank them for their service. (In order to let the officials get off work by 6 p.m., this small ceremony took place at 5 p.m.)

At 5 p.m. I walked out to Seoul Plaza. The summer breeze was pleasant. After a while, a considerable number of city officials had gathered to bid me farewell. I stood in front of the microphone and thanked them for doing a remarkable job. I talked about how one of them had told me that he couldn't remember working so hard in his seventeen years at City Hall. I told them that I was grateful to all of them because I knew that I wouldn't have been able to do any of this if it weren't for their dedication, commitment, and energy.

Female secretaries were huddled together listening to my remarks. Many of them had been working at City Hall for years. I noticed that all of them had tears in their eyes. I went up to them and thanked them for enduring the long hours and grueling work. After I was done thanking everyone, the secretaries came up to me and asked if they could take pictures with me. Soon, everyone came in groups and I took photos with all of them. People passing by stopped and congratulated me and took photos as well.

When our small farewell party was over, my driver, who has been with my family for many years, came to pick me up. I got in the car, waved good-bye, and went home.

New Journey

I left the mayor's office in June 2006, immensely proud of what we had achieved as a team. I still find it a pure joy just to stroll along Cheonggyecheon and to see so many people enjoying life. Seoul has transformed itself into an international city of style and substance. Being mayor of Seoul allowed me to serve the great city that gave me so much. I was glad to be able to repay its wonderful people, who welcomed a poor farm boy from Pohang more than forty years ago.

Once again I was an ordinary private citizen, but my abiding interest and passion in sustainable development and the environment continued. I read as many books as I could on the subject and talked to experts. I also embarked on a nationwide policy tour, which afforded me an excellent opportunity to engage directly with the wider public to find out what their issues were. My sights were now set on Korea and its future.

My staff would join me on these field trips, which took us all across Korea. My small entourage included Mr. Kim Hee-joong and Mr. Im Jae-hyun, both indispensable aides who have been with me for many years, taking care of everything, both personal and professional. Others included Ms. Lee Jin-young and Ms. Kim Yoon-kyung, who improved and polished my messages, kept exhaustive journals of our meetings, and provided me with valuable advice on a wide range of issues. Once we had established a schedule, we would hop into our minivan and visit factories, meet with the workers and owners, hold town hall meetings, and listen to the concerns of the people.

We would join volunteers helping flood victims, and oftentimes visited institutes conducting research in such next-generation science as information-, bio-, and nano-technology. Later on, more people joined our team, armed with ideas and specific plans. These policy guys would fine-tune the many ideas that we gathered from our earlier trips, and I was able to implement many of these ideas when I became president. We were able to personally hear the people's passions, frustrations, aspirations, and hopes and to incorporate them into our vision for a new Korea. Our vision was becoming clearer. In order to further expand our horizon and learn about what was going on abroad, we visited Germany, the Netherlands, Japan, India, and the United Arab Emirates. We wanted to find out what others were doing to survive and thrive in the twenty-first century.

On a more personal level, it was also during this period that I moved into a traditional Korean-style house, a *han-ok* (Korean mansion). *Han-ok* architecture features slanted roofs covered with tiles; high ceilings; and large, inviting front lawns. I found it enchanting. It was evocative of the rural home that we once lived in years ago (although more spacious, and with modern amenities). I could hear the raindrops and feel the wind; strangers would drop in just to ask for a glass of water. I was amazed that such friendliness and openness were still alive in the heart of Seoul. Such is the rich diversity that Seoul offers its people.

Meanwhile, the country was slowly gearing up for the next presidential election, which was scheduled to take place in December 2007. I was keeping myself busy with my new ventures and finding out how I could best serve my country in a new capacity.

On December 19, 2007, I was given another chance to serve my country. I was elected as the Republic of Korea's 17th term president[32].

December 19 happens to be my birthday as well as my wedding anniversary. It is a very special day with much to celebrate. When people ask me what I celebrate on that day—my birthday, our wedding anniversary, or my election as president—I tell them that in a sense, they are all related: I celebrate my life and my marriage and the opportunity these have afforded me to serve my country.

EPILOGUE

For a poor boy from Pohang, it's been a great adventure and, most of all, a great privilege.

My presidential inauguration took place on February 25, 2008, in front of the National Assembly building. It was an unusually frigid day, but the sky was clear and blue. After attending all the official functions following the inauguration—the car parade, receptions, luncheon, and separate meetings with visiting dignitaries—I stepped into the building that would be my office for the next five years. The main building had been built by Hyundai Construction back when I was CEO; I had no idea then that I would one day be its occupant.

After signing my first official document as president—approving the appointment of my senior staff—I sat behind the large wooden desk. I knew being president of the world's thirteenth-largest economy was going to be quite different from being CEO or mayor. I also reminded myself that I should be prepared for unexpected events that were beyond my control. I just didn't think they would happen so soon.

When the 2008 global economic crisis struck, many said that it was the worst crisis to hit the global economy since the Great Depression of the 1930s. I never dreamed that barely a year after taking office, I would have to struggle to keep the Korean economy from sinking. It was a chilling reminder of how fragile our world is, how ill-prepared we can sometimes be, and how in this era of connectivity our collective fates—for better or worse—are tied together.

Beginning in Washington, D.C. in November 2008, the G-20 leaders from developed and developing countries came together to resolve this global crisis. Korea took part in the G-20 while doing its best to weather the turmoil at home. For many Koreans who had vivid memories of the 1997–98 Asian financial crisis, the 2008 global crisis seemed ominous. Throughout subsequent G-20 meetings, the international community came up with specific solutions and action plans. By the time Korea hosted the fifth G-20 Summit in November 2010, the global economy showed encouraging signs. Many were hopeful that the worst was over. However, as much as there is hope for recovery and growth, instability and uncertainty remain; much work still needs to be done.

The global economic crisis tested our commitment to international cooperation, and equally pressing global concerns are just as difficult to resolve and require cooperation. Climate change is one such. On August 15, 2008 I outlined our new vision for the future—Low Carbon Green Growth—as we celebrated the sixtieth anniversary of the founding of the Republic of Korea. This vision is about ensuring sustainable growth and prosperity while protecting our planet.

For a country like Korea, and for many others, coming up with a viable solution to this global issue is directly related to our survival in the twenty-first century. The Global Green Growth Institute (GGGI) was founded by Korea for this purpose. It is an international body that is dedicated to pioneering a new paradigm of economic growth by supporting developing and emerging countries in the design and implementation of green-growth economic plans; facilitating public-private partnership in green investments and innovation; and supporting research to advance the theory and practice of green growth. Another key objective is sharing these relevant technologies, because without sharing new technologies and know-how, climate change and related issues cannot be dealt with in any meaningful way. As we know, climate change isn't simply about rising temperatures or sea levels, although these are very serious consequences that threaten countries like the Maldives and many island states in the Pacific region. Climate change will fundamentally alter our way of life; we must come up with solutions that are effective and long-lasting. And for these solutions to bear fruit, we must be willing to work together.

Security and stability are vital as we work toward such common goals. However, threats such as terrorism, piracy, human trafficking, and proliferation of nuclear weapons—to name a few—still remain and are likely to increase if we fail to respond collectively. The North Korean nuclear issue is one such challenge; it must be peacefully resolved, and stakeholders must work together to ensure stability and prosperity for the Korean Peninsula. A peaceful peninsula will have enormous benefits that will go far beyond the region. It is not surprising that the question I get asked most often is whether I see the Korean Peninsula eventually reuniting, and if so, when I expect that to happen. I honestly do not know when, but I do know that it will happen. Permanent peace is possible on the Korean Peninsula, and a stable and unified Korea will contribute to global peace and prosperity.

It has already been more than three years since I was elected to this office. I remember the thrill of winning the election, but also feeling the immense weight of my responsibilities. I promised myself that I would not seek quick success or easy victories, but that I would always do what was right. There were painful moments to endure and difficult decisions to make. But there have also been proud achievements and joyous celebrations.

For example, I was proud when Korea successfully hosted the G-20 Seoul Summit, thereby contributing to charting a new path forward. When launching World Friends Korea, a volunteer program similar to the Peace Corps that will send more than 20,000 volunteers overseas, I felt proud of what these Koreans were doing in remote parts of the world. When I met an Ethiopian lady who thanked me for what she was able to do because of help from Korean volunteers, I felt happy that we were giving back. When I met Korean War veterans from Australia, Denmark, the United States, and elsewhere who came to Korea to commemorate the sixtieth anniversary of the war, I could see in the eyes of these old warriors how proud they were to see Korea doing so well.

I will spend my remaining days in office always remembering what a great honor it is to serve. And after I leave office, I will continue to serve. I will visit my friends abroad and work with them so that all of us can enjoy a more sustainable and greener future. I will take part in educating our children about the importance of sustainability, green growth, and protecting our environment. And through my foundation, The Lee & Kim Foundation, I will continue to help the next generation of leaders, especially those who struggle to succeed amidst poverty and other difficulties, like I did fifty years ago. I hope to watch these children grow up to become scientists, musicians, engineers, entrepreneurs, and maybe even president. Whatever they become, I hope they will contribute to the betterment of mankind.

For a poor boy from Pohang, it's been a great adventure and, most of all, a great privilege. And my journey is not over yet.

NOTES

1. Japan colonized the Republic of Korea from 1910 until
Japan's surrender and ultimate defeat in 1945, at the end of the
Second World War. Japan was a brutal conqueror, and during
this time a number of independence movements occurred within
Korea, the most famous of which is the March 1 Independence
Movement that took place in 1919. During Japan's occupation of
Korea, life for ordinary Koreans was harsh; historical records
show that hundreds of thousands were arrested, tortured, and
killed. Japan sought to systematically wipe away any traces of
Korean culture and tried to force the Korean people to adopt
Japanese culture, for example by forcing Koreans to change
their names into Japanese, banning the use and study of the
Korean language, and making Koreans pledge allegiance to the
Japanese emperor. Also, many Koreans were forcibly conscripted
into the Japanese army and killed in battles overseas. Korean
women (as well as those from other countries occupied by
Japan) were sold into sexual slavery and euphemistically called
"comfort women."

2. North Korea invaded the Republic of Korea early on the
morning of June 25, 1950. Shortly after the outbreak of the Korean

War, on July 7, 1950, the United Nations Security Council adopted Resolution 84, in which the Security Council condemned the attack and recommended that the members of the United Nations provide assistance to the Republic of Korea (ROK) "to repel the attack and restore peace and security to the area." Although the South Korean government was aware of an imminent attack by North Korea, the ROK military was nevertheless overwhelmed, and within days of the invasion, its armed forces were in full retreat all the way down to Busan, South Korea's southernmost city. It was here that UN forces fought the Battle of Busan Perimeter, which is considered one of the fiercest battles that took place during the war. U.S. forces alone suffered more than 37,000 deaths, and other members of the UN coalition suffered heavily as well.

3.   From 1955 until its abolishment by the Korean government in 1982, a statewide curfew forbade anyone to roam the streets between midnight and 4 a.m. Anybody caught out after midnight was forced to stay overnight at a nearby police station until the curfew was lifted. Due to this draconian measure, buses, trams, and taxis were jammed with passengers between 11 p.m. and midnight every night.

4.   The May 16 Coup occurred in 1961 when Lieutenant General Park Chung-hee and a group of young army officers overthrew the unpopular civilian government (Second Republic) that had been established after Syngman Rhee stepped down from the presidency. Following the coup, General Park created the Supreme Council for National Reconstruction, promoted himself to a four-star general, and assumed absolute control over the country. At first, General Park vowed that he would return to the military once a civilian government was put in place; however,

when the constitution for the Third Republic was enacted, General Park discharged himself from the military, ran for the presidency as a civilian candidate, and won. As president, he is credited with modernizing Korea and halting the spread of communism, but he is also criticized for stifling democracy and abusing human rights. After two consecutive terms in office, he attempted to prolong his presidency into a third term, which the constitution prohibited. He sought to amend the constitution. This was met by vehement opposition from the public, but he successfully amended the constitution, allowing for a third term.

5.   Kim Jong-pil is famous for being one of the "Three Kims" (the other two being former Presidents Kim Dae-jung and Kim Young-sam) who were at the center of modern Korean politics for close to four decades. As an army major during the May 16 Coup and a kinsman to President Park Chung-hee, Kim Jong-pil was one of President Park's closest aides and was subsequently appointed to many high-profile government positions, including prime minister (twice) and head of the ruling party, among others. He was the founder and the first director of the Korean Central Intelligence Agency (later renamed National Intelligence Service) which was much feared and loathed by Koreans. He ran for president in 1987, finishing a poor third, but his influence in Korean politics remained strong until he retired in 2004.

6.   Seodaemun (West Gate) Prison, located in west-central Seoul, opened in 1907. At first, the prison was used by the Japanese to incarcerate those who took part in anticolonial activities; later, it was used by Korea's authoritarian regime to house democracy activists and other civil-rights leaders. It was closed in 1987 and has been designated as a historical site and museum.

7.   My original five-year sentence was a request made by the state; the court's sentence was the final verdict. Although I was sentenced to two years, the sentence was suspended for three years, and in Korea, such a suspension means the person doesn't have to serve a prison term. The reason I spent time in prison was because I was arrested on charges of "inciting rebellion," and back then, when a person was accused of a crime, he was sent to prison while the trials took place. If a person who is released from prison with a suspended sentence commits another serious crime, then they are prosecuted and must serve time in jail.

8.   Chung Ju-yung (1915–2001) was the legendary founder and patriarch of what later became the Hyundai Group, one of Korea's largest conglomerates. He was the oldest of six children born during the Japanese occupation of Korea. He displayed a keen business sense early in life and was known throughout his career for his creative and (some would say) quixotic business sense. He built Hyundai from scratch, and later would own world-class companies engaged in shipbuilding (the world's largest), automobiles, finance, and construction, among other endeavors. He also played a pivotal role in winning the 1988 Summer Olympics bid for Korea and famously sent five hundred "unification cows" to North Korea, temporarily paving the way for easing tensions between South and North Korea.

9.   The Kyung-bu Expressway (or Seoul-Busan Expressway) was Korea's first expressway, spanning 416 kilometers and connecting many of South Korea's major cities. Construction began in 1968, following orders from President Park Chung-hee, and was completed two years later. Sixteen companies took part in the massive public engineering project; seventy-seven workers

were killed, and from the outset the project generated controversy and faced opposition from the public sector, businesses, and even members of the cabinet and the ruling party, as being reckless and unnecessary. Upon completion, however, the expressway was credited with greatly increasing efficiency in distribution and contributing to the overall growth of the economy. For this, the expressway is regarded as a symbol of the miraculous growth of the Korean economy and is called the "lifeline of Korea."

10.   In 1975 Hyundai built Korea's first automobile, the Pony, a small, four-door, rear-wheel-drive sedan with a 1.4L four-cylinder engine. It was the first car to be developed indigenously by a Korean manufacturer (design was done by an Italian company), making Korea the second country in Asia, following Japan, and the sixteenth country in the world to possess the technology to develop and manufacture automobiles. The Pony was later exported overseas, beginning with Ecuador and ultimately to many countries, including those in Europe. The follow-up model, the Pony II, underwent a face-lift and continued to reign as Korea's top seller before being retired in 1987.

11.   Chung In-yung (1920–2006) was the younger brother of Hyundai founder Chung Ju-yung and played a pivotal role in developing Korea's heavy-industry sector. He graduated from a university in Japan with a major in English and worked as a newspaper reporter before joining Hyundai Construction at the request of Chung Ju-yung. After his departure from Hyundai Construction, he went on to found Halla Construction, which later became Halla Group, one of Korea's top conglomerates in heavy industries.

12.   Samsung (which means "three stars"), most famous for its cell phones, flat-screen 3D televisions, and other high-end electronic appliances, is Korea's largest conglomerate, with annual revenue of more than US$180 billion. It has numerous subsidiaries, including shipbuilding, semiconductors, construction, finance, and life insurance, and its business accounts for approximately a fifth of Korea's total exports. It was founded in 1938 by Lee Byung-chull (1910–1987) who, along with Chung Ju-yung, played a pivotal role in industrializing Korea. Samsung started off as a small trading company, then diversified into textiles, retail, and securities. Beginning in the late 1960s, Samsung started manufacturing televisions and other electronic appliances; today it is the world's second-largest memory chip maker and its cell phones are some of the most popular in the world. Lee Byung-chull's son, Lee Kun-hee, is the current chairman.

13.   *Joong-ang Ilbo* was first published by Lee Byung-chull in 1965 and is now owned by the Hong family. In 1968, Hong Jin-kee (1917–1986), who served as President Syngman Rhee's Minister of Justice, became chairman, and his daughter, Hong Ra-hee, married Lee Kun-hee, Lee Byung-chull's son, who is the current chairman of the Samsung Group. Hong Jin-kee's eldest son, Hong Seok-hyun, is the current chairman of *Joong-ang Ilbo*, and he also served as Korean ambassador to the United States in 2005.

14.   In Korea (and also in Japan), *salaryman* is a word used to describe a white-collar employee who works for a private company and whose sole source of income is his salary (for women, the term *career woman* is used). Doctors, lawyers, bankers, and other types of specialists who may also receive

salaries are not referred to as salarymen. The term is used as a sort of caricature of the tired office worker with no prospects and little income; in Korea, a salaryman is normally understood to be someone who is middle-aged with a wife and two children, who works late all the time, and who may be forced into retirement at an early age.

15. Yushin ("Revitalization Reform") was basically a new constitution that President Park promulgated after dissolving the national assembly and suspending the existing constitution. This "new" constitution allowed the president to be elected for an unlimited number of six-year terms, and made it a capital offense to criticize the president or the state in any way, severely restricting freedom of speech and vastly increasing the authority of the state security apparatus. This was an attempt by Park to extend—indefinitely—his rule, and ultimately led to his assassination by his Chief of Intelligence, Kim Jae-kyu, who shot and killed President Park on October 26, 1979, while Park was having a private drinking party with his close associates (Kim was one of those attending). Following the death of President Park, General Chun Doo-hwan assumed control of the country (the December 12 coup or 12-12 coup) and subsequently was elected president.

16. Chung Mong-koo is the current chairman of Hyundai-Kia Motor Company.

17. President Park Chung-hee was killed by Kim Jae-kyu, one of his closest aides, who was then chief of the Korean Central Intelligence Agency (KCIA). President Park was known to hold small, private dinners in one of his many private residences

situated around the Blue House (president's office). Such dinners became more frequent after the assassination of First Lady Yook Young-soo in 1974. On the day he was assassinated, President Park was having dinner with Kim Jae-kyu, Cha Chi-chul (Chief of Presidential Security Service), his chief of staff, and two young female companions, one of whom was Shim Soo-bong, one of Korea's most famous pop singers at the time. Kim Jae-kyu later testified that his motive was to stop Park Chung-hee's dictatorship, but others claim that his initial intention was to kill his archrival, Cha Chi-chul, and that killing the president was unplanned. The story goes that during dinner, Kim Jae-kyu became agitated over derogatory comments made by Cha and that Kim then pulled out his pistol and shot Cha; the bullet pierced Cha's wrist and Cha hid in the bathroom. With Cha gone, Kim then shot President Park in the chest, and when Kim attempted to shoot the incapacitated president in the head, his revolver got stuck; he went out of the room to fetch another revolver from one of his KCIA aides and shot Park Chung-hee in the head—a shot that proved fatal. Cha was subsequently shot and killed as he attempted to escape. Kim Jae-kyu was later executed.

18.   Cha Chi-chul was an army captain during President Park Chung-hee's military coup in 1961; he later became one of the president's most loyal aides. Cha was elected to the National Assembly for four consecutive terms before becoming the chief of presidential security. He was known to be fanatically devoted to and fiercely protective of Park Chung-hee; he had a poster on his office wall that read "President Park is the State." He was notorious for being a megalomaniac. He considered cabinet ministers and other high-ranking officials his subordinates and treated them as such.

19.   The Fifth Republic (1981–1988) was the period during which Chun Doo-hwan was president. Following the death of President Park Chung-hee in October 1979, Major-General Chun Doo-hwan led the December Twelfth Coup, effectively taking control of the country. However, labor unrest and student demonstrations calling for democracy continued, which led Chun to declare martial law on May 17, 1980, triggering massive protests. On May 18, demonstrations took place in the southwestern city of Gwangju; Chun then ordered the deployment of special forces to quell the demonstrators, and the military brutally and indiscriminately attacked civilians, including women and children, killing hundreds in what would become known as the Gwangju Massacre. After Chun became president in March 1981 through indirect elections, he implemented various reforms and attempted to strengthen ties with countries such as the United States and Japan; however, the Fifth Republic also saw grave human-rights abuses, rampant corruption, and curtailment of the press. Demonstrations calling for democracy continued and finally, on June 29, 1987, Chun agreed to a constitutional reform allowing for direct elections (the June 29 Declaration). In 1988 Roh Tae-woo (Chun's military academy classmate and hand-picked successor) was elected president, beginning the Sixth Republic (1988–1993). Later, both former presidents were tried and found guilty for their role in the Gwangju Massacre as well as the 1979 coup and for accepting bribes while in office. Both served jail sentences and were pardoned by then-President-elect Kim Dae-jung in 1997.

20.   The statewide curfew applied only to Koreans.

21.   Kim Il-sung (1912–1994) was a communist who ruled North Korea from its founding in 1948 until his death in 1994. Kim

was a member of the Chinese Communist Party during his early twenties, and during the Japanese occupation of Korea he took part in anti-Japanese guerilla activities in northern China. His accomplishments as a guerilla fighter were undistinguished; however, his feats were greatly exaggerated later by the North Korean regime. In 1945, when Japan was defeated during the Second World War, Stalin's Red Army marched into North Korea, facing little resistance, and Stalin installed Kim as the head of the provisional government. Kim's return to North Korea thus began the de facto division of the Korean Peninsula with a communist North Korea and Syngman Rhee's South Korea, which was backed by the United States. In 1950, Kim invaded South Korea, starting the Korean War, and after three years of conflict and millions killed, the peninsula was divided along the 38th parallel (the two countries are technically still at war). Kim was an autocratic ruler who cultivated a cult of personality unlike any other on earth; he was regarded as a savior and divine ruler who had supernatural powers. His philosophy of *Juche* (self-reliance) was practiced throughout North Korea, and he is referred to as the "Great Leader." His son Kim Jong-il ("Dear Leader") assumed control of the country after Kim Il-sung's sudden death in 1994 (supposedly from heart failure), and his youngest son, Kim Jong-eun (age twenty-seven) has been designated his heir.

22.   While trying to win the contract for the Jubail housing project in Saudi Arabia, two of our executives were falsely charged and jailed. We later found out that a member of the Saudi royal family who had close business ties with one of our competitors had framed our executives. Following this unfortunate incident, we began exploring other markets in the Middle East.

23.   The "turtle ship" was the world's first battleship that made use of steel; it was successfully deployed by Admiral Yi Sun-shin during his victorious naval battles against the Japanese during the sixteenth century. Admiral Yi is considered a brilliant tactician and leader; he won twenty-three naval battles against the Japanese before being killed in action in 1598. The turtle ship is regarded as part of Korea's proud heritage, a symbol of resistance to Japanese aggression, and an example of Korean ingenuity and technical innovation.

24.   Mahathir bin Mohamad (b. 1925) was Malaysia's fourth Prime Minister, from 1981 until 2001, making him the longest-serving prime minister in Malaysia's history. Mahathir is credited with bringing about the rapid industrialization and modernization of Malaysia with bold reforms and massive infrastructure projects. He has dominated Malaysian politics for more than forty years and still wields considerable influence, even after his retirement. He has also been a strong advocate for and a tireless representative of Third World development throughout his career.

25.   North Korean agents, acting on direct orders from Kim Jong-il, planted the bombs inside their overhead compartments after boarding Korean Air flight 858 (from Iraq to Korea) at Saddam Hussein International Airport in Baghdad, Iraq. When the plane arrived at Abu Dhabi for refueling, the two agents—a male and a female—disembarked the plane, and the flight continued on to its next destination, which was Bangkok, Thailand, before blowing up over the Andaman Sea. The two North Korean agents attempted to escape to Amman, Jordan but failed and were detained in Bahrain when authorities detected their fake Japanese passports; when South Korean agents caught up with them, the

North Koreans each smoked a cigarette laced with lethal cyanide. The male agent died, but the female agent—Kim Hyun-hee—failed in the suicide attempt when authorities forcefully pulled the cigarette out of her mouth. Kim was taken back to Korea and sentenced to death, but was pardoned by President Roh Tae-woo. She still resides in Korea under tight surveillance.

26. Today, the Yakutia Republic (or Sakha Republic) is a federal subject of Russia. Its land stretches north to the Henrietta Islands in the Arctic Ocean. Its total area is slightly smaller than that of India, or roughly a third of China, and its population is less than one million. Yakutia Republic is famous for being well endowed with an abundance of natural resources, including oil, gas, tin, diamonds, gold, silver, and tungsten.

27. One hundred and sixty nations took part in the 1988 Seoul Summer Olympic Games, making it one of the largest gatherings at the time. Unlike the 1984 Summer Olympic Games in Los Angeles, the Eastern communist bloc decided not to boycott the Seoul games. As a result, the former Soviet Union and East Germany, as well as other members of the Eastern bloc, attended. The Seoul Olympic Games would be the last for the Soviet Union and East Germany.

28. During the 1992 presidential primaries, Kim Young-sam and Lee Jong-chan agreed to take part in a primary race in order to determine who would become the party's candidate. However, on the day of the primary, Lee Jong-chan decided not to show up and Kim Young-sam clinched the party nomination. Soon after, Lee Jong-chan founded his own political party and subsequently merged his party with that of Chung Ju-yung. In 1996 I ran against Lee

Jong-chan for the National Assembly seat representing the Jongno district and won. In 1998 President Kim Dae-jung appointed Mr. Lee as Director for the National Intelligence Service (NIS; formerly known as the Korea Central Intelligence Agency or KCIA).

29.   Such neighborhoods are called moon towns because most of them are built on hilltops overlooking the city, not because of the commanding view but because the land is cheap. The name may sound romantic, but the reality is far from it; moon towns were so called because these scraggly neighborhoods were deemed to be closer to the moon, and lacked many of the basic amenities of urban life, running water and adequate roads among them.

30.   Roh Moo-hyun was my predecessor, Korea's 16th–term president.

31.   Chung Myung-whun is a pianist and conductor. His two sisters, Kyung-wha and Myung-wha, are also accomplished musicians. The three performed as the Chung Trio, winning worldwide acclaim. Chung has won numerous awards as a recording artist and has successfully conducted many of the world's leading orchestras. For his service as the music director of the Paris Opera, he has been honored with the highest decoration in France, the Légion d'honneur.

32.   Unlike in the United States, where a president is often identified by his chronological place in the order of presidents (e.g. George W. Bush, 43), Korean presidents are known by the term which they serve. For example, I am known as the 17th-term President, but this doesn't mean that I had 16 predecessors, only that I am serving out the seventeenth term. Korea has had nine

presidents, some of them serving multiple terms under military dictatorships. I am currently serving out the 17th term while my predecessor, Mr. Roh Moo-hyun, served as our 16th-term President. Under a constitutional amendment following the end of military dictatorship, Korean presidents are elected for one five-year term and cannot run for reelection.